Enterprise, Entrepreneurship *and* Small Business

D0528269

Enterprise, Entrepreneurship *and* Small Business

Simon Down

Los Angeles | London | New Delhi
Singapore | Washington DC

SAGE Publications Ltd
1 Oliver's Yard
55 City Road
London EC1Y 1SP

SAGE Publications Inc.
2455 Teller Road
Thousand Oaks, California 91320

SAGE Publications India Pvt Ltd
B 1/I 1 Mohan Cooperative Industrial Area
Mathura Road
New Delhi 110 044

SAGE Publications Asia-Pacific Pte Ltd
33 Pekin Street #02-01
Far East Square
Singapore 048763

Library of Congress Control Number: 2009935765

British Library Cataloguing in Publication data

A catalogue record for this book is available from
the British Library

ISBN 978-1-4129-0884-9
ISBN 978-1-4129-1012-5 (pbk)

Typeset by C&M Digitals (P) Ltd, Chennai, India
Printed and bound in Great Britain by TJ International Ltd, Padstow, Cornwall
Printed on paper from sustainable resources

Mixed Sources
Product group from well-managed
forests and other controlled sources
www.fsc.org Cert no. SGS-COC-2482
© 1996 Forest Stewardship Council
FSC

To Linda, Anton and Jacob, with love.

Contents

Acknowledgements

I wasn't sure the book would get written for a while, but we got there in the end. Special thanks to Kiren Shomen for her belief in me and inspiring this project, and to Alan Maloney, Kate Wood and all at Sage for their professionalism. Thanks also to Andrew Simpson, Mike Taylor, Steven Pinch, Stuart Basefsky, Chris Steyaert, Bill Gartner, Tony Watson and Sara Carter for their help.

Reader's guide and features of this text

Many business studies texts today break the text into such small chunks that they cease to become books that are meant to be read, but rather become pages to be scanned: gobbits of mere information, rather than the meaningful, contextualised knowledge that is the real stuff of a degree in higher education. I believe that reading widely and deeply is still the key to learning to become an independent thinker, whether it is a book or the web that is being read. Lists of facts and bland presentations of theories as if they were facts – stuff to be memorised and regurgitated – fail the student and demean intelligence. I challenge you to engage and think about the topics discussed in this book. You will find more questions than definite answers: more diverging views than unchallenged perspectives. You will decide things for yourself. You might disagree with me but the text does provoke a view. I am no ghostly, distant author, but, like the lecturer or tutor that is using this book on your enterprise course or module, a real life presence.

Each chapter provides an introduction to a core theme or area of interest within the study of enterprise, entrepreneurship and small business, and successively builds a strong sense of purpose: to place its subject in the context of the world we live in. When you finish using the book you will not know everything these is to know. Your lecturer or tutor will along the way explain there are some strange omissions and some odder inclusions. Some of your other reading will no doubt unmask the pretentions to neutrality, or some other intellectual blind spot, that I have failed to note. These are my words, not the last word. The book is, I hope, a fresh look at entrepreneurship and small business studies, one that will provide for a stimulating learning environment.

Concept guide

Every now and then I shall highlight a particular word or concept in bold that may be unfamiliar. On the same page, in a box, there is an explanation of what it means.

Fenderco case studies

Most chapters have at least one or two case studies based on Fenderco, a small firm operating as part of an international joint venture in the port infrastructure industry. The company, located in the fictional town of Maltonbury, somewhere in the middle of England, manufactures and distributes rubber and steel products designed to stop ships damaging themselves upon berthing. These semi-fictionalised accounts are derived from my book *Narratives of Enterprise: Crafting Entrepreneurial Self-identity in a Small Firm* (Down 2006), an account of my three years of research on the firm. In the case studies the firm's entrepreneurs (Paul and John) and employees (Mark and Will) reflect on issues relevant to the chapter or section where they occur. Questions and exercises prompt you to reflect upon what they are saying.

Fenderco logo

Other features

Each chapter begins with an overview, highlighting what I hope you will learn, and ends with a short summary. There are some suggestions for both in-class seminar or tutorial activities and discussions, and suggestions for home-based activities such as watching films. There is however more reading than doing in the text, and I have shied away from incorporating too many interruptions to the flow of the narrative. Your lecturer or tutor will want to devise their own exercises and activities that perhaps will connect you more directly to your own enterprise context. Each chapter ends with a short list of key references for further reading. At the end there is a full list of references of the sources I have used in the book, and a subject index.

Part I

Studying Enterprise, Entrepreneurship and Small Business

The book is split into three main parts. Part II looks 'inside' the enterprise (Chapters 3–8). Part III focuses more on the 'outside', the broader context in which enterprising activity takes place (Chapters 9–11). Chapter 12 concludes the book. However, this part – Part I – comprises Chapters 1 and 2 and introduces the topic. The first chapter provides an intellectual overview of the major themes and topics we will look at throughout the book. Chapter 2 provides a map to studying enterprise, and explains the sort of tools – theories, methods, concepts, and so on – we will use.

1

Introduction

Overview

This chapter has the following objectives:

- To explain the need for a contextualised appreciation of enterprise, entrepreneurship and small business.
- To demonstrate the growing contemporary importance of enterprise through a brief historical analysis of its development.
- To introduce competing perspectives explaining the rise of enterprise, entrepreneurship and small business.
- To explain the orientation, content and plan of the book.

Why 'Enterprise'?

Enterprise is becoming more and more an important part of our experience of life and work. Many students will find themselves, one way or another, having to 'create' their own jobs after graduation. Even within large organisations employees are increasingly being asked to work in entrepreneurial ways. Governments, corporations, even churches and universities all clamour to sing the praises of the enterprising spirit. My own university has 'entrepreneurs in residence' and 'professors of practice' that also run successful business ventures. You may even be taking a course where you are running your own business as part of your degree. Entrepreneurs like Richard Branson are seen as world heroes by many. Television shows make minor celebrities of minor entrepreneurs: putting aspiring innovators and chancers and their business ideas through the mill of questions and tests, for the voyeuristic pleasure of the viewer to see who has won, lost or made a fool of themselves. It seems that everyone has plans to be his or her own boss someday. Enterprise is everywhere.

If this is the first time you have studied enterprise, entrepreneurship or small business studies you won't know how different this book is from other textbooks that have come before. It's straightforward, thought-provoking and broad in its intellectual outlook. Most enterprise or entrepreneurship texts are huge and heavy bricks of books, with an emphasis on facts and advice about how to run a business. This book is about enterprising people, the enterprising things they do, and the environment in which it all takes place: we are studying business, not learning how to run one.

This book could have been called an *Introduction to Small Business Studies* or *Entrepreneurship Studies*. The choice of the word *Enterprise* in the main title, and as the organising principle of the book, is for a good reason. As will become apparent there are a lot of different, sometimes contradictory, behaviours and forms of activity that can be described as enterprising. The study of enterprise encompasses the criminal *and* corporate, as well as the classical small business entrepreneur. It comprises of entrepreneurship, small business, micro-business, the self-employed and all manner of contexts in which these are found. Even whole organisations can be described as operating in an enterprising manner. In Chapter 2 we will learn that this breadth of meaning can cause a lot of debate and disagreement about what we really should be studying and researching under the banner of 'enterprise'. These thorny definitional and boundary issues can wait until later. What should be noted now is that the common factor between the classical entrepreneur, the criminal wheeler-dealer and the entrepreneurially-minded corporate financier is a go-getting, can-do attitude. They all share an ethos – a distinctive and habitual way of thinking and doing – about the role of the individual in the world, and the way to get on in it. It is looking at enterprise as a moral outlook that provides an occasional but uniting theme running through this text.

As I suggested above, the enterprise ethos is currently very popular and common in many parts of the world today. It wasn't always the case. Thirty years ago the Western nations thought the way to economic and social prosperity was through **economies of scale** and large organisations, where competitive pressures could be absorbed easily, and job security, and hence social stability, ensured. Weren't small firms supposed to die out, as the economy became more efficiently organised in large organisations? Thirty years ago much of the world didn't even have capitalist economies (communist China and Russia both had largely closed and planned economies). Thirty years ago it was rare for universities to have business schools, and where business was taught they did not offer courses in enterprise, entrepreneurship and small business. That you are now taking a course in enterprise reflects its perceived importance. This book will offer answers to why this is the case.

We will then need to have a small grasp of history to understand these changes. But there are many other subjects we'll have to engage with to understand our topic. We shall look at business studies sub-disciplines such as entrepreneurship and small business studies for sure, but we will also learn about economics, psychology, sociology, and management and organisation theory, even philosophy. This is another of the differences of this textbook from others in the area. We will look at enterprise from a broad intellectual perspective. The boundaries between things are often where all the interesting stuff goes on. It's the same with academic disciplines too.

Our text also emphasises the generic elements of the subject, downplaying the tendency for national and intellectual parochialism. Being British this has been

Economies of scale are the savings that organisations make because they can produce large numbers of things or provide services in the same standardised and repeated manner, using capital investment efficiently.

hard for me sometimes. Like most people I see what goes on in my backyard as crucially important. But as my overseas friends remind me, the United Kingdom doesn't have an empire anymore and isn't the centre of the universe: we live in a global space. Whilst different nations have particular types of enterprising environments (governments have different tax laws and different approaches to enterprise support, for instance), the commonalities between nations are stronger and more relevant than the differences.

If this is a set textbook for your enterprise course, then it is because your professor, lecturer or tutor feels that the book covers the range of the topics in a way which is appropriate to the aims of your degree. But textbooks can't do everything. This is not a book that will prove practically useful to working out how to run a business. There are hundreds, probably thousands, of books designed to do this. Hopefully you will also have an opportunity to take a course to see what running a business is like first hand. Maybe, like me (when I was younger I ran a very small independent music record label in London) you have already run your own business, or maybe you hope to do so.

If you have seen the value in getting a university education, you will no doubt see the value in studying enterprise in an academic way. It is not just entrepreneurs that the world needs. Many of you may build careers in IT, banks and other financial institutions, or in the public or voluntary sectors. In all of these careers understanding how enterprise works is important. The argument of this book is that enterprise is far more than simply the activity of entrepreneurs and small business owners. It is about the defining ethos or morality of our time. Understanding the implications, manifestations and context of enterprise is vital to being a knowledgeable and sophisticated worker citizen of the twenty-first century.

The place of enterprise in the twenty-first century

The evidence is diverse, globally uneven and often contradictory, but that enterprise represents a significant and distinct facet of the developed world that in many ways is different from the past, is perhaps crushingly obvious. This section explores why this is the case and introduces some of the major themes covered in this book.

How about we start with a dictionary definition? Enterprise is: 'an undertaking or new project, *esp* when bold or dangerous; readiness, initiative and daring in undertaking; a business concern' (*Chambers* 1993: 561). We can see that in addition to its meaning a business entity – an enterprise – it also denotes an orientation: a way of doing things that is active, creative, positive, and occasionally dangerous. The words enterprise and enterprising can be ascribed to both individuals and collectives, such as organisations: both Bill Gates and Microsoft might be described as enterprising.

It is not surprising that we start with a dictionary definition. The language we use to explain ourselves is important. In the developed economies the processing of knowledge and information – words and numbers, and even more words and numbers – has become the main driver for economic and social change, replacing manufacturing and the primary industries which dominated the nineteenth and twentieth centuries. The importance of enterprise as a way of describing the character of these changes is essentially the point of this book.

One of its main themes is that amongst all the facts and statistics relating to the growth and importance of small entrepreneurial enterprises, or the facts and statistics showing that this growth and importance is over-emphasised, one central fact stands tall. What is definitely the case amongst all the hype and counter-hype, is that people everywhere talk and write about enterprise. This is interesting, and academics have for some time been researching why we talk and write so much about certain things and not other things. As it relates to enterprise the main location of these debates has been in a discussion of the 'enterprise culture' (C. Gray 1998).

Originating in the early 1980s this debate focused on the political response in the US and UK to the earlier economic and social problems of the 1970s, and the desire by politicians to create environments that would encourage people to take the economic initiative. Oil prices, inflation, interest rates and unemployment were all high in much of the West, and the resultant social instabilities created a mood for profound political change. The policies of Ronald Reagan in the US and Margaret Thatcher in the UK (Figure 1.1) were radical in many ways and sought to change the very purpose of government. The ethos of most post-Second World War Western governments had been to care for citizens, providing structures and environments to meet everyone's needs as equally and fairly as possible. Some have called this period the 'managed economy' (Audretsch 2007: 7). Above all the state took a central role in organising many, if not most aspects of the nation, including nationalised industries. The problems of the 1970s were perceived as being caused by such a *statist* approach and the 1980s saw political programmes on both sides of the Atlantic which attempted to 'roll back' the state. These new political and moral outlooks saw society and the economy made up of individuals, not collectives. Government's new role would be to enable and facilitate the freedom of the individual. In exchange for the protection of those rights, individuals would have to learn or be encouraged to be more self-dependent. They could no longer rely on the state for all their needs and direction. If the economies of nations were to be strong, individuals would need to be enterprising. A key policy element of this new direction was to re-regulate employment and corporate legislation in order to encourage more enterprising behaviour in the economy. As a result, it was hoped an entrepreneurial society (Audretsch 2007) would emerge.

Though the failure of the European communist states and the marketisation of communist China seemed to underline the fundamental error of state centralism, the extent to which both the original diagnosis of failure in the 1970s and the prescription of enterprise as the solution to the problems are true, remains debated to this day. The state has certainly not disappeared and remains central to the social and economic management of all nations. It is also true that economic activity is freer than it once was. But an enterprise culture, at least taken narrowly in the sense of people depending on themselves for work, is only partly the case, and not in the sense of the majority running their own small businesses. Large corporations still dominate

Figure 1.1   Margaret Thatcher (UK Prime Minister 1979–1990) and Ronald Reagan (US president 1981–1989)

Archives UPI/AFP/Getty Images

economies, the majority of people in work are still employees, and governments in the US and the rest of the world still have a profound effect on business. It is however certainly the case that in terms of how people perceive and talk about work and the economy notions of enterprise dominate.

What though is the nature of the evidence for the rise of enterprise? Surely the facts and statistics will speak for themselves? If only it were that simple. A famous historian once wrote, 'a fact is like a sack – it won't stand up till you've put something in it' (Carr 1972: 11). As you'll know from watching or listening to the news, the same facts and statistics often get used to make different and opposing arguments. They are inert, and need effort to be of use. The same happens in research. So although many of the numbers produced regarding small firms, self-employment and levels of entrepreneurship show the increasing growth of small-scale economic activity and definite shifts in the composition and balance of the workforce and economic structure, the issues remain complex and contested. This is because statistics don't seem to resolve debates on their own, and can be marshalled, presented and analysed in many ways. The bare facts still need to be interpreted and understood in relation to their social and economic contexts: you still need a theory; a point of view; a reason for explaining why something is morally or economically or socially or politically more or less important, better or worse.

An example of these complexities – and one which points to various debates of forthcoming chapters – can be seen in the story of research into job creation. Jobs – where they come from, why there are not enough and their changing characteristics – have been at the centre of many debates in the social sciences concerned with work and business. This is because they are often seen as indicators of a healthy economy and society.

Until the 1980s it was thought that large corporations and public organisations created most jobs. An influential study in the US by David Birch (1979) began a change to all that, and has spurred a continuing debate. His research into job creation in the 1970s concluded that small and medium sized enterprises (SMEs) created 80 per cent of the net new jobs. The significance of this is that if you see job growth as a good indicator, then clearly economic policies emphasising the support of larger corporations was misplaced. Similar research followed Birch's study and eventually a new academic and political orthodoxy was established which also claimed to show that networks of smaller enterprises were also where much of the innovation in the economy took place.

More recently the orthodoxy that Birch initiated has come under scrutiny from a number of different quarters. Bennett Harrison (1994) in particular has synthesised criticisms of the new logic and has argued that the whole 'small firms myth' simplifies and detracts from the realities of a corporate dominated economy.

Harrison argues that Birch's study was flawed from the start and better statistical research indicates that there has not been a growth in the numbers of jobs created by small firms. Though the criticism of Birch's methods may be something of a straw man (see Kirchhoff and Greene 1998), his broad-ranging assertion that the focus on small firms obscures more important changes which have occurred to the power relationship between smaller and larger organisations, is less easily dispensed with. Harrison and many others, argue that large organisations today practise *concentration without centralisation*. What he means is that big firms have decentralised, but because they engage in lean and flexible production methods, with small numbers of core workers and dispersed peripheral employees (either directly employed or subcontracted through small or other large firms), the control over their resources is still maintained. This power over their widely dispersed activities is facilitated by new information technologies and by new management methods. For example, a large corporation will control its outlying or subcontracted suppliers by maintaining a supplier quality partnership, whereby the supplier must provide products or services at a certain quality level, and also provide certain information to the corporation in direct information transfers: the control is held by the corporation despite the supplier being a separate enterprise.

How does this benefit the large enterprise? If a large corporation out-sources 50 per cent of its activity, reducing the numbers of people it employs directly by half as well, it might create a number of new enterprises (or create new business for existing ones). These new companies will employ people, but perhaps at lower wages and with lower benefits than the previous jobs in the corporation. The net effect has been an increase in productivity for the corporation and a reduction of the total labour and resource input cost. On the surface this looks as though both more wealth and more jobs have been created, but it might mean that all the corporation has done is shift the more costly and risky elements of its activity to other parts of the global economy. Whatever way you interpret this, it is clear that it is driven by the needs and behaviour of large business, and not the behaviour of entrepreneurial individuals creating more enterprises. The enthusiasm for all small firms (as a distinct **unit of analysis**) as a universal engine of economic growth is misplaced.

The job creationists' argument emphasises the *numbers* of jobs created by small firms, and in particular high-tech, high-growth firms, and downplays the more *structural* arguments about where the power to shape the economy lies. These arguments turn on the analytical frame of analysis: one on aggregate numbers of specific entities – 'SMEs' – the other on the structures and relationships of all entities.

| Activity |

Read the short article on this topic from the *Washington Post* at http://www.webcitation. org/5jLAxBUSf [.]

Fenderco case study

Paul, entrepreneur and owner-manager of Fenderco, is talking with Simon (researcher and current author) over a beer one night:

In retrospect it was a big mistake to take on the manufacturing plant. Before we bought Steel Applications we simply contracted them to make all of our fenders. Their business was going through some problems and David, the managing director, made us what looked like a really attractive proposal. I always loved going there seeing the designs I had drawn up being turned into real things. It was great talking to these guys – they were so skilled and knowledgeable – and I learnt a great deal about what works in the real world. I had always quite fancied being the owner of a manufacturing business. So anyway, John, my business partner at Fenderco, thought it was a good idea too and we did the deal. In most respects nothing really changed. The relationship was the same, but we, Fenderco, were now the owners. We didn't get overly involved in the management of the business; David continued as the MD. Changes we'd agreed as part of the deal were made and for a while things did improve.

Then we went through our own bad patch and orders slowed down for a while. The rise in the price of rubber hit us quite hard. Steel Applications was a better business in lots of ways, but if anything it was even more reliant on our business than before. Then there were the new welding regulations following that dreadful passenger walkway collapse at Fishguard harbour: seven or eight people died and the welding standards were ultimately at fault. I am glad we weren't behind that contract: we would have probably done the job in the same way. It was tough that winter any which way. We should have taken on a more hands-on approach from the start. We should never have bought it. The crunch came and David phoned me up out of the blue saying that unless we laid some people off the business would likely go under. It was really scary. Honestly I'd never really thought about the implications before. Fenderco only employed Will, Mark and Joan at our offices in Maltonbury. Then it just hit me. The responsibility of it all: 18 grown men relying on me for their livelihood. I feel pretty bad about what happened. We just couldn't commit Fenderco to keeping the business afloat and we had to wind the business up. David handled it mostly and a new business started up almost immediately, but with less staff. We weren't financially involved in this new company. They still do the majority of our manufacturing work. I was pretty naïve about it all. I've lost all my romantic feelings about running a manufacturing business; employing that amount of people is just too much of a headache.

Activity

1 What does this passage reveal about Paul's attitude to growing Fenderco?
2 Why might employing people be a headache and something some entrepreneurs avoid if they can?
3 Why can a business like Fenderco still grow without employing manufacturing, distribution and installation functions directly? Does this approach create more or less jobs for the economy as a whole?
4 In terms of the level or unit of analysis, discuss in groups different single level explanations (individual, firm, industry, and society/economy) for the failure of Steel Applications under Fenderco's management. Which is the most convincing explanation and why? Then look at multi-level explanations and individually ascribe percentages to each of the four levels: e.g. 50 per cent individual, 30 per cent firm, 10 per cent industry, and 10 per cent society/economy. Give reasons for the weightings, compare with others in the group and come to a consensus.

Case Study

So if the economic dominance of small firms is a myth, why has it become so pervasive and persuasive? Harrison doesn't deny the importance of enterprise as such. Rather he tries to place its growing importance as a way of describing the world by emphasising the underlying historical, political and ideological reasons for the prominence of enterprise. The reality of the small firm is more complex and mundane.

Harrison also dispels some of the other myths that have grown up around the small firm. There is a perception that smaller firms are better, more harmonious places to work than larger organisations. Research that we will explore in more detail in Chapters 5 and 6 shows that many small enterprise workers lack representation from unions and work in businesses that are less able to adhere to best practice in environmental and health and safety. They generally provide less pay and poorer conditions, and are often found at the margins, providing lower skill peripheral labour for larger firms.

After Birch claimed so much for small firms others started to explore the benefits of small enterprise, and found that when many different firms were concentrated in an industrial district in a dynamic network the impact for innovative economic and technological development could be profoundly positive. As a result of this particular and specialised form of innovative networks of enterprises, many people started to believe and promote the idea that small firms in general are inherently innovative as a form of business. This tail wagging the dog type thinking has been common among those who uncritically enthuse about small firms, and this book aims to cut through some of these myths. In Chapter 9 we will look at enterprise and innovation in its more complex detail.

What does all this criticism mean to how we study small firms and enterprise? Should we not bother looking at small firms at all? No. Small firms are very important – if we include the self-employed, most people still work in smaller enterprises – but it is better to look at them along with their broader economic, political and social contexts. Other research has put this more directly and argues that if you only look at small firms that is all you will see (Scott and Rosa 1996). Later, in Chapter 2 we will look in more detail at how the way we look at the different actors (small and large firms, governments, consumers and so on) and their roles affects the interpretations we make. By over focusing on the small enterprise as a unit or level of analysis we run the risk of ignoring other more important factors.

Other types of analyses critical of orthodox enthusiasms for enterprise rhetoric look at government and corporate behaviour in promoting enterprise and ask what the motivations might be. Most developed nations are currently carrying out policies which would support Birch's analysis, but these same governments also help structure the economy in a way which supports corporate behaviour in the way that Harrison describes. And anyway, governments do not an economy make. We live in a global economy, both in terms of the internationalisation of markets, but also in terms of its regulation. Indeed, if support for job creation via smaller enterprise was so fundamentally a part of government activity and had been successful in creating new dominant economic structures, why is it that there is so much vociferous opposition to the power, lack of accountability and scope of large corporations? If Harrison is right, and by and large this text agrees with his more sceptical approach to the hype surrounding enterprise, the responses of governments in promoting small firms in particular and enterprise more generally need to be explained. We look at government support more directly in Chapter 11.

What these debates indicate is that reality is complex and that the place of enterprise in the twenty-first century is more diverse than simply looking at it as a function of job creation. Enterprise is not just about numbers of people running their own business. There are too many public servants and too many corporate employees who are behaving, talking and being asked to manage their work in entrepreneurial ways. Any look at the recruiting literature of the major corporations will show that they too promote an enterprising way of talking and doing (Barrett 2003).

As a result, some scholars – we will meet them later – have sought to combine the analyses of the culture of enterprise, with an explicit emphasis on the language of enterprise. This shift to an interest in how people talk and write about what they are doing is not just restricted to enterprise studies. The turn towards language has been adopted in many social sciences, and for good reasons. Not only has the world itself become more organised around communication, information and textual knowledge, but also serious debates about the nature of knowledge have been raging in many social sciences. Put simply the answers that traditional social science research tends to produce – generally information based on counting things – do not seem to answer some of the questions that people want answers to. As famous anthropologist Clifford Geertz has written: 'It is not worth it [...] to go round the world to count the cats in

Zanzibar' (1973: 16). The new approaches – both the theories and the research methodologies they imply – seem to offer a way to understand the meaning behind the bare facts, and a variety of different theoretical approaches have emerged to compete with (but also to complement) the more traditional. Are cats important in Zanzibar? Do they have any religious significance? Why do people keep cats in … etc.? We will look at the **discourse/narrative** approaches in more depth at various points in the text. For now it is enough to say that they argue that the language that people have available to use to describe and control activity is vitally important in understanding enterprise activity.

Enterprise is not just about words though. We have seen that since the 1970s the behaviour of large corporations has changed. Economies of scale were not producing the same amounts of profits. Like governments, big business was in trouble. Large organisations began to restructure themselves, creating flatter hierarchies (and less managers), and smaller autonomous business units responsible for producing their own profits (which has created more entrepreneurial managers). These new forms of large fragmented organisations employed less and less people, as new technologies and new lean and mean techniques for managing their activities such as subcontracting, outsourcing and just-in-time stock inventory, were introduced. Labour laws changed: either to encourage these new corporate behaviours, or as job saving responses to corporate regime shopping (moving activities to cheaper labour cost areas and/or more liberal legal environments). There has been a fundamental decline in primary and secondary industry and a rise in the tertiary or service (or knowledge) economy. The increasing global interconnectedness of financial institutions and markets has meant that these political responses – generally called neo-liberalism – to the economic stress of the 1970s and 1980s remain a dominant political ethos today, though the recent crash may be the start of a new era.

Changes have not just occurred at the structural level. The nature of individual and social behaviour has also changed. The exact relationship between cause and effect between large structural changes to the economy/society and individual behaviour is a complex problem, but clearly there is a relationship. People are different now compared to what they were in the past: they think and behave differently. The beliefs, attitudes and moral outlooks are different, and the choices and opportunities available to make decisions about are also different. Watch any film about everyday life from the 1960s and you will see what I mean: that's why we find them funny or strange.

Home-based exercise

Watch a black and white film set in the mid-twentieth century one afternoon, read up about the film on IMDB (www.imdb.com) or wikipedia (http://www.wikipedia.org), and note down your thoughts about the type of work people are doing, the characters' attitude to the work and how it is represented in the film. Alternatively talk to your grandfather/ grandmother about their work when they were young. In class if time allows show clips from the film from YouTube (www.youtube.com) and discuss the differences between work in the mid-twentieth century and today.

Social attitudes to work, government, even the nature of what it means to be individual have changed. For most people the differences with the past are n startling but they do exist. Work is still central to establishing a sense of identity f many. Many of us are free to create **portfolio/boundaryless careers** in a world whic requires our skill and effort in short bursts on transient projects. Or, if we are less we educated we are likely to have to choose between different periods of fleeting an low-skilled casual employment. For both, work is punctuated with periods of 'leisure . This type of work isn't as secure as the 'jobs for life' of the past. As a result, along with an increasing need for self-reliance comes a greater degree of personal risk. Taken as a whole, work and the relationships surrounding it are becoming increasingly transitory. Concepts such as employee loyalty and commitment are declining in importance: it is the individual who must make his or her own way in the world. And this way of working is having profound social consequences. If the popularity of self-help and therapy books and the rise in mental health problems are anything to go by, not all individuals are necessarily happy with all the flexibility, freedom to choose, self-regard and self-achievement on offer in the enterprise society.

It's not just at work that enterprising individualism rules. As consumers we find ourselves at the focal point of a whole range of competing pressures for our attention. We are told that we are unique and important individuals. As internet consumers, where as the saying goes, the world is at our fingertips, we become active, enterprising agents/consumers, looking for ever-cheaper and more specialised products and services. Aside from the new markets and enterprising opportunities that these new individual horizons provide for us, there is also some disquiet about the relentless focus on the individual that our enterprising world presents to us.

Contemporary philosophers and social scientists from a variety of stances argue that some of the problems of the modern world are attributable to the excessive regard for individualised values that the enterprise society represents and promotes. What is seen as good or leading a good life – one that is valued and attractive both individually and broadly as an aspiration in society – revolves too much around individual, material and achievement-based values; values that the ethos of enterprise seems to encourage and support.

We will not resolve these debates. However, it is instructive that we have engaged with it here at the beginning of this book. I wanted to highlight early on that the stuff of enterprise studies is not a parochial backwater of business studies. Nor is it a defined and agreed upon fixed body of knowledge. Studying enterprise in this book does not make its subject boring through erecting tight and closed boundaries: narrow views make for narrow understandings. An eclectic and critical approach is vital to produce thorough useful knowledge. Let's see what the rest of the book has in store for us.

Portfolio/ boundaryless careers are employment biographies or histories where people do a number of related (or unrelated) things in their lives, which may include paid and professional employment, but might also include being self-employed, running a business, or even volunteering or taking time out to travel. More and more we need to construct and present convincing 'stories' that link the various activities of our careers to potential employers. In itself this is a more self-reliant and enterprising form of work.

Plan and style of the book

The book is organised in three main parts, I to III. Part I looks at the different ways in which enterprise has been research, studied and taught, and shows the advantages in studying it in the broad way I have suggested above. Parts II and III make a distinction between the human activity that goes on inside the enterprise (the hard work, rewards and challenges of managing and working in enterprises) and how that fits into the broader social, economic and organisational contexts outside the enterprise. Then in the final chapter we have a conclusion which restates and summarises the insights generated and the approach taken throughout the book.

Along the way we will look at a diverse range of concepts, theories and subjects including most of what you would expect in a textbook on enterprise, entrepreneurship and small business. We will also look at subjects that get ignored: criminal entrepreneurs big and small; what happens to an organisation when there is too much entrepreneurship; the significance of the ageing population of Western nations; the global diversity of enterprise including the world's ethnic and Indigenous entrepreneurs. Why? Because a view of enterprise that sees only the archetypical fat, white, balding male entrepreneurs of small manufacturing firms, is not tenable today, if it ever was. We need to see enterprise in all its glory and all its ugliness. We need the whole picture.

The variety of academic disciplines looking at enterprise is very broad. This is because people are interested and excited by different things, have different problems to solve and different views about the world: some want to count cats, others understand why they are important. Chapter 2 concludes Part I and sorts out the mess a fair bit and defines what enterprise is about, what the different academic tribes think, how where you live in the world might have a bearing on how you view enterprise, and introduces the different theoretical approaches to the subject. It summarises the arguments in favour of using the concept of enterprise broadly, and elaborates on the advantages for the student and the field more generally. I argue that the use of enterprise creates a far more multi- and interdisciplinary subject of study: more challenging, engaging and more appropriate for an expanding and exciting field.

Chapters 3 and 4 start Part II, which looks 'inside' enterprise: both at the level of the organisation, the level of the individual and the processes of 'entrepreneuring' (Steyaert 2007). Chapter 3 looks at how both the enterprise and the entrepreneur have attracted the attentions of many writers from economic traditions. Their ideas are explained and critically assessed. There is more to the enterprise and the entrepreneur than economics can tell us and different traditions from other areas of the social sciences, such as psychology and sociology, are discussed to produce a much fuller picture of the entrepreneurial process in Chapter 4.

Chapters 5 and 6 look at the people who actually manage and work in smaller and entrepreneurial enterprises. Firstly, we look at the distinctive characteristics of managing smaller and entrepreneurial enterprises. This includes an assessment of research looking at both internally (training, discipline, control and so on) and externally (relations with suppliers/customers) focused activity. Secondly, we look at the distinctive aspects of working in smaller/entrepreneurial enterprises. This could mean quite a narrow focus on employee relations research, but in Chapter 6 we will look at a broader range of material. Both chapters emphasise the particular importance and implications of the informal social relations that constitute the employment relationship in smaller/entrepreneurial enterprises.

Earlier I suggested that even if you were to work all your life in a corporate environment it was likely that there would be much talk and exhortation to be enterprising, to take the initiative, to be an entrepreneur. This is so common a feature of organisations these days that people who run sections or business units within corporations as if they were independent businesses have their own name: they are intrapreneurs. Chapter 7 addresses intrapreneurship, and the implications of working in the entrepreneurial corporation, both for the individual, for the organisation and the rest of society.

Though this is not a *how to* book, any text in the enterprise studies area needs to have an appreciation of the practices of financing, marketing, networking and strategy and growth. Chapter 8 reflects on these management processes and the contexts in which they take place.

Chapter 9 begins Part III and discusses the economic contexts of enterprise, which are crucial to any sophisticated understanding. As earlier chapters will have shown, enterprise is not an isolated set of activities, but a complex web of individual and collective initiatives contingent on a variety of structural and environmental factors. This chapter deepens the proceeding analysis and locates enterprise in the pattern of market relationships that has emerged in the last few decades. We will ask further questions of the more glib notions of enterprise which are touted as an economic panacea for all the world's ills. The chapter is in two parts, the first of which will focus on flexibility, globalisation and changing organisational relationships, and the second takes a look at the relationship between enterprise, innovation and technology. Both sections will present evidence which seeks to deflate the sometimes gung-ho rendition of enterprise, and shows that, as with much else in life, there are diverging views regarding the reality, relevance and wisdom of seeing enterprise, in whatever form it takes, as a universal curative.

Chapter 10 looks at the social contexts and diversity inherent in enterprise. The shifting social mores of developed nations are assessed for their impact on the propensity and manner in which people engage with enterprising activity. Specifically, changes in class, family and gender structures are examined. The characteristics and impact of immigrant, ethnic and Indigenous enterprise; the persistence and development of family enterprise; the influence of religion; the characteristics of illicit or criminal enterprise; and the shifting generational demographic of enterprise (the impact of ageing populations) are also considered. Though not exclusively so, much of this chapter is discussed using the concept of marginality.

Chapter 11 looks at how governments around the world adopt a stance to enterprise activity. In the main governmental activity is subsumed within broader economic and social policy, which, even in the freest of the free market economies, has profound and significant impacts on how people go about doing business. In recent decades in the developed economies and in the previously planned economies of Eastern Europe, governments have to varying degrees and for a variety of reasons supported specific policies targeted at enhancing enterprise. In certain countries enterprise support 'industries' have emerged. This chapter seeks to characterise different approaches to enterprise support, and explain the generic reasons for and against adoption of such policies, and the broader political, economic and social trends underlying their adoption.

Finally, Chapter 12 restates and summarises the main themes of the book.

Before we get started I should say something further about the style of the book. In lectures I will often see students unloading their bags of the many brick-sized encyclopaedic textbooks they have to carry, and I wonder at the necessity of all those strained shoulder muscles. This text is meant to counter this trend. True knowledge and learning is not about amassing facts, it is about developing an understanding and confidence to be able to use and apply knowledge. It's about relating what you are learning to the experiences of your own life: the life already lived and the life to come. I presume that you are already active participants in the world: people who use knowledge to do things for yourself and for other people. If you are studying this book for a course and you don't say 'hey, this sounds inter-esting' or 'hey, this is making me think about the world and *my* life in a different way', or 'hey, this means something to me', then really you should think about why you are studying it, or why you are studying business studies (or whatever it is) at all. Life is too short to be doing things for boring reasons. Be enterprising!

I do not shy away from an intellectual and properly social scientific style. It seems to me that other fact-obsessed texts are demeaning to your intelligence. If there are some difficult but pertinent ideas we will have a look at them. Hopefully this will be done in an accessible and clear way. I have ~~striven~~ (no cross that out, a better simpler word is 'tried') to make sure the writing is in plain accessible English.

Each chapter draws on different and appropriate literatures. The sources I have selected do not come exclusively from the small business and entrepreneurial academic journals, because often the best and most interesting work is done elsewhere in the core disciplines of economics, sociology, and management and organisation studies more generally. The chapters are not swamped with distracting references and superfluous theories and concepts. Instead at the chapter ends there will be a list of suggestions for further reading. These will normally be the articles or books which have inspired or provoked the central ideas of the chapter.

Another reason why the book is not swamped by academic references is because the nature of studying a topic is different from researching it. Academics tend towards very narrow interests, and as a consequence tend also to get a little precious about their interpretation of facts, or view of particular topics, theories or concepts. This causes a lot of argument and debate, which is obviously and gener-ally a Good Thing. If you are trying to get to the bottom of something, it's a good idea to make sure all views, facts, theories and concepts are considered carefully. Many of the details of these debates are fought over very technical and theoreti-cal issues which occasionally exist as much to support the egos of the academic experts, obscure the flaws in their argumentation and keep non-expert opinion out and thus preserve their expert status, as they do to advance an understanding of the specific issue. Underlying this flippancy regarding academic research is a serious point, which we will return to elsewhere in the book. The world is not simple and straightforward. It is made up of people with different views, interests and reasons for believing in things in particular ways. Part of the point of this book is to point these differences out; to outline the choices if you like. But I am not suggesting that I am some omnipotent and objective guru who sits neutrally above all the arguments. I too have a perspective, and obviously it will structure and inform this book. I have tried to avoid going into the details of these debates which are found in the journals where academics publish their research. Instead, research into enterprise is drawn upon judiciously and presented in a way that makes the key issues obvious and accessible.

The perspective presented in this book is one that cautiously welcomes the moral perspective that enterprise – in all its diversity – brings to human relations. It neither rejects and lambastes, nor heaps hyperbole on individuals or organisations that seek to label their activities as enterprising. What it does is ask you to consider carefully and thoughtfully the place of enterprise, entrepreneurship and small business in the twenty-first century. Some of the conclusions about the moral nature of enterprise that I draw might be somewhat surprising, or at times somewhat difficult to grasp (I said accessible and clear, not free of complexity), but our exploration of enterprise will definitely involve you considering your own outlook on the world: this is not the book for you if you prefer the rote learning of uncontroversial facts.

So, let's get to work!

Summary

The basis for studying small business and entrepreneurship under the banner of enterprise was explained. The growing significance of enterprise was discussed in its historical context. Different arguments used for the importance of small and entrepreneurial organisations were presented. The plan and style of the book were outlined, and each chapter briefly described.

▇ ▇ Further reading ▇

Harrison, B. (1994) 'The small firms myth', *California Management Review* 36(3): 142.

Kirchhoff, B.A. and Greene, P.G. (1998) 'Understanding the theoretical and empirical content of critiques of US job creation research', *Small Business Economics* 10: 153–169.

2

Studying Enterprise:
What, Where, When, Who and How?

Overview

This chapter has the following objectives:

- To provide a 'map' or guide to how different academic disciplines and approaches relate to each other.
- To introduce six dimensions (or specification decisions) of enterprise research – purpose, theoretical perspective, focus, level of analysis, time frame and methodology – which form the basis for knowledge claims about entrepreneurship and small business.
- To show that these dimensions have geographical aspects, whereby European and US scholars tend to adopt consistently different approaches to producing knowledge about enterprise.
- To argue for a pragmatic and inclusive approach to theorising enterprise.

Introduction

To be human is to be connected with many separate and overlapping spheres of life. Those that research human activity in academic disciplines tend to erect formal and precise boundaries in seeking to describe and explain that activity. And whilst scientific work should be precise, textbooks are works of synthesis and should draw inclusively and broadly from the range of pertinent disciplines. Boundaries need setting though. Chapter 2 does this. It is not about enterprise, it's about studying enterprise. Imagine this chapter as a map – its an old cliché, but an appropriate one – explaining different territorial boundaries; the places of particular interest; the major connecting routes; the dangerous marshes where people can get bogged down; and the mysterious, exciting places yet to be explored. What maps do is tell you what's in and what's out. You have ten more chapters to go. You need a map.

One aspect of maps is how quickly they become obsolete. The territory of entrepreneurship is growing fast, and it re-shapes as it grows. The number of academic articles with entrepreneur/ship in the title published in 1990 was about 50, in 2006 it was 370 (Sorenson and Stuart 2008: 518). Ever more topics are added to the sub-disciplinary field of entrepreneurship and small firms. Blackburn and Smallbone, writing about the UK research scene, suggest that this growth is due to the same structural changes in the economy I discussed in Chapter 1 and 'reflects an increasing interest in the field on the part of policy makers at local, national, and the European Union levels, as well as by the media and society at large' (2008: 267). Not only is the study of enterprise growing in size, but also in importance. We imagine that research into entrepreneurship is clearly serving an important need in society, answering vital questions. Many of these questions will be debated in this textbook. But don't expect clear cut answers. Enterprise scholars do not agree on the discipline's purpose or on what theoretical perspectives are relevant; on what questions need answering. We don't agree on what should be studied or how it is defined, what time frame is relevant, or even how the research should be conducted (Gartner 2001; Low and MacMillan 1988). This chapter explains why we disagree, but also shows how the territory connects. The study of enterprise might be more like the European Union than the United States of America in terms of its constitutive coherence, but it does cohere.

Many of the ideas, theories and concepts I allude to here are described in fuller detail in subsequent chapters. In order to make sense of the messy map of enterprise some simplification is necessary. The argumentation metaphor I use to do this is a common one, again, almost a cliché. It is the notion of positions on a line, stretching from one pole to another. Inevitably the tendency here with this form of argumentation is to stress the distinctive and the extreme. Positions at the end of the line, or poles, are clearer, easier to grasp. This form of argumentation smooths the peaks and troughs in order to tell a coherent story. The dimensions of that story are provided to us by an important article by Low and MacMillan (1988). They specified six things – purpose, theoretical perspective, focus, level of analysis, time frame, and methodology – that enterprise researchers need to consider when doing research (Gartner 2001: 27). This research when written up into articles and books becomes knowledge about enterprise. These six dimensions, six lines if you like, present us with a way of thinking about the what, where, when, who and how of enterprise research. They give us a map explaining where things are, so that we can better study enterprise.

The next section addresses five of the six decisions researchers make to do enterprise research. Who – the way enterprise is organised into specific subject based disciplines – and where – the geographical distinctions which characterise enterprise studies – each have their own sections, before we come back and address the sixth Low and MacMillan decision – theoretical perspective – which we discuss in the last section.

What? When? How?

Purpose and focus

Why research and study entrepreneurship? For many in the field there seems little purpose in researching the topic unless it seeks to 'explain and facilitate the role of new enterprise in furthering economic progress' (Low and MacMillan 1988: 141). The majority of entrepreneurship scholars seem to support this through their research practice, but others have noted that this has led to a 'narrow focus on financial and economic measures of performance' (Brush et al. 2008: 262). I agree. There are lots of important and interesting things that happen in and around smaller and entrepreneurial firms that may have little to do with furthering economic progress. And anyway, how are we to define economic progress?

Progress as an exclusive purpose seems to place the study of entrepreneurship at a disadvantage compared to most other subjects. Engineers study the properties of bridges, geographers, coastal erosion, and historians, the French revolution. All do this for a wide range of reasons, some of which might be of direct relevance and utility to problems we have today (safer bridges, how best to build barriers, understanding contemporary revolutions). But utility is not the only purpose of the disciplines. Nor should it be in enterprise. What about the relationships between culture, **ideology** and entrepreneurial processes? Are these not important? Are these relationships only interesting insofar as they further economic progress? Ideas – about markets, value, equality, property, morality, and so on – and not calculations about progress lie at the heart of how and why economies and societies function (Curran 2000b: 215). Research should be useful, but it needn't only be because it adds to our wallets.

Ideology refers to a set of ideas and beliefs that underpin particular approaches to a political, economic, religious (and so on) system.

It is therefore important that the purpose of research is explicitly articulated. The knowledge you are learning about enterprise has been created for a purpose. You need to understand what that purpose is. For many things you will read that a purpose becomes apparent through the way that things are defined. As there are many purposes for research, there are many definitions of entrepreneurship. As a work of synthesis this textbook will not settle on one, nor will it list many. Definitional issues are important but are often overplayed (often to fix the purpose). They are framing devices, and as this text is intent on being inclusive – enterprise and entrepreneuring rather than entrepreneurship – we will simply accept that no single definition will suffice, and push on with competing descriptions and explanations. Your understanding of enterprise, entrepreneurship and small firms will build up over the course of the book and over the course you are studying. Even those such as Low and MacMillan (1988: 141) who want entrepreneurship scholars to share a 'common purpose' have acknowledged that it is unlikely that any one statement can capture all there is to say. There are just too many different angles to be incorporated and too many disciplines to view them from.

There has however been some progress towards a common purpose since Low and MacMillan's (1988) article. Chief among these is the shift away from seeing entrepreneurship as situated exclusively in the acts of individual entrepreneurs, towards seeing it as a process within specific and general contexts. The purpose of entrepreneurship research is not to unveil the entrepreneurial person, but the entrepreneurial process. Thus Gartner (1985) defines entrepreneurship as the creation of new ventures in a process combining the influence of environment, individual(s) and organising. Shane and Venkataraman (2000: 218) reckon it's the 'study of *sources* of opportunities'; the processes by which opportunities are discovered and exploited. Chris Steyaert (2007) prefers the verb *entrepreneuring*, reflecting an emphasis on the emergent and creative process of being enterprising and the inherent relational, social and historical context in which it takes place. These definitions are inclusive, not just of individual entrepreneurs, but also of the environment or context in which entrepreneuring is done. These different process-oriented definitions have had a positive impact on our understanding of entrepreneurship. We look at the notion of opportunities in more detail in Chapter 3, and Gartner and Steyaert's approaches pervade the whole book, and specifically the discussion below, focused on the 'European' school of entrepreneurship.

Levels of analysis

According to Low and MacMillan entrepreneurship researchers 'may choose among five *levels of analysis*: individual, group, organization, industry, and societal levels' (1988: 151). Historically there has been too much emphasis on single level factors such as the attributes and personality of the entrepreneur, or at the level of the firm, and not on the different levels in which entrepreneurship takes place. Recent years have seen increasing recognition of the important of multi-level research (Brush et al. 2008: 259). This likely reflects significant efforts pointing out the inherent problems in single level analysis (Davidsson and Wiklund 2001; Gartner 1985, 1988; Scott and Rosa 1996; Shane and Venkataraman 2000). In order to explain the behaviour of entrepreneurs it is simply not sufficient to look at the individual level. Human activity is inherently interconnected to other individuals and groups in different forms of interaction, and entrepreneurship is constrained and enabled by different organisations, industrial sectors and the cultures, laws and **norms** of different societies.

Similarly, the firm is only one type of vehicle for enterprising behaviour, and the life and death of a firm may not be the best way to describe the emergence, success or failure of an entrepreneurial opportunity. Many ideas emerge whilst the wannabe entrepreneur is still employed. Many entrepreneurs have more than one firm and try to make their ideas work through successive ventures over time; multiple firms can contribute particular aspects to an overall enterprise.

Moreover, which level we look at has a profound impact on how we view the success of an enterprising idea. What might be good for the entrepreneur might be very bad news for the society or other businesses in the locality. Different interests can gain and lose from entrepreneurial activity depending on where you are looking from. As Davidsson and Wiklund note 'it is fully conceivable that successful new enterprise at the micro level translates into economic regress at the societal level and that failed entrepreneurship at the micro level contributes to economic development' (2001: 90). Figure 2.1 illustrates the importance of level of analysis, showing how different types of enterprises can have both positive and negative outcomes. *Hero* enterprise reflects genuine and broad benefits to society through entrepreneurial activity (i.e. Google). *Robber* enterprise reflects

Norms and **Normative**: Norms are common expectations we share about proper, appropriate behaviour, but 'normative behaviour is not simply the most frequently occurring pattern', it also implies 'the presence of legitimacy, consent and prescription' (Abercrombie et al. 2000: 243).

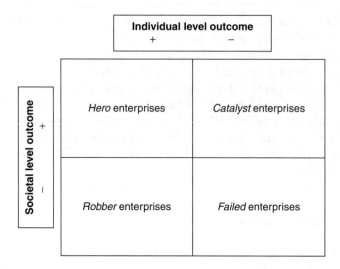

Figure 2.1   New enterprise outcomes on different levels (adapted from Davidsson and Wiklund 2001: 91)

activity that may be extremely entrepreneurial but of little broader value to society as a whole, economically or otherwise (Enron's disastrously criminal entrepreneurialism or illegal drugs businesses are examples). *Catalyst* enterprise reflects those genuine failed businesses, the ideas of which are picked up and made successful by others. And, of course there are *failed* businesses: 'enterprise attempts that fail and lack positive spillover effects on other actors' (Davidsson and Wiklund 2001: 90).

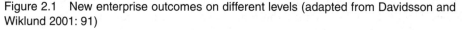

_____ Time frame _____

Another aspect of understanding knowledge about entrepreneurship and how it is created is the time frame selected by researchers. Enterprise scholars need to be efficient and get value for money when conducting research. This means that research is often a simple snapshot of what is happening. Obviously, businesses change and develop over time and single snapshots cannot capture change. Depending on the sort of question you want to answer, knowledge about enterprise should illuminate what happens over time. Sometimes longitudinal research methods are needed. Oftentimes a series of snapshots will do the job. But the time frame is not simply a methodological issue. Decisions also need to be made about when in the life of a business is it best to do research?

Entrepreneurship research is currently over-focused on the business start-up. Is this the most important time in the formation of a business? 'Where can one draw the line between entrepreneurial activity and non-entrepreneurial activity? Does it end after the first year of an organization's existence? Or, perhaps it ends when a company sells its shares on the public markets?' (Sorenson and Stuart

2008: 524). When does entrepreneurship start? Are there identifiable stages that all enterprises go through? Or are stages too ridged and sequential a way of thinking about what can be an extremely non-linear process.

Others see our current knowledge about enterprise as lacking enough of a historical time frame. Whilst a great deal of effort is made in understanding real time everyday processes, the impression that can be given is that the issues being discussed are happening for the very first time. Much entrepreneurship research is ahistorical, bound up in the moment. Jones and Wadhwani suggest that there needs to be more historically literate enterprise knowledge: 'By embedding entrepreneurship within the broader process of historical change in industries and economies, historical research provides insights for other social scientists into how contemporary entrepreneurial activity may be better contextualised in time and place' (2006a: 32). What might look like significant increases in rates of entrepreneurialism over a short period might look like a small insignificant blip in a longer period of overall decline. Time frames matter.

Methods

Back in the mid-1960s Bob Dylan was seen by many as a symbol of change and hope, a force for creative destruction if you like. At a press conference in Los Angeles in 1965 (as shown in the Martin Scorsese film *No Direction Home*, 2005) a reporter asked a question:

> *Reporter:* **How many people who labor in the same musical vineyard in which you toil – how many are protest singers? That is, people who use their music, and use the songs to protest the, uh, social state in which we live today: the matter of war, the matter of crime, or whatever it might be.**
>
> *Bob Dylan:* **Um ... how *many*?**
>
> *Reporter:* **Yes. How many?**
>
> *Bob Dylan:* **Uh, I think there's about, uh ... 136.**
>
> *Reporter:* **You say *about* 136, or you mean *exactly* 136?**
>
> *Bob Dylan:* **Uh, it's either 136 or 142.**

The reporter looked somewhat mystified by the howls of laughter that followed Dylan's quip. But the failure of his ridiculous question illustrates a critical limit of enumerating for enumeration sake. Within the study of entrepreneurship too, many work on arcane problems with the same mind set. This is not to suggest that enumeration is wrong. For many problems you need to have some idea of the proportion of which type of people do this or that. Numbers matter, but not for all possible problems.

Broadly put we see two traditions of doing entrepreneurship research that frame the methods decision. The first is what's called normal science. This apes natural science philosophy and procedures and seeks to build an 'accumulation of **empirically** tested hypotheses and well grounded generalisations, developed through quantitative data,

Empirical refers to knowledge about phenomena that is derived from experiment, experience and observation rather than from theory or logic.

rigorous design, and statistical techniques' (Brush et al. 2008: 250). This approach is currently more popular within the field, such that Brush and her colleagues found that less than 10 per cent of studies adopted the case study, a methodological technique typical of the alternative tradition (2008: 259). The majority of entrepreneurship scholars either use questionnaire surveys or readily available secondary data, such as the Global Entrepreneurship Monitor or government statistics. Brush et al. also explain that the trend in recent years has been towards secondary data which reflects ease of access on the internet, and survey fatigue from entrepreneurs and small business owners and managers.

The second tradition of doing research takes an eclectic, diverse and pragmatic approach to methods. Whilst the normal science approach has the advantage of producing very reliable knowledge, it can also be somewhat divorced from everyday reality. The second tradition draws on different scientific and philosophical assumptions which place particular events under the researcher's gaze, using observational, reported speech and textual methods to illuminate the practices of everyday life. Methods and approaches in this *interpretive* or *qualitative* tradition include **ethnography**, case study, and interviewing.

Ethnography is a research method that embeds the researcher in the 'world' or culture being studied and collects (commonly through interviews and observation) a thick description of practices and behaviour usually over a sustained period of time.

Welter and Lasch agree that both traditions have much to offer and are critical of the 'taken-for-granted assumptions that rigor is "only" achieved by using multivariate data techniques' (2008: 245). Unthinking adherence to quantitative methods as the only properly scientific approach can lead to myopia. What should simply be a tool can often become an objective in itself: methodology tends to shape all else. Kaplan's 'law of the instrument' describes this intellectual trap well: 'give a small child a hammer, and he will find that everything he encounters needs pounding. It comes as no particular surprise to discover that a scientist formulates problems in a way which requires for their solution just those techniques in which he himself is especially skilled' (1964: 28 cited in Weick 1996: 302; cited also in Brush et al. 2008: 261). The interpretive tradition produces insightful and contextualised knowledge about enterprise, and tends to include a greater range of behaviour. However, it doesn't easily build consistent, comparable and unified knowledge. The sociologist Howard Becker formulates the respective problems of these methodological approaches, which often centre on the merits of qualitative and quantitative research methodologies, in the following way:

> **Qualitative research – we might better say research that is designed in the doing, that therefore is not systematic in any impersonal way, that leaves room for, indeed insists on, individual judgment, that takes account of historical, situated detail, and context and all that – research of that kind is faulted for being exactly all of those things and therefore not able to produce 'scientific,' objective, reliable knowledge that will support prediction and control. Research which tries to be systematic and impersonal, arithmetic and precise, and thereby scientific, is faulted for leaving out too much that needs to be included, for failing to take account of crucial aspects of human behaviour and social life, for being unable to advance our understanding, for promising much more in the way of prediction and control than it ever delivers. (1993: 219)**

Research methods are only tools, and are never going to solve problems by themselves. Some research questions need quantitative tools, others qualitative. Many problems need both. The answers to questions come from the contributions of many different researchers, each taking a different methodological route to illuminate the problem.

Each of these dimensions of doing enterprise research – what Low and MacMillan (1988) call specification decisions – produce choices about which group to be part of; to place you somewhere – whether it's stuck in some technically important but dull bog, or exploring exciting new territory – on the enterprise map. In other words by making choices about how to do research and what tools to adopt, allegiances to different groups are made. Later we will look at the choice of theoretical perspective. First we shall examine how these choices also influence the shape of academic disciplines.

Who? Academic tribes

The famous historian E.H. Carr advised students to 'Study the historian before you begin to study the facts' (1972: 23). This instruction counts for all academic disciplines including the student of enterprise. How so? His point is that in order to understand the knowledge that is being presented, you need to know *who* is doing the presenting and what assumptions he or she or they have made about the issue or problem at hand. Which group is the scholar part of? Where on the map can you find them? A historian will be interested in the entrepreneurial process in different ways to an economist. Approaches to *what* is being studied and what is deemed interesting are the product of academic differences. These are shaped by the education, socialisation and institutional norms associated with different academic disciplines. Figure 2.2 explains the basic organisation of the sub-disciplinary field of entrepreneurship. Each knowledge domain and social science discipline by and large adheres to certain commonly understood norms. Business studies has its own set of norms – political and moral, as well as academic – but in some respects it is a mini-university of knowledge in itself, drawing on a wide range of academic disciplines, but chiefly the social sciences; economics, psychology and sociology. Each of these disciplines informs and shapes a range of sub-disciplines, topics and issues as depicted in Figure 2.2.

These institutionalised disciplinary and sub-disciplinary groupings find expression through academic departments or faculty groups, journals, conferences and workshops. But it's much messier than the table implies. There are many business and management academics that publish work in two or more sub-disciplines: I attend both entrepreneurship and organisational theory conferences.

There are also other differences that separate knowledge production into 'tribes' (Becher and Trowler 2001). There are the different topics that interest and excite scholars. These change slowly over time as their topicality and

Knowledge domain	Business Studies			
Relevant social science disciplines	Economics	Psychology	Sociology	Other social sciences: geography, politics, law, etc.
Sub-discipline	Economics Accountancy and finance Marketing Strategy/Logistics/Operations management Innovation/Entrepreneurship/Small business HRM/Personnel/Industrial relations Organisational Behaviour/Theory[1]			
Enterprise sub-disciplinary field; topics and issues	Entrepreneurship and Regional Development. Entrepreneurship Education. The role of universities in fostering entrepreneurship. Spin off processes and knowledge transfer. Support infrastructure for entrepreneurial ventures and business incubation. Entrepreneurial Process: From Creation to Growth. Entrepreneurial Finance and Venture Capital. Innovation and Technological Entrepreneurship. Corporate entrepreneurship/intrapreneurship. Technology Commercialisation and its impact on entrepreneurial activities. Globalisation and SMEs. Family firms. International Entrepreneurship. Networks and Entrepreneurship. Social Entrepreneurship and Corporate Social Responsibility. Green Entrepreneurship. Historical and Cultural 'Milieu' and Entrepreneurial Culture. Entrepreneurship and Regional Open Innovation Systems. Entrepreneurship and special interest groups. Regulation and Entrepreneurship.[2]			

Figure 2.2   Organisation of entrepreneurship knowledge

[1]The horizontal position of these sub-disciplines more or less corresponds to the influence of the 'parent' social science discipline. The closer to the centre each sub-discipline lays the more eclectic the influences.

[2]Taken from RENT XXII – Research in Entrepreneurship and Small business Conference 2008. This particular conference was chosen as it happened to have the longest list of topics and issues. Conference themes will change slightly from year to year.

relevance for broader debates ebb and flow. In the case of entrepreneurship topics such as green and social entrepreneurship have emerged relatively recently. Topics will also change, broaden or narrow. The study of gender and enterprise shows how a specific focus on female entrepreneurs can develop into a cross-cutting perspective on enterprise studies as a whole. Studies of enterprise from a gendered perspective have served to highlight and question the inherently male stereotypical assumptions within the field (Ahl 2006; de Bruin et al. 2006). Many of the topics however, finance and growth for instance, have hardened into what Gartner (2001: 35) has termed 'informal communities'. Entrepreneurship has become so large a sub-discipline of business studies that many scholars rarely stray out of their topic or interest group, and indeed in many cases will explore their topic in other disciplines and sub-disciplines.

There is also a distinction between those enterprise scholars that are interested in entrepreneurship who have no particular interest in smaller firms, and those small business scholars that have little interest in entrepreneurship. The former tend to be economically oriented and are generally concerned with growth and, obviously, corporate entrepreneurship. One of the reasons for this narrower focus is an aim of establishing a more or less agreed general integrated theory explaining the processes inherent and exclusively related to entrepreneurship (Casson 2005; Davidsson 2003; Davidsson and Wiklund 2001; Low and Macmillan 1988; Shane 2003): we look at this in more detail in the section looking at theory. Those that focus on small firms are more likely to have sociological or geographical interests and often a policy orientation. A US (entrepreneurship) and European (small firm) split along these lines is also discernable, though the distinction is declining as the study of enterprise becomes internationalised. We deal with geographical differ-ences in more detail in the next section.

One of the more important but subtle things to look for when reading academic work is whether the author is doing the research *for* enterprise: does the research seek to promote the benefits of enterprise or to enhance firm performance? Or, is the research being reported simply *about* enterprise, with no direct intention to 'help' enterprise? This book, as I explained in Chapter 1, is *about* business, not *for* it. It's not a 'how to' book, nor do I promote enterprise. This is not the same as being against it, but it might imply being critical of what businesses, entrepreneurs or economic systems do.

Criticism is both inherent and unavoidable in good scholarship. Even those who wish to promote enterprise have to make critical judgements about how best to achieve their aims. Researchers are critical of the practices they study either for performative (**Enron** was managed badly and failed) or moral/political reasons (Enron's managers were bad people/the system that allowed Enron to operate that way is wrong). Or, they are critical of their own practices: of the different approaches taken to, or interpretations made of, research data, and of the theories offered to explain enterprise phenomena. As it happens criticism is also inherent to the practices of entrepreneurs. In identifying and acting on imbalances of supply and demand, identifying and exploiting opportunities,

The **Enron** Corporation was an energy conglomerate with a range of businesses in natural gas, electricity, communications, commodities trading and financial services. At the time of its collapse in December 2001 it was the seventh largest US corporation (Seeger and Ulmer 2003: 59). Following bankruptcy senior executives were convicted for fraud, insider trading, and other crimes. The Enron case is discussed in Chapter 7.

entrepreneurs are inevitably going to be critical of existing business practices. To destroy old routines, a notion of what's wrong with the existing situation is needed in order to create something better.

The distinction between being *for* or *about* enterprise is a real one, and it is indicative of a major fissure between what might be called a normative school (the school defines the common standards, norms or expectations about how to study and research enterprise) which tends to define its purpose in terms of being helpful to businesses in terms of boosting their performance in some way (Brush et al. 2008). The 'European' school either claims neutrality of purpose, distancing itself from supporting business aims, or, alternatively criticises business practices for progressive social, moral or political reasons. Either way, entrepreneurship and small business is in my mind 'a subject to be studied rather than a phenomenon to be promoted' (Blackburn and Smallbone 2008: 279). However, it is important to stress that these distinctions are polar positions I am characterising. Most academics will adopt stances along a spectrum of possible positions, not just at the poles. The important thing to realise is that despite these divisions, conversations between even the most resolute and dogmatic can and do take place. It is however crucial to grasp that conflicts and debates *do* exist.

Where? Geographical differences

Academic conversations (literal ones as well as those that take place in journal articles and books) are like any other, subject to misunderstandings due to language and cultural differences (Welter and Lasch 2008: 242). Remember: study the scholar – and where they come from – before you study the research. Though I stress the differences between US and European scholarship in this section, the diversity of orientations amongst scholars in national contexts should be noted (Anderson et al. 2009). Bill Gartner is to many a scholar in the European tradition (Hjorth et al. 2008), but works in Clemson University, South Carolina, USA and publishes in both European and American journals. More unites enterprise scholars than separates them. Thus European should really be 'European', as it reflects more than which side of the Atlantic you happen to be on. Rather, 'European' refers to a more or less consistent approach to a theoretical perspective, purpose, focus, levels of analysis, time frame and methodology that is different to the predominantly US based normative school.

The study of enterprise, entrepreneurship and small business is no longer immature but it is diversified and fragmented (Blackburn and Smallbone 2008: 274). A weak **paradigm** operates with permeated and fluid boundaries. The US school is dominant and founded on an economic and individualist notion of entre-preneurship, and tends to be *for* entrepreneurship. In contrast the European school tends to be focused on enterprise as a creative and historically contextualised

Paradigm is the set of assumptions, ideas, principles and practices that make up a particular view of reality for the group – for example an academic discipline – which shares them.

process, and to be *about* enterprise. These alignments are definitely too tidy though. But the distinctions do exist. For instance Brush et al. (2008: 261) emphasise the tendency for European journals to publish articles that see enterprise as a collective endeavour. As a consequence more multilevel analysis is conducted looking at the environment, the firm and the individual entrepreneur. US entrepreneurship journals tend to publish articles taking an individualistic view of the entrepreneurship process, and looking singly at individuals or firms. This distinction is also reproduced methodologically: 'the picture emerging is one of a variety of qualitative research methods and combinations used by European researchers and a more quantitative orientation of US researchers' (Welter and Lasch 2008: 244).

Hjorth et al. (2008) have identified three distinctive attributes of the European school. First, explicit attention is paid to the socio-economic, historical and cultural context. This means a connection with real life practices of enterprise is achieved. The loss of realism that one sees in much statistical analyses is avoided. Second, ideas and theories, often from outside business and management, are drawn from a broad social science base including, but not dominated by, economics. Third, innovative concepts can be accommodated including the novel demands prompted by the spread and penetration of enterprise and entrepreneurialism in society and (popular) culture, which normative business entrepreneurship, with its narrow focus on performance, growth and new venture creation, generally ignores.

What about the rest of the world? By and large scholars in other parts of the world associate with *for*/normative or *about*/European traditions. Enterprise studies has become more international over the last decade or so (Blackburn and Smallbone 2008: 279), and as a result, along with diversity, a greater degree of commonality between the two broad camps has emerged. Particular nations will of course have their own traditions. In the UK for instance, historically the emphasis has been on small firm research (Blackburn and Smallbone 2008; Welter and Lasch include 'Nordic' countries here, 2008: 243). But UK scholarship has gradually become less distinctive as it has become more international, with most scholars now sharing broad interests in enterprise and entrepreneurship, whilst also sharing a predominantly European orientation. Australia is more mixed, and India and China tend to adopt positions aligned to US norms. However, given the growth of China, India and other newer economies and their growing influence, we can expect to see even more diversity, or indeed the growth of alternative scholarly traditions applied to thinking about enterprise.

How (again)? What is theory for?

Gartner implies that a sixth specification decision – the theoretical perspective – 'hinges on assumptions' (2001: 27) made about the other five, seemingly the more technical decisions that we discussed above. He is implying that the theoretical perspective is the most important of these decisions. He's right. But this section will not seek to explain the key theoretical approaches to enterprise. The proper place for discussing how scholars have been theorising enterprise, entrepreneurship and small business is over the course of the book alongside the 'specific set of problems and issues' (Gartner 2001: 34) that excite and engage different communities of enterprise scholars. What is more useful here is to describe what theories are and what they are for.

'Theory is a dangerous, greedy animal, and we need to be alert to keep it in its cage' (Becker 1993: 221). Becker is warning us that just as methods can become heavy tools that get in the way of finding stuff out, so too can theory. But just what is a theory? A theory is a set of statements or principles that aim to help explain real life events, facts or phenomena in a generalised and consistent manner. Theories are abstractions. They attempt to take away all the stuff that is particular and idiosyncratic, and get to the nub of the matter, so that when other similar but puzzling events, facts or phenomena emerge, the theory can help explain what is going on. Without these ways of reducing the clutter of real life it would be very difficult to have meaningful – that is, easily 'translatable' to a wide range of people – conversations about problems. We would simply rely on telling stories – which are themselves a form of theory or abstraction; very useful for many purposes – or worse, randomly listing and describing facts, about what we have seen and heard. Both stories and theories order and structure and select information and present it for specific purposes: stories to charm and amuse; theories to simplify and aid understanding.

One of the problems with theory, why it can become a 'dangerous, greedy animal', consuming energy, is that people can spend too much time on trying to devise the perfect house of cards; perfect structures and models that attempt to answer too much. They get trapped in a boggy marsh. Theories are supposed to be useful, not as complicated as the world itself. Theories like cards can never stand up for long however, because life moves on and wriggles around continuously. People change their behaviours. Societies and economies restructure themselves. Perfect theories don't exist in the social sciences, unless you can stop people and organisations doing stuff. At best, the best theories help us even though they are incomplete. At worse, the worse theories do nothing. Theories succeed because people think they are useful and interesting: a bit like stories really.

The search for grand, meta- or universal theories infects the language of the social sciences despite the obvious flaw in reasoning. Some that study entrepreneurship support a natural science approach, and treat entrepreneurship as if it were an atom or molecule. They want to stop the world and seek perfection. In the view of the European school, a manifestation of this thinking can be seen in the language used in journal articles. Authors will often talk about the purpose of research in terms of our knowledge being incomplete. The implication is that we could have a complete knowledge of entrepreneurship if only we had better methods, more facts and better theories. To imagine that a theory of entrepreneurship might be devised and that all entrepreneurship scholars would then be able to predict behaviour without fail or perhaps simply pack up their laptops and find others things to think about is naïve. The notion of 'developing an integrated, theoretical approach' is to many European scholars 'unachievable' (Blackburn and

Smallbone 2008: 279; Steyaert 2007). Gartner puts it just as emphatically and suggests that 'entrepreneurship research espouses a diverse range of theories applied to various kind of phenomena. There is no theory of entrepreneurship that can account for the diversity of topics that are currently pursued by entrepreneurship scholars' (2001: 34). Jones and Wadhwani also argue that entrepreneurship scholars such as Shane and Casson have gone too far in their attempts to identify 'the *essential* and *universal* elements of entrepreneurial behaviour and **cognition**' in that their general theories become so abstract that they 'explain relatively little when they are held up against specific, grounded entrepreneurial cases' (2006b: 10, emphasis in the original). They are not suggesting that theoretical generalisations aren't possible, but that they cannot transcend history and place. Context matters and 'general theory explains very little of the most interesting and important variation in entrepreneurial behaviour' (ibid.). Hence according to Sorenson and Stuart, Shane and Venkataraman's (2000) call for a focus on the 'novelty of the entrepreneurial act' would exclude 'all but a small (maybe even minuscule) fraction of the many millions of firms founded' (Sorenson and Stuart 2008: 525). When one is intent on distilling down to the purest elements of what entrepreneurship is or might be, inevitably only the rarest examples fit the model. This is a problem because there are always new behaviours and new contexts in which entrepreneurial creativity will emerge. Hence theories are always contingent and transient, something that the European school accepts and embraces.

> **Cognition** is the mental process of knowing and thinking, including aspects such as awareness, perception, reasoning, and judgement. Derived from psychology and used by entrepreneurship studies to investigate if entrepreneurs process information and think differently from other non-entrepreneurs.

As with the boy with the method's hammer, theories can also become ends in themselves. Academics work very hard at creating new theories, and there does need to be a conversation about how best to explain phenomena. But as Karl Weick notes of some academics, there is a tendency 'to pursue either abstractions [theories] or particulars [facts] by themselves, independently, as if they had a life of their own and self-contained meaning' (1996: 309). Whether you place too much energy into producing abstract theories, or indeed, produce particular stories with little means of connecting to an understanding of other similar stories, both fail the test of building useful knowledge.

The desire to construct narrowly defined slices of life – or high consensus research paradigms where all agree with the problems and how to go about answering them – in order to more easily theorise them is contagious and other fields periodically undergo such anxieties. A particularly famous exchange between Jeffrey Pfeffer, who was in favour of a normal/natural science strong paradigm approach to organisation studies, and John Van Maanen (1995), who wasn't, showed us the problems. At its heart Van Maanen's critique of the strong paradigm view of social scientific theorising is that theory making is constructing reality, not simply reflecting it (1995: 135). For Van Maanen '[t]heory is a matter of words, not worlds; of maps, not territories; of representations, not realities' (1995: 134). His view is analogous to a European school version of the study of enterprise, and suspicious of those who argue for a narrowly bounded, high-consensus paradigm, and a universal theory of entrepreneurship.

Perhaps a good way to think of this is to imagine the difference between a debating competition and a conversation at a dinner party. Those that like a debate are keen to win it. In such winning the ideas and contributions of the loser are made redundant. Only the winner's knowledge counts. Those that like conversing are keen to share different possibilities, build knowledge and a genuine consensus on the topic. What are you, a lover of debate or conversation?

Theory means different things to different people. To purveyors of the normal science approach a theory is an abstract attempt to explain phenomena that can be tested by research. The European perspective sees theory slightly differently in that it can be based on middle range theories; those that attempt 'to understand and explain a limited aspect of social life' (Bryman and Bell 2003: 8, cited in Blackburn and Smallbone 2008: 281). These two traditions – the normative and the European – constitute separate 'communit[ies] of scholars in dialogue about a specific set of problems and issues, and who hold similar beliefs about the relevance of certain methods for solving these problems' (Gartner 2001: 34). Entrepreneurship as a whole is not a single disciplinary community in this sense. Rather there are 'informal homogeneous communities' (Brush et al. 2008: 261; Gartner 2001: 35) that congregate around the specific topics and subjects detailed in Figure 2.2. Hence, whilst entrepreneurship as a field of study cannot agree on a single theoretical perspective, there are both conversations and debates, and theories, not a single agreed theory.

Fenderco case study

The ethnographic researcher/author (Simon Down) on how he approached the six specification decisions in researching Fenderco.

The Fenderco case study was based on a three-year ethnographic research project. At the time – the project began in 1998 – there had been very little ethnographic research into small firms. Books by Dick Hobbs (1988), Monder Ram (1994), and Ruth Holliday (1995) all showed how effective the method could be at illuminating the detailed, real life aspects of, respectively, petty criminal enterprise, immigrant small business, and employee relations in small firms, and I was determined to use the *method* to address the behaviour of entrepreneur/owner-managers. The *purpose* of the research was thus to add and build on to a detailed, descriptive knowledge of what entrepreneurs/owner managers actually do, something that according to the literature on entrepreneurship was needed to progress knowledge about entrepreneurship and small firms.

All projects need a *focus*, even ethnographic ones, which tend to start with a broad, fairly hazy idea and then narrow down as patterns of behaviour emerge, and the researcher gets to know the people and the environment better. At the outset the focus of the project was to investigate how entrepreneurs learnt (Down 1999). This eventually shifted to a focus on self-identity construction when I realised that how they learnt from their environment, depended on how they constructed a sense of self. Conceptually therefore a shift in a level of analysis had taken place: learning became a subset of self-identity.

Case Study

The ethnographic method implies a broad engagement with different *levels of analysis*, and though empirically the setting is at the individual and group/firm levels, the general approach calls for a significant engagement with contextual factors at the broader organisational and socio-economic levels. Similarly, part of the raison d'être of ethnography is to spend a significant length of time in the environment being researched. Traditionally when ethnographers study tribal societies (the method came from anthropology) this would mean permanent emersion. In my case the research was conducted in a series of regular, punctuated visits over three years. This elongated *time frame* of engagement and observation provides a means to see how behaviours, lives and activities develop: over time confidence and the rapport between researcher and research grow. Finally, a commitment to ethnography as a methodology has certain implications for which *theoretical perspectives* are adopted. The commitment to particular, rather than universal, aspects of human behaviour – an interest in thick descriptions, rather than generalised ones – obviously favours middle range theorising and concept building about the processes researched, rather than grand general theorising.

In-class activity

In small groups discuss the questions below. They are aimed at getting you to think about specification decision choices – purpose, theoretical perspective, focus, level of analysis, time frame, and methodology – and their impact on the sort of knowledge that is produced.

What sort of knowledge would emerge from a project on small firms adopting quantitative, questionnaire-based, methods?

What would a researcher do to examine the broader socio-economic environment (industrial sector and societal levels of analysis) surrounding a small firm? Who would the researcher talk too? What might the researcher read? What secondary statistical data would be useful?

What methods other than ethnography could provide data about small firms over longer periods of time?

What sorts of research problems/questions about small firms or entrepreneurs would not benefit from the ethnographic methodological approach?

Conclusion: integration without losing diversity

The message of this chapter is that diversity is strength. Ultimately the notion of enterprise is the more appropriate framing concept for studying entrepreneurship and small business in all of its many varieties. The book accepts Allan Gibb's (2002) view that small business and entrepreneurship should move away from heroic, individualised notions of the entrepreneur and towards a wider notion of enterprise. Accepting diversity means of course that a science of entrepreneurship

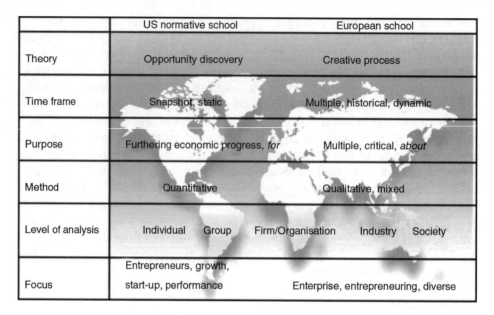

	US normative school	European school
Theory	Opportunity discovery	Creative process
Time frame	Snapshot, static	Multiple, historical, dynamic
Purpose	Furthering economic progress, *for*	Multiple, critical, *about*
Method	Quantitative	Qualitative, mixed
Level of analysis	Individual Group Firm/Organisation Industry Society	
Focus	Entrepreneurs, growth, start-up, performance	Enterprise, entrepreneuring, diverse

Figure 2.3   A rough map of enterprise

cannot be achieved, but this is an impossible goal anyway. Social scientific knowledge can be achieved through many forms of enquiry. Both the normative and the European traditions add to our knowledge, in spite of the limits and imperfections of theory and method. Theory and method both need to be kept in a cage. They are tools to solve problems, not ends themselves. Pragmatism is the order of the day. Moreover, too close a fascination with furthering economic progress runs the risk of being blind to that diversity, and of course, of failing to be independent and critical of the phenomena being researched and studied. A crucial aspect of any research is that it is reliable. I don't just mean in the sense of statistical reliability, but more in the sense of does the analysis, interpretations and conclusions being drawn from research by whatever tradition, theory or method, sound plausible? Do they chime with and connect us to our everyday sense of the world? It is important therefore that whilst enterprise research should be relevant to businesses and policy makers, it should also be independent. If enterprise academics are saying the same things as those who practise what is being studied then it is likely that the academics are dispensable (Weick 1996: 310).

The chapter has also provided a map to the study of enterprise (see Figure 2.3). It's very much my map, or rather one that sides with the European school of enterprise. It is not neutral. But this is the same even with real maps. There are different ways of projecting the surface of the earth onto the pages of atlases which have implications for the size of particular countries and their relationship to each other. There are different ways to fit curved realities onto flat surfaces. It's the same with spheres of knowledge. But having any map is better than being lost.

Summary

Overall the chapter has provided a guide to studying enterprise, entrepreneurship and small business studies. The disciplinary structure of enterprise was explained. Specifically two major approaches – a predominantly US based 'normative', and a 'European' school – were identified. Researchers following these traditions tend to make different specification decisions regarding the sort of research undertaken and why. The implications of the six specification decisions – purpose, theoretical perspective, focus, level of analysis, time frame, and methodology – for understanding knowledge claims about enterprise were discussed. It was argued that a pragmatic and inclusive approach to studying, theorising and researching enterprise was the most appropriate.

▓ ▓ Further reading ▓

Blackburn, R.A. and Smallbone, D. (2008) 'Researching small firms in the UK: Developments and distinctiveness', *Entrepreneurship Theory and Practice* 32(2): 267–288.

Brush, C.G., Manolova, T.S. and Edelman, L.F. (2008) 'Separated by a common language: Entrepreneurship research across the Atlantic', *Entrepreneurship Theory and Practice* 32(2): 249–266.

Gartner, W.B. (1985) 'A conceptual framework for describing the phenomenon of new venture creation', *Academy of Management Review* 10(4): 696–706.

Gartner, W.B. (2001) 'Is there an elephant in entrepreneurship? Blind assumptions in theory development', *Entrepreneurship Theory and Practice* 25(4): 27–39.

Hjorth, D., Jones, C. and Gartner, W.B. (2008) 'Introduction for "recreating/recontextualising entrepreneurship"', *Scandinavian Journal of Management* 24(2): 81–84.

Low, M.B. and MacMillan, I.C. (1988) 'Entrepreneurship: Past research and future challenges', *Journal of Management* 35: 139–161.

Shane, S. and Venkataraman, S. (2000) 'The promise of entrepreneurship as a field of research', *The Academy of Management Review* 25(1): 217–226.

Steyaert, C. (2007) '"Entrepreneuring" as a conceptual attractor? A review of process theories in 20 years of entrepreneurship studies', *Entrepreneurship and Regional Development* 19(6): 453–477.

Welter, F. and Lasch, F. (2008) 'Entrepreneurship research in Europe: Taking stock and looking forward', *Entrepreneurship Theory and Practice* 32(2): 241–246.

Part II

Inside Enterprise

Part I sought to set out the store of enterprise studies. As should now be apparent it is something of an out-of-town shopping mall in its breadth and scope. You should be confident now about the sort of intellectual tools and resources that are required to understand enterprise, entrepreneurship and small business. We have defined the territory and established the boundaries. You have a map. And, whilst the differences between entrepreneurship and small business are substantial, a broad approach which recognises that their combination under the notion of enterprise is extremely useful as it allows for the inclusion of modes of thought and domains of activity that tell us more about its contemporary extent and importance. Researchers may have good analytical and methodological reasons for quarantining aspects of enterprise, but for a textbook this is unnecessary and likely to lead to an overly narrow view.

The six chapters of Part II are very much the core of our book and look at the 'inside' of enterprise. What does this mean? My use of the word 'inside' is actually a little disingenuous in that we do not studiously avoid discussing the various historical, social and economic factors which lie outside enterprise. Chapter 3 in particular has little to do with the goings on of actual firms, or indeed the every-day practice of entrepreneurs. That said the main objects of interest are the 'entities' that make up the enterprising environment as understood by economists. Part III explicitly focuses on the 'outside' contexts in which enterprise takes place. In truth the world is not so easy to split up in this way and there will be many overlaps.

Over the next six chapters we look at how people have explained the existence of firms and new venture creation, particularly from an economic perspective (Chapter 3); Chapter 4 focuses on how we account for the behaviours of people that create them; we describe and analyse the way that people – entrepreneurs and owner-managers – manage enterprising entities (Chapter 5); we see what the consequences of these management practices are for the people working in them (Chapter 6); in Chapter 7 we look at the world of corporate entrepreneurship; and finally we reflect on the specific financial, marketing and networking practices and knowledge needed to survive and prosper, and how firms grow and strategies (Chapter 8).

3

Entrepreneuring: Firms, Organisations and the Entrepreneur

Overview

This chapter has the following objectives:

- To introduce and explain the contribution classical, neo-classical and contemporary economics has made to understanding entrepreneurship and enterprise.
- To introduce and explain contemporary entrepreneurship process theorists influenced by economics and explain their powerful influence.
- To understand and critique the underlying assumptions of the economic world view.

Introduction

For a chapter that is aimed at what might appear as quite simple entities – the firm and the entrepreneur – what comes below may seem like unremittingly hard work. Blame the economists! Unsurprisingly given their key place in the world there has been a lot of thinking and writing about the firm and the entrepreneur. There is also no doubt that historically economics has dominated the study of enterprise. Both the firm and the entrepreneur are chiefly economic actors, but the chapter addresses economics with a broader concern for social science and business studies. Remember that one of the basic principles underlying this book is that the firm and the individual – entrepreneur or owner-manager – are not solely economic, but also social and moral actors. But the influence of economics is profound and it is important to have a good grounding.

Most texts fudge the economic origins of ideas with enterprise. Homage is paid to the economic classics to help legitimise their texts by reference to the original **canonical** sources, but they rarely get to grips with what it really means to current thinking. The basic ideas of long dead and mostly irrelevant economic theorists are trotted out without any real reference to the historical context of their ideas. As a consequence it is often difficult to present and understand the reasons underlying the different theories explaining enterprise today. Entrepreneurship and small business studies as academic disciplines are often depicted as the young, unruly and

Canonical is derived from the word 'canon' which in this case refers to an established widely accepted or dominant body of knowledge.

immature baby brothers of economics, but as we shall see in recent years there has been a growing sophistication in the development of theories specifically aimed at explaining the behaviour of entrepreneurs and the new organisations they help create. This can be explained by the growth of interest in enterprise by those disciplines more interested in a pragmatic and engaged level of theorising, a re-examination of the classic fundamental economic foundations on the part of enterprise scholars, and developments in economic theory itself which has seen the firm and the entrepreneur re-examined. This chapter will explore all these developments.

Thus, in the first section we develop a potted history of economic thought about both the firm and the entrepreneur. It is important that their thinking is seen in the context of what economists were and remain interested in. They have only quite specific interests in the firm and entrepreneur and these are not necessarily the same as those of enterprise studies. This section addresses the contribution of economic thinking, and assesses their contemporary relevance for entrepreneurship and small business studies today. Next we continue this history but shift away from mainstream neo-classical economics to look at more recent economic theories of organisations and entrepreneurship, which have emerged partly as a result of frustrations with mainstream economics, and partly as a desire by economists to colonise the other social sciences. We then leave economics proper behind us, and steer the discussion towards more process-based views of the enterprising organisation and individual prevalent in contemporary enterprise and entrepreneurship studies.

Classical and neo-classical approaches to the firm and the entrepreneur

Rationality is the quality of behaving in ways consistent with or based on logic and reason.

Back in the Enlightenment – a period of eighteenth-century European history where reason, **rationalism** and science began to shake off the fetters of religious and secular superstitious thinking, and move beyond the scientific and pseudo-scientific knowledge of the ancients – a variety of what were called philosophers began to think about how markets, exchange and value were becoming more complex and important. They were interested in broad aspects of the economy and included the law, politics, moral philosophy and much else besides in their writing. The economy of this period was growing strongly, and began its long epochal shift away from the land towards the factory and beyond, a process that is still taking place today. Farming and industry both became more efficient in producing more things and greater profits. This was achieved through greater use of clock time to better organise production and labour resources and also greater use of mechanised technical innovations, both of which reduced the skill and costs of labour inputs. Trade was increasingly globalised (the slave trade and the commodities it produced were key components of this new economy), and new products, such as sugar, tea and tobacco were finding mass markets. Huge profits were being made: many European stately homes, villas and châteaus were built at this time. Farmers, merchants and traders were turning into capitalists and entrepreneurs. Instead of people simply buying and selling, entrepreneurs were building factories, investing capital, and setting up industries. The

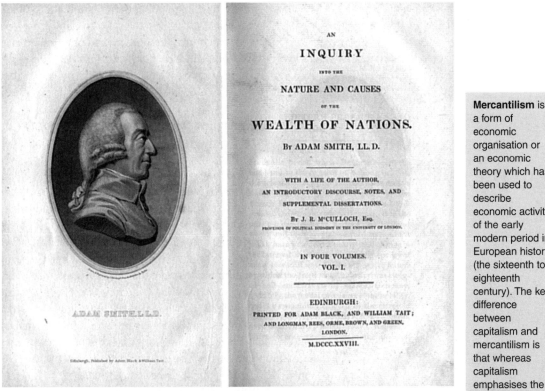

Figure 3.1   Frontispiece of *An Inquiry into the Nature and Causes of the Wealth of Nations*

Etching created from enamel paste medallion by James Tassie (1787)

social stigma against elites making money from mere commerce was abating. **Mercantilism** was becoming capitalism. But with growth came new problems about how to organise, about how to explain what was happening, and about what, if anything, to do to keep it happening. These problems were discussed, debated and solved by the *classical* school of economics.

Perhaps the most famous of these philosophers is Adam Smith, who published *An Inquiry into the Nature and Causes of the Wealth of Nations* in 1776 (Figure 3.1). He argued that the new capitalist economy was a virtuous system of trade, where if people were left to pursue their own interests the 'invisable hand' of the market would produce a healthy and balanced economy and a good and prosperous society. Smith did not mean that greed was morally good, but that the processes of demand, supply and price formation would find an equilibrium – because things in nature always found a balance – in free markets and thereby as if by magic do good for the wealth of nations. The economic system did not require people to do good things, just to engage in free commerce. He was also one of the first to describe the efficiency benefits to be derived from the division of labour: the process of increased specialisation which meant that any given work task could be achieved quicker and with less inherent skill, and at less cost. With these and other deliberations Smith founded

Mercantilism is a form of economic organisation or an economic theory which has been used to describe economic activity of the early modern period in European history (the sixteenth to eighteenth century). The key difference between capitalism and mercantilism is that whereas capitalism emphasises the freedom and expansiveness of markets, mercantilism focuses on the benefits of trading to the nation and building up a large reserve of gold. A nation's economy should be based on strong exports and restricted imports. The theory was based on the assumption that the economy is a finite resource that the nation seeks to maximise if it wants to prosper.

modern economics. His ideas about human nature and economics still form the basis of the world economy today.

There were many others who followed, extending, disagreeing and opening up new areas of economic thinking, some emphasising the role of the entrepreneur as a recipient of profit as an income for their distinctive contribution. For our purposes we need not elaborate further here. We can fast-forward to the beginnings of the modern economy, where the association of entrepreneurial endeavour, ownership and organisational form began to become more complex. Whereas the role of the entrepreneur/manager/capitalist in Smith's era was normally combined in one individual, increasing growth, complexity and specialisation in the economy meant the specific role of the entrepreneur and the nature of the firm began to provoke more debate. And this was not only because of changes to the structure of capitalism brought about by the birth and growth of large global corporations and capital investment markets (in Chapter 7 we look at this history in more detail). Along with globalisation, increasing economic prosperity, population growth and urbanisation of the nineteenth century, the amount and diversity of what constituted science was also expanding. Whereas in Adam Smith's day it was at least vaguely feasible that a scholar might have a passing acquaintance with *all* scientific knowledge, in the late nineteenth century this was no longer possible.

Adam Smith

Epistemology refers to the theory of knowledge, 'or the theory of how it is that people come to have knowledge of the external world' (Abercrombie et al. 2000: 120). Different research methodologies or approaches (say interviewing vs. questionnaires) are based on different epistemologies, different understandings of what counts as valid and useful knowledge.

Academic disciplines grew large and schisms broke out everywhere over fundamental issues about **epistemology** or what counts as knowledge. Some felt that all natural and human behaviour – both gravity and Smith's 'invisible hand' – was subject to universal laws. Others, such as the Austrian School who saw history and actual human action as vital to understanding economic behaviour, felt that in the human and social sciences laws didn't exist and reality was contingent on historical and situational factors. Neo-classical 'mainstream' economists by and large agreed with the former and began erecting intellectual and institutional barriers in order to set about the business of 'finding' or establishing these laws. Neo-classical economics was like physics, or at least it tried to be. As Keynes, a great economist of the early twentieth-century observed, the economist 'must contemplate the particular in terms of the general, and touch abstract and concrete in the same flight of thought' (cited in Heilbronner 1961: 250). Better to have abstract, limited, but indubitably true knowledge, than the essentially subjective, particular and contingent. Those writers and thinkers who believed that economic matters could only be properly explained by describing the human actions of the historical situation continued but did their work on the margins of economics proper, or, in the case of some of the economic greats, separated their work out into texts for the general reader and mathematics for the mainstream economic specialist.

What then do neo-classical economists think about the firm and the entrepreneur? Strangely enough economists are not really interested in the business firm or individuals as such. Economists are interested in the way whole economic systems function. To achieve their insights they will make certain assumptions. Chief among these is that individuals in pursuing their self-interests make rational choices and engage in self-optimising behaviour in relation to their economic activity. This behaviour is good for all of us because in pursuing our self-interest equilibrium is achieved. All business activity – the 'firm' is shorthand for this – is similarly treated as an abstract single point acting rationally in pursuit of wealth optimisation. Economic knowledge is based on these assumptions, which simplifies the everyday complexities of actual people and organisations. Systemic issues about how prices are arrived at in markets are well dealt with by traditional economic reasoning, as are many other questions relating to the way whole economies behave. As Sidney Winter has put it, 'If your purpose is to understand the main system-level regularities, which are in any case are substantially obscured by their complexity and by random noise, you need not and should not invest in precision at the actor levels' (2003: 13). To answer the big questions you need to simplify the world, and in this way economists add much. When it comes to the behaviours of complex or even simple organisations and the decision-making processes that take place within them, it is less successful. This is important to the study of small firms and entrepreneurship. Whilst one might be able to determine between entrepreneurial and non-entrepreneurial firms via systemic economic analysis (how they perform in the market), it is a different matter to understand the behaviour that produces these differences. As Ricketts has suggested, 'the emphasis [of neo-classical economics] on the final state rather than the process of getting there inevitably diverts attention from the distinctive contribution of the entrepreneur' (2002: 54–55). For this we have to look inside the firm which we shall do in more detail in the next sections.

Schumpeter

Nevertheless there have been many economists who have written about the entrepreneur, and we consider the contributions of economists Joseph Schumpeter, Frank Knight, and Israel Kirzner. You should bear in mind that each of these men has written many books and articles and to reduce their writing to a few paragraphs cannot but simplify their contribution. Remember too that their original objective was to explain the behaviour of the economic system at a particular time in history. Their inclusion here is because they happened to expound a theory of economics which had the entrepreneur as an important component, one that continues to influence entrepreneurship theory today.

Perhaps the most famous is Joseph *Schumpeter* (1883–1950; Figure 3.2). Schumpeter's work was notably interested in the broad sweep of history, sociology and the economy, and he wrote in the Austrian School tradition emphasising the historical and situated context. Specifically Schumpeter disagreed with the virtuous and altruistic equilibrium thesis. Rather he argued that economic systems tended towards disequilibrium. In order to avoid the fate of a stagnating economy constant innovations are required, and it is entrepreneurs that provide them (we will revisit his theory relating to innovations in more detail in Chapter 9). Like Karl Marx (1818–1883) – a nineteenth-century economist whose name and ideas were being

Figure 3.2   Joseph Schumpeter

Harvard University Archives, call # HUGBS 276.90 p (3)

used, when Schumpeter was in his prime, to set up an alternative social and economic system which threatened the dominance of capitalism (i.e. Soviet Russian and international communism) – Schumpeter felt that capitalism had an inbuilt tendency to depression and stagnation, and eventual demise. Unlike Marx however he felt capitalism was worth saving. It was only the dynamism of capitalism and the acts of entrepreneurs in breaking down the old failing routine ways of doing things that gave new life to the system. He described this process as *creative destruction*.

What a great way to think about entrepreneurship! Of course that is what entrepreneurs do: they create new ways of doing things in starting innovative businesses, which bring them rewards in the form of profits from the brief monopolies they create in these new markets. They kill off all the old dinosaurs, destroying old and moribund industries. Notwithstanding his broad contribution to economics, what is important to us about Schumpeter – and he has been and is still vigorously debated by enterprise scholars (Goss 2005) – is the vivid language that he has given us. Schumpeter's entrepreneur really is a true hero. Listen to this:

> There is the dream and the will to found a private kingdom, usually, though not necessarily, also a dynasty. The modern world really does not know any such positions, but what may be attained by industrial or commercial success is still the nearest approach to medieval lordship possible to modern man. Its fascination is specially strong for people who have no other chance of achieving social distinction. [...] Then there is the will to conquer: the impulse to fight, to prove oneself superior to others, to succeed for the sake, not the fruits of success, but of success itself[:] economic action becomes akin to sport [.] [...] there is the joy of creating, of getting things done, or simply of exercising one's energy and ingenuity. [...] Our type seeks out difficulties, changes in order to change, delights in ventures. (1934 [originally published in German in 1911]: 93)

No one before or since has quite captured this commonsense feel of the entrepreneur. His description tallies with our sense of the extraordinary people we hear about. Indeed it is arguable that Schumpeter has provided us with an **ideal typical** language to be able to do this, something that likely explains his enduring popularity. But even Schumpeter became aware of the idealised nature of his entrepreneur and later modified his ideas. The industrial world in 1911 was dominated by individual oligarchs who had in the late nineteenth and early twentieth century created new industries and transformed old ones. After leaving Germany to move to the US in the 1930s, Schumpeter revised his view of the entrepreneur and recognised that dynamic corporations, not just individuals, could create whilst destroying, reflecting the increasing ability of large business to institutionalise its fight against routine and stagnation through an investment in innovation. Discussion and criticism of his ideas continue today and form the basis of a major tension in the enterprise field: the degree to which the extraordinary-ness should define what entrepreneurship is. Should you really need to form or transform whole industries in order to qualify as an entrepreneur? Clearly there is much that does not transform whole industries or economic systems that today we would describe as entrepreneurial. And, though there are some that promote a narrow extraordinary view, most enterprise scholars will increasingly take a broad, inclusive and mundane view of the entrepreneurial process.

Ideal typical – an ideal type is a description of something that whilst it is unlikely that the exact example will ever actually be found anywhere, includes all the characteristics one might expect to find associated with the thing in question. 'Ideal types are hypothetical constructions, formed from real phenomena, which have explanatory value. "Ideal" signifies "pure" or "abstract" rather than normatively desirable' (Abercrombie et al. 2000: 170).

Knight

Two other mainstream economists have had a significant impact on contemporary enterprise studies. A contemporary of Schumpeter, Frank *Knight* (1885–1972) worked within the neo-classical school and is important today because of the continuing relevance of uncertainty and deficits in information about the future. He highlighted the distinction between risk which can be known, and uncertainty which is unknowable. For Knight the entrepreneur accrues rewards in the form of profits because she is able to make a judgement and decide on a course of action in the face of uncertainty. This emphasis on the ability to make judgements stresses a view of the entrepreneur which highlights the creative abilities of those engaged in entrepreneurship. A problem or perhaps an advantage with this, and one that arises in many theories relating to the entrepreneur, is that capitalist investors and managers also do this. Investors bear risk, and managers make judgements; are they then both entrepreneurs? This emphasis of the active judgement in creating opportunities implicitly recognises the possibility that entrepreneurship is a process that many can engage in. Notwithstanding the mundane implications of Knight's entrepreneur, in other ways his ideas are similar to Schumpeter's. They both straddled the fundamental methodological and theoretical divisions that beset economics in the first half of the twentieth century and were against the over-simplification inherent to mathematical modelling, chose to take an eclectic 'middle way', and were intimately concerned with the ethical and moral consequences of capitalism. And, as with Schumpeter, enterprise scholars continue to acknowledge the distinction between risk and uncertainty.

A more contemporary economist Israel *Kirzner* (1930–) is useful because he showed that one of the major tenets of neo-classical economics was unrealistic. In order that people can act rationally there is an implicit assumption that perfect (full and correct) knowledge is available, and that this will lead to the best possible decisions about what to purchase and about what is made, and will thereby lead to perfect competition: equilibrium. This sounds a little too neat and tidy to me, and there would be few economists who believe this describes actual human behaviour. What it does do for economists is give them a mechanism for understanding how markets and exchange work in theory, and anyhow economists have also developed many other ideas – Kirzner's is one of them – whereby the lack of and search for knowledge and information can be 'costed'. What Kirzner realised was that the differential alertness to the opportunities provided by possessing certain knowledge and information was something that marked out entrepreneurs as special actors in the economy. As Ricketts has written: 'an entrepreneur is any person who is "alert" to hitherto unexploited possibilities for exchange' (2002: 59). What the entrepreneur does – because she is alert – is discover the opportunities for making money that are just sitting there in the knowledge and information that is all around us. In contrast to Knight and Schumpeter, Kirzner's entrepreneur is relatively passive: 'I view the entrepreneur not as a source of innovative ideas *ex nihilo* [out of nothing], but as being alert to the opportunities that exist already and are waiting to be noticed' (Kirzner 1973: 74). This doesn't sound very heroic, but it does reflect the economic functionality of the entrepreneur in establishing equilibrium. This leads us on to a key point.

I have been at pains to stress throughout that Schumpeter, Knight and Kirzner, and other economists as well have all developed their theories for economists and held different objectives relating to major technical and theoretical problems in economics: Schumpeter was interested in the business cycles of capitalism and the role innovation plays in this process; Knight focused on interest and profit, and how profit was a reward for the bearers of uncertainty (entrepreneurs); and Kirzner was interested in the convergence toward equilibrium (Foss et al. 2007; Swedberg 2000: 21). How they arrived at creative destruction, judgement in the face of uncertainty and alertness to discovering opportunity is a product of economic theory and not a serious investigation of entrepreneurial processes by empirical research. That they remain powerful ideas is testament both to the power of economics as a discipline and the inherent intuitive qualities of the ideas, even if there are good arguments for their having occasionally been taken out of context in enterprise studies.

This then has also been a cruelly partial view of economics. The view hopefully just about stands – like the wooden block tower in a Jenga game moments before it falls – but there is much that is missing. However, as this is not a text in political economy or economics, we are less interested in the economist's objective of finding or establishing universal laws of behaviour in terms of economic systems, markets and human behaviour in respect of value, exchange and price.

Contemporary economic theories
of organisations and entrepreneurship

Following the Second World War (1939–1945) and the growing need for knowledge about how best to run and explain the behaviour of large organisations, the students of the great economists set about becoming great economists themselves and developed economic theories that could meet the need for more realism whilst not giving up entirely on economics as a paradigm. Although not entrepreneurship theories in themselves two ideas continue to have a significant influence on current thinking: neo-institutional economics (NIE) and evolutionary economics.

Neo-institutional economics (NIE)

In order to exchange something some time and effort is required to make the transaction. This might be the time taken to get information, the time lost when you could be doing something else, the time and effort involved in actually making the exchange, and so on. According to neo-institutional theory, 'institutions' are formed in order to reduce the costs of these transactions by the application of rules, routines and other controls. The 'institution' here is not synonymous with 'organisation' or firms: they might be both the UK legal system and the 'market' or the Law Society and the London Stock Exchange. Instead of the notional 'single production functions' of neo-classical economics NIE suggests it is the transaction that is the base unit of analysis from which all economic organisation functions (Rowlinson 1997: 24). NIE thus represents an attempt to introduce informal social norms and formal legal rules into economic thinking: the sort of norms and rules that economic institutions rely on to function.

The notion of transactions emerged when economists – such as Oliver Williamson (1986) – started asking tricky questions about the real nature of the firm and realised that organisations needed to be taken seriously as economic actors. Some of these economists asked why some transactions took place within organisations (in organisational 'hierarchies') and some between them (in 'markets'). At root the question relates to an assumption about markets as tending towards equilibrium: that is, at some point the cost of transacting within the firm will cost more than the same transaction in the marketplace.

In addition to the notion of the transaction, the key difference from neo-classical economics is in the way that rationality is 'bounded' rather than notionally absolute. Clearly individuals cannot know all the information that would likely have a bearing on their decision about a particular transaction. Furthermore – economists being surer about these things than most of us – Williamson felt that human nature was prone to what he called 'opportunism': the tendency not just towards a self-interest, but 'to incomplete or distorted disclosure of information, especially to calculated efforts to mislead, distort, disguise, obfuscate, or otherwise confuse' (Williamson 1986: 26 cited in Rowlinson 1997: 26). Williamson argued that organisations attempted to reduce the costs of making transactions, but there was always a danger that some individuals in a firm might see opportunities to advance their own self-interest and thus reduce the cost-saving to the firm. An important employee might for instance pass on important information to a competitor in the hope of securing better employment. Or they might set up their own entrepreneurial venture and take expert employees and clients with them.

Transaction cost savings are achieved by monitoring or governing the behaviour of employees within the firm such that they share the same objectives as the firm owners, and thus are steered away from the 'opportunistic, hidden pursuit of separate interests [...] at the expense of the firm' (Witt 1999: 107). This monitoring or governing activity is also affected by certain environmental factors such as uncertainty caused by unforeseen events and human behaviour. As we saw when we discussed Knight above, dealing successfully with uncertainty is one of the attributes of entrepreneurial behaviour, but in other ways, as Witt has written 'the transaction cost approach [NIE] disregards the role of the entrepreneurial imagination in setting up the firm' (1999: 100). How so? NIE under-emphasises the agency involved in 'imagining' the business and its future: the organisation in other words is not just an opportunity controlling, efficiency maximising mechanism. As Rowlinson notes, transaction costs theory doesn't adequately 'take account of the importance of actors' competing pictures of the future, their "subjective models"' (2001: 4).

The problems inherent to NIE haven't stopped the likes of Witt and others from attempting to apply it to other aspects of economic theory (in his case evolutionary economics, 1999) in addressing the question of entrepreneurship. What Witt doesn't make explicit is that the entrepreneurial imagination itself is potentially an aspect of opportunism that needs to be controlled. As in the example above, there are many firms where the wellsprings of entrepreneurialism will emerge from the opportunistic behaviour of employees. My own research has shown how nascent entrepreneurs can emerge from the frustrations and opportunism of 'young gun' entrepreneurial employees who ultimately and opportunistically break free from their 'old fart' employers and start their own firm (Down and Reveley 2004).

Neo-institutional economics is currently a very active field with each prominent economist interested in the entrepreneur vying for his or her particular combination of economic thinking. Inevitably critics of NIE point to the difficulty in actually identifying 'the transaction': what is it exactly? More broadly the problem with Williamson's approach is that the notion of markets and hierarchies is very black and white. Economic decisions are not simply made in markets or hierarchies (Rowlinson 1997): the choices that people and organisations make and the coordinating mechanisms constraining and enabling these activities are extremely diverse and nuanced. Notwithstanding this criticism, neo-institutional economics has been very successful and can be seen as part of the growth and expansion of economic thinking: it is an attempt to expand the methods (i.e. the quantification) and underlying philosophy (the rationality and so on) of economics to encompass broader social, legal, and historical topics.

As with much of social science, economics has been deeply influenced by Charles Darwin's theory of evolution: or rather the extension of his ideas into social science (Sewell 2004: 947). The notion of the economy as a brutal struggle for survival certainly underpins Schumpeter's notion of creative destruction: the entrepreneur is a survivor and a force for change. Evolutionary theory explains the development of *organisms*, and economists and other social scientists use this idea and apply it to populations of organisations or firms, the people that act within them and the environment, as if they too exist in a large organic system. By contrast neo-classical economics has at its root a mechanistic system metaphor; it seeks to discover fundamental laws of nature much like physics and then predict what will happen in the future.

Nelson and Winter are normally associated with the formation of evolutionary economics. They argued that the market selects the best behaviours of economic actors – in the form of standardised activity patterns or routines, which if successful would be imitated, and would lead to struggles amongst those that shared the same routines – and rewards those behaviours with survival. Their (1982) theory differs from neo-classical norms in that neither the notion of firm and individual maximisation nor rationality is accepted. Rational behaviour in their model is bounded by the routines of organisations and maximisation is a product of the struggle for organisational survival, not an inherent motivation.

Following these economic foundations, entrepreneurship and sociology scholar Howard Aldrich (1979; Aldrich and Ruef 2006) applied evolutionary theory to the emergence of organisations, arguing that they evolve like organisms fighting for survival in a process of natural selection. Aldrich developed an organisational model whereby the four components – variation, selection, retention and struggle – of natural selection describe the process for why some organisations succeed and others don't. An infinite variety of behaviours are likely to take place in organisations: some of these will be chosen as useful to the organisation, and some will then be retained and used as part of the routines by which organisations struggle over scarce resources, compete and make alliances in order to become the fittest and survive. Thus, in terms of entrepreneurship – which for many, whether it is evolutionary or not, is at root the process of organisational emergence (Curran and Burrows 1986: 269; Gartner 1985) – the approach is a way of taking the emphasis away from the entrepreneur as an individual and concentrating on processes and environmental context (Aldrich and Argelia Martinez 2001). Aldrich has also rightly criticised entrepreneurship researchers for being overly fixated on the successful cases of entrepreneurship, which, as is well known, is very much the rarity as far and away most new organisations fail. Aldrich uses the evolutionary approach to highlight the importance of the 'entrepreneurial cycle' – conception, gestation, infancy and adolescence – as a vehicle for ensuring a view of all entrepreneurial activity over time.

Evolutionary approaches to economics and organisation do however attract a good deal of criticism (Sewell 2004). These focus on the exact relationship between the use of evolutionary ideas of natural selection, and the life cycle and behaviour of organisms. Is the idea used for real or as a *metaphor*? Do entrepreneurial organisations actually function like organisms, or is there something quite different between the biological and the socio-economic? Are the infinite historical and situational possibilities for variation and selection within organisations really comparable to the relatively rule-bound nature of biological reproduction? Dynamic evolutionary theories of entrepreneurial change tend to downplay the role of intentional strategic action, the everyday purposive human activity that is the life and soul of why economic activity actually takes place (Rowlinson 1997: 65–69; Schumpeter's own use of the evolutionary analogy was fairly loose: one can't accuse him of under-emphasising the influence of individuals!). As Rowlinson has it, 'although evolutionary theory has predicted the mechanisms of change, it cannot predict the outcome of change itself' (1997: 80). In other words entrepreneurs don't do what they do so that their firms can survive in an evolutionary battle, or to maintain the functionality of the capitalist engine. They do it to make money, because of the will to conquer, to change society, to prove their worth to their fathers, and a whole host of other reasons.

Ultimately evolutionary approaches to economics and economic organisation have introduced a metaphor for thinking better about issues of change, emergence, and process, which is clearly an advance on the fixation with the hero entrepreneur. Given the complexity and ambiguities of social and organisational behaviour, perhaps it does not matter that the use of biological analogies may be wrong so long as the analytical tools aid understanding (that is, conduct research which can lead to useful practical outcomes). What Aldrich has definitely achieved in his application of evolutionary theory is to have made ideas about process, history and context palatable and understandable to orthodox economists. Whereas more thorough-going social constructionist/interpretivist arguments are beyond the pale to economists, Aldrich's approach is fairly normative in the sense that it is in part derived from an economic perspective (e.g. Nelson and Winter 1982), and that he sees entrepreneurship as a fully scientific endeavour where a full integrated academic field is achievable. As we saw in Chapter 2 there are those that seek order and certainty and want their social science to be as much like the natural sciences as possible, and others who don't and see it as more about descriptive and pragmatic commentary and analysis, eschewing general theories because they deny a fundamental pluralism in social matters.

We confront these opposing world-scientific views again in the next chapter, when we look at explanations of entrepreneurial behaviour in individuals. Neo-institutional and evolutionary theory have both undermined some of the foundations of neo-classical economics by bringing the historical and situated squarely back into economic analysis. With these two ideas we can at least begin to look exclusively at entrepreneurship, something that economics had struggled to do both theoretically and empirically. Both approaches continue to influence a wide range of social-scientific research including entrepreneurship, and it is very much the case that they have acted as a bridge to the formation of the two dominant general economic theories in entrepreneurship today, which we look at now.

Economic process theories of entrepreneurship

We first discussed process theories of entrepreneurship in Chapter 2. The process theories we discuss below derive from predominantly economic thinking, and have emerged from an attempt to reform some of the more unsustainable tenets of neo-classical theory. But before getting to grips with the work of Mark Casson and Scott Shane should we ask again what we mean by process?

What this means is that the activity and behaviour of people involved in enterprise should be seen as the ongoing, dynamic and continuous activity that exists within situated historical, social, economic, political and moral contexts. This means that entrepreneurship becomes a more realistic, connected and integrated process that sits within an environment rather than something that notional and abstract individuals do as the function of an economic system. The rise of process views of many topics has reflected a tug of war in the social sciences more generally between those that cede too much emphasis on the individual (agency) or the environment (structure) in isolation. It is obvious that what's needed are explanations of what happens between these poles, as well as descriptions and ideas about what happens at them. There are still arguments regarding the extent to which processes can be generalised, or whether all that can be done is to build up complex and rich pictures of processes by looking at the particular, but the majority of enterprise scholars would accept the need to look at processes, even if they disagree about what they are. For those scholars like Casson and Shane, influenced by the economic thinking described above, there is a tendency to search for an objective and general theory which can describe the processes of entrepreneurship wherever they are found. Let's see what they have to offer.

Casson's judgement model

Mark Casson has applied and synthesised economic and managerial theories of the firm and placed the entrepreneur in a pivotal position of coordinating resources and establishing organisations that identify and monitor new information relevant to exploiting market-making entrepreneurial opportunity (2005: 332, 335). He believes, following Knight, that entrepreneurship is '"judgemental decision making" about the coordination of scare resources under conditions of uncertainty' (Cassis and Pepelasis Minoglou 2005: 4). Entrepreneurs are special because they have different access to, and/or interpretations of, information which leads them to be able to make profit-making judgements. He takes the ideas of Schumpeter, Knight and Kirzner and combines them to create a theory which allows us to predict under what circumstances, both personal and environmental, entrepreneurial resources will be in demand or what will enhance or stifle their supply: he is interested in 'a theory of the aggregate behaviour of a population of entrepreneurs' (Ricketts 2002: 73). His market for entrepreneurs model suggests that the environment for entrepreneurial opportunities is dependent on the dynamism of the economy (the pace of change in the economy), and that each change in the circumstances of the economy will create further opportunities. However, this dynamism is negatively affected by the numbers of entrepreneurs that enter the chase, and the reward for these entrepreneurs declines because of the competition for profit-making opportunities. The supply of qualified entrepreneurs who are able to do something about their opportunity recognition due to their access to investment resources, will increase insofar as the expected reward from entrepreneurship exceeds the expected reward from being an employee (i.e. wages). Casson's objective is to be able to measure the demand and supply of entrepreneurs to ascertain the ideal – or equilibrium – situation for a thriving entrepreneurial economy (Figure 3.3).

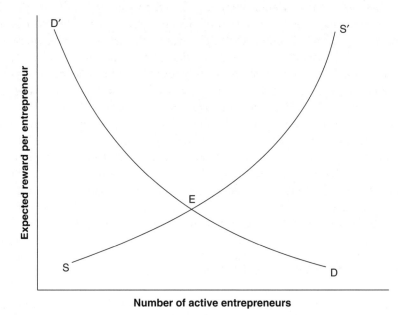

Figure 3.3 A simplified model for a market for entrepreneurs (adapted from, and with apologies to, Casson 1991: 196)

The problems with his ideas are familiar to all economic models. Can all the different factors influencing the reward given to good judgements or the supply of entrepreneurs (e.g. education, ideology, social attitudes, government policy, and so on) really be usefully measured? Can one really measure the 'pace of change' in the economy? Casson also assumes that entrepreneurs are able to work out their expected reward in relation to the changing nature of the economy: like Schumpeter's hero, perhaps too much is expected of the *individual* entrepreneur. Casson's vision of the entrepreneur, though ostensibly very broad because it is 'anyone who specialises in taking judgemental decisions' (2005: 339), in practice favours a grander, more corporate, more qualified 'true' entrepreneur, who is as likely to operate in a corporate environment as an SME. In my view Gartner's (1985) new venture creation model of entrepreneurship goes further in combining both the methodological pluralism (insights from economic, sociology, psychology, and so on) and the complexity and variety of the process. Moreover, the broader salience of the mobilisation of enterprise and entrepreneurial ideology in society and for individuals is lost in this *economic* analysis. For this we need to turn to sociological and psychological explanations, the topics of the next chapter. However, with Casson we do enter the entrepreneurship discipline proper, and his process-based analysis is rightly very popular because it combines an economic model which can say useful things about the systemic role of populations of entrepreneurs, with managerial ideas of how entrepreneurs actually behave. Our final section looks at another view about the process of entrepreneurship that has been strongly influenced by economic thinking.

Shane's opportunities

Scott Shane offers us *A General Theory of Entrepreneurship*, the rather grand title of his 2003 book. Shane is widely regarded as having made important advances, placing entrepreneurial *opportunity* at the centre of the study of entrepreneurship. Whereas Schumpeter ascribed opportunities to the ability of entrepreneurs to create them, Shane supports the view of Kirzner and argues that opportunities are *discovered* by individuals: he believes in the objective existence of entrepreneurial opportunities. Shane emphasises the interaction of the individual and the opportunity, and his ideas complement and extend Casson's by focusing on the cognitive aspect of entrepreneurship and opportunity recognition (we look at cognition in more detail in the next chapter). As Davidsson (2004: 208) suggests, Shane is important because 'his fresh perspective on entrepreneurship emphasises the *interacting* explanations for the *processes* of emergence of new and [(…)] *innovative* economic activity regardless of organisational or ownership context'. Shane has successfully convinced many scholars that it is 'the process of opportunity discovery [that is] distinctive or unique to entrepreneurship' (Fletcher 2006: 424). However, Davidsson (2004) feels that he has used research evidence which is incompatible with his argument. This is echoed in Casson's own assessment: 'Despite various protestations to the contrary, he relies heavily on economic logic in developing his argument' (2005: 429). Davidsson (2003) also suggests that despite opportunities having become a central concept in entrepreneurship there is a continuing fuzziness about what they are. It is as if we have shifted from one catch-all term, entrepreneurship, to another that sounds less emotive and more scientific without actually gaining any greater insight. In the light of this criticism Casson, as a key player in the synthesis of the new economic orthodoxy about entrepreneurship, rather pats himself on the back by claiming that Shane's 'book demonstrates not only the success of the theory of entrepreneurship, but the success of a theory grounded in fundamental economic principles' (2005: 428–430). A case of economics rules, OK.

There are more fundamental critiques of Shane and Casson's adherence to mainstream economics. We have already seen in Chapter 2 Jones and Wadhwani's criticism that the level of abstraction required means that their theories 'explain relatively little when they are held up against specific, grounded entrepreneurial cases' (2006b: 10). A different critique, but one similarly based on an appeal to the context in which entrepreneurship takes place, is based on a different theoretical base largely at odds with many of the central ideas of economics. Whereas contemporary economics sees opportunities as existing 'out there' waiting to be found, or in Schumpeter's case, as the product of creation and new knowledge, there are those enterprise scholars who think the economic approach generally ascribes too much to individuals and ignores the 'relationally and communally constituted' nature of life (Fletcher 2006: 421). Thus Fletcher rejects the 'structurally-determinist and cognitive agency-oriented views' of opportunity recognition: opportunities are not out there waiting to be found, nor are they exclusively located in people's heads. From the creative process paradigm (we read about this earlier in Chapter 2) people *create* opportunities together. This does not mean (as critics often claim) that the outside world doesn't exist. That would be silly. The point is that in this view economic and social life, and opportunities, are produced via the relations 'between people, institutions, material objects, physical entities and language' (2006: 422). The creative process view is very different from economics, and we will discuss it again in the next chapter. For now we will conclude by making some general observations about this chapter.

Conclusion

Taken as whole the story of the economic approach has been one of an increasing willingness to get to grips with actual human behaviour, whilst holding on to the fundamental notions of self-interest, individualism, and rationalism and a search for a general theory. We have seen that economics offers a great deal to our understanding of enterprise. Shane and Casson and others who claim to offer a general theory of entrepreneurship have essentially used ready-made models to fill what has been something of a theoretical vacuum at the heart of entrepreneurship. In the absence of prior strong theoretical formulations, it is not so surprising that enterprise scholars largely ignore the inherent problems of the economic approach. They offer certainties where others offer more questions. To achieve these certainties, assumptions and simplifications about the disputed nature of human behaviour are made. The chapter has shown how economists and enterprise scholars have tried to deal with these. But as with any social science the assumptions remain, and are worth some further consideration, particularly as our interest in enterprise is broader than economics.

As we saw in Chapter 2, for most entrepreneurship scholars who work within a broadly economic paradigm, a key purpose is to help further economic progress. If we continue with this narrow, instrumental and utilitarian view of enterprise, we might fail to see beyond the light cast by the 'streetlight of existing belief' (Winter 2003: 18) and be unable to appreciate alternative ways of seeing our topic. This is not the same as saying that economic growth is not a useful and important social and moral objective: though some would say that we are currently over-fixated on material ends and that the current obsession with high rates of economic growth – and the nature of the social, political and economic systems that support it – is too damaging to be socially, politically, environmentally or even ultimately economically sustainable. The issue is that not all aspects of our topic need have a direct impact on whether the economy and small and entrepreneurial firms perform better. And anyway, we might ask, better for whom? Owners? Consumers? Employees? Society? Is this the best of all worlds that we live in today?

In a less emotive and political sense this criticism is simply a matter of disputes about appropriate levels of analysis and boundary definitions: what exactly constitutes entrepreneurship? Economists are generally interested in the big picture, and they want a universal tool that can do all the work in explaining it. I don't really agree with this and would prefer to use a range of different, perhaps incompatible and messily arranged tools, and to look at the topic in a broader, but theoretically more eclectic and less dogmatic sense. The resulting picture might be richer and less coherent, but then so is the world. We don't all have to aspire to Casson's or Schumpeter's mythic hero and make our fortunes in the corporate world to be acting entrepreneurially: 'there can be any number of socially situated definitions of entrepreneurship' (Rehn and Taalas 2004a: 237) and being entrepreneurial is not limited to the market-economy or 'normal' business world, nor does it have to be especially exciting.

Finally there is another even deeper moral assumption with economic approaches to entrepreneurship. Is the entrepreneur a good person? Do they do good things? Do they deserve the rewards they get? We mostly assume that they are and do and economists variously ascribe a very important role and high value to the 'true' entrepreneur. We have seen that different economists see this role and its contribution to the good society and the rewards it should accrue in different ways. When economists position the entrepreneur in this way, they are not simply arguing over facts (how they see the world functioning), they are also asserting a moral value to the entrepreneur (about how the world should be if it is to be a good and prosperous society). And because powerful people listen to economists these positions about who should be valued and rewarded as a result of their contributions end up influencing and structuring the distribution of rewards we actually do receive. Thus 'economics does not simply describe the reality of value-production but is actively implicated in the act of sharing out the value that is rewarded to each actor' (Jones and Spicer 2005: 191). We might structure society – its laws, its hierarchies, its rewards and so on – in many different ways, emphasising people who *own resources* (capitalists), or those that own and *supply labour* (workers), or those that make good judgements and *combine things* (entrepreneurs). Economics attempts to describe a permanent natural order relating to the value of things, and it does so by simplifying the essence of individual human behaviour into a series of laws, as if it were akin to the behaviour of atoms. It is an essentially conservative outlook on human matters which relies on there being little new under the sun. We definitely live our everyday lives with the consequence of this way of thinking. Whether it's true or the best of all worlds is for you to decide.

Summary

The chapter builds a history of economics as it relates to the entrepreneur and entrepreneurship. Overall economics is interested in the nature of economic systems and a search for generalised and unified theories more than it is in the particular behaviour of economic actors. Some branches of economics have shifted inexorably toward more realistic assumptions regarding the behaviour of individuals, including entrepreneurs and others engaged in enterprising behaviour. Contemporary entrepreneurship theorists therefore use a combination of mainstream economics, management/organisation theory and other social science concepts to explain the entrepreneurship process. Economic thinking is the dominant disciplinary influence on entrepreneurship, particularly in the normative US approach. The chapter criticises the underlying assumptions that hamper economic thinking about entrepreneurship for negating the diversity of motives and human intentions, which go beyond individual rational instrumentalism.

■ ■ Further reading ■

Casson, M. (1991) *The Entrepreneur: An Economic Theory*, Oxford: Oxford University Press.

Fletcher, D.E. (2006) 'Entrepreneurial processes and the social construction of opportunity', *Entrepreneurship and Regional Development* 18(5): 421–440.

Rowlinson, M. (1997) *Organisations and Institutions*, London: Macmillan.

Schumpeter, J.A. (1934/1911) *Theory of Economic Development: An Inquiry into Profits, Capital, Credit, Interest, and the Business Cycle*, Cambridge, MA: Harvard University Press.

Shane, S. (2003) *A General Theory of Entrepreneurship: The Individual–Opportunity Nexus*, Cheltenham: Edward Elgar.

4

Entrepreneuring: Explanations of the Entrepreneurial Self

Overview

This chapter has the following objectives:

- To understand the contribution of different psychological and sociological approaches to the entrepreneur and the entrepreneurial process.
- To describe the historical development of theories and concepts.
- To critique the focus on the individual as the most appropriate conceptual level of analysis.
- To show the limits of the personality traits and cognition approaches to understanding the entrepreneurial process, highlighting the benefits of the creative process approach.

Introduction

In the last chapter we followed the story of economics and its engagement with management, entrepreneurship and the social sciences. In this chapter we debate the contribution of psychology and sociology. The story follows a similar pattern; the development of ideas and research about entrepreneurship has slowly shifted from one focused on the psychological and sociological characteristics of specific individuals – an interest in *the* entrepreneur – to a view which emphasises many different processes which are involved in entrepreneurship, or as Chris Steyaert (2007) has put it emphasising the verb, *entrepreneuring*. Explanations of human behaviour are our focus.

We have seen that economics has a useful but rather narrow and purposefully unrealistic concept of human agency or action, and that many entrepreneurship scholars turned away from an individual focus towards more process-oriented and structural economic explanations (e.g. evolutionary economics, neo-institutionalism). Others stuck with *the* entrepreneur and turned towards psychology, which shares with economics an attachment to fixed categorical entities, in this case universal aspects of the individual such as their personality traits. They would ask the question 'who is an entrepreneur?' and see understanding entrepreneurship as synonymous with *the* entrepreneur, their behaviour and ways of thinking.

We shall see that there is a fundamental problem with this individual focus. Culturally – in the West at least – we give great status to the ability of individuals. Whilst it is obvious that '*the* entrepreneur' is a key aspect of the enterprise process, we also know that it wasn't really the pharaohs that built the pyramids or Bill Gates who built Microsoft. Entrepreneurs are necessary, but perhaps not sufficient in understanding enterprise processes. And ever since Bill Gartner (1988) suggested that '"Who is an entrepreneur?" Is the wrong question', the theoretical focus on individual entrepreneurs has generally declined. Gartner was attempting to close a chapter on an increasingly fruitless period of research in entrepreneurship that placed the personality of the entrepreneur at the centre of the discipline. He stressed two important and fundamental problems. Firstly, an individual focus closed off a great deal of what was interesting about enterprise and the contexts in which it happens. Secondly, personality theory didn't even address the issue of individual behaviour particularly well. We'll look at these problems in more depth as we work our way through this chapter, but first it is worth making a broader point about the way science works.

By 1988 personality traits theory in many areas of psychology had long been understood as a flawed theoretical approach: that it was not answering the right questions. Why do some people continue to find it useful?

When a challenge to a theory or idea is made, it doesn't necessarily mean that everyone suddenly stops using it. Academics build careers around popular theories and communities develop, with their conferences, journals, and institutes. People with different beliefs and commitments debate and dispute each other's claims about different theories. Facts are gathered, interpreted and contested. Even today in entrepreneurship a few people still do research on personality traits (Korunka et al. 2003). It takes time for advances in one field to be adopted in others.

Science often finds itself going down what become dead ends. Back in the early twentieth century scholars were convinced by eugenics. Eugenics was the science devoted to improving the human species. Though interventions such as the forced sterilisation of 'unfortunates' (the mentally 'deficient', the disabled, the criminal and 'fallen' women) were enthusiastically adopted in the UK, the US (Figure 4.1) and other Western nations to weed out the 'weak' (Burleigh and Wippermann 1991: 33), the application of such policies (supported by 'scientific' evidence) in Nazi Germany towards more explicit racial ends meant that the science was eventually discredited after the Second World War. Eugenics became a pseudo-science. At its height though, it had all the paraphernalia, pomp and circumstance of a real science: it possessed esteemed journals, prestigious professorial chairs, international institutes and conferences. Ideas used to explain phenomena are products of their time and science ultimately reflects the views and aspirations of the societies they operate within.

It was Thomas Kuhn (1962) who wrote about how science experienced paradigm shifts from time to time as a result of the accumulation of evidence which strained the credibility of the normal way of thinking about a problem.

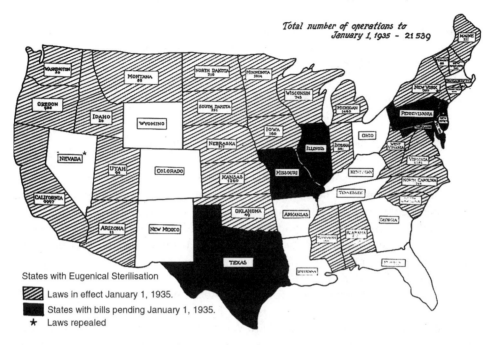

Figure 4.1   Map showing the extent of sterilisation laws and numbers of people sterilised by US states in the 1930s

Courtesy DNA Learning Center

Arguably the social sciences experience this process even more acutely as different paradigms can and do co-exist. 'Normal science' in most areas of the social sciences – where all participants agree on the basic nature of the problems of the discipline – is unlikely to occur, though particular paradigms will tend to dominate: in business and management it is economics and psychology. Hence, just as different psychologies coexist alongside each other (Harré and Gillett 1994: 2), personality research into entrepreneurship is published and coexists uneasily alongside cognitive and creative process approaches.

The next four sections show the historical development of thinking about agency and entrepreneurship. First we look at the key paradigms within psychology and social-psychology and discuss the early applications of psychology and personality traits theory in the field of entrepreneurship. With this knowledge we will be able to better assess the competing claims of the two key paradigms in entrepreneurship today: entrepreneurial cognition, and the social constructionist or 'creative process' approach (Steyaert 2007; of course as I have mentioned in Chapter 1, I am not neutral in these debates and my own work falls firmly into this latter tradition). The chapter concludes with a discussion of how more recent developments in philosophy, the science of the mind/consciousness and discursive psychology might influence entrepreneurship research in the future.

The early days of entrepreneurial psychology and personality theory

In order to understand the competing contemporary perspectives in entrepreneurship we need to get a feel for the shape of psychology itself and how it perceives individual behaviour. Note that there isn't just one psychology. It's a big field, each strand of which has influenced business and management and other social sciences in a myriad of ways.

Psychologies plural, not psychology singular

Key to understanding mainstream psychology is its general adherence to a physical or natural science model ('normal science') of seeing people and doing research. In the experimental *behaviourist* school of thought only what is observable and controllable is admissible as evidence: we can only understand the observable behaviour of organisms. Like physics or biology behavioural psychologists are interested in discerning universal laws pertaining to human (and animal) behaviour. Because of this focus on observation, the emphasis of much research has been on the stimulus–response experiment (prod a rat and see what happens), and on generating mathematical data to prove or disprove hypotheses and theories (classify and count what rats do after being prodded). What is not considered so much are the contexts in which human beings and rats exist. Nor are the subjective experiences, thoughts and views of people taken into account very much. Rats, of course, can't tell us what they feel.

Underlying this approach is an assumption of a split between the mind and the body: 'The body with its chemical, pneumatic, mechanical, and electrical mechanisms was made of physical stuff; the mind with its thoughts, feelings, recollections, and images was made of mental stuff' (Harré and Gillett 1994: 4). Behaviourism largely ignored mental stuff because you couldn't see it and then prod it.

As a result of the self-imposed limitations of behaviourism this form of psychology was eventually joined and challenged by two others. The key challenge came from *cognitive* psychology in the late 1950s. This rejected experimental behaviourism and its limiting focus on the observable, and instead emphasised mental processes. The cognitivists agreed with the behaviourists on the mind/body split, and they saw the machinery of the human mind as something universal, common to all. They overcame their lack of knowledge about mental stuff by applying indirect scientific methods of theory testing and deduction that physicists or biologists would use with matter they can't see. Whilst what happens in the subjective mind is not directly observable (though today some would infer a great many things from the new brain scanning and monitoring technologies), certain formulations, explanations or hypotheses can be seen to be more likely by careful and rigorous testing of the different possibilities. The psychologist in this paradigm becomes a detective of the mind, and the mind a rule-following *machine* that is a lot like a computer (Figure 4.2). Later we critique this approach in relation to entrepreneurial cognition.

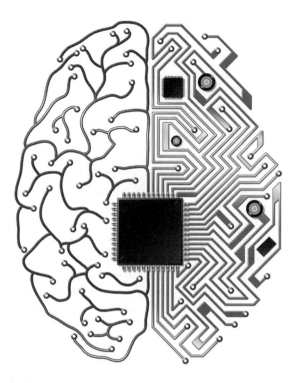

Figure 4.2   The brain as a computer

© iStockPhoto

The other important development in the 1950s was the emergence of *social-psychology*, which despite solidifying into a rather specific and narrow disciplinary focus on experimental approaches (see Shaver 2003) is also related to a range of other approaches – including the more explicitly sociological – that have emerged since and which emphasise the social dimensions of individual action. Human beings in this psychology are recognised as having **subjectivity**, and that behaviour should be seen as much as a social achievement as an individual one. In other words psychology was about the ways people *interacted* with each other in their social context: the psychology of the individual was socially constructed, part of a creative process. In this paradigm, one strand of which was popularised by the symbolic interactionism of Erving Goffman (1959), the cultural meanings held in language, body language and the use of social space became centrally important to understanding human psychology. These ideas form the basis of contemporary 'creative process' theories of entrepreneurial identity formation which we also critically discuss in the final section.

This difference between cognitivism and the more socially-oriented psychologies more or less describes the ends of two poles which typify the study of the individual in entrepreneurship today. Psychology like economics has fractured between those who see the study of human behaviour as a natural or social science, between a desire to create universal laws which enable prediction but force classification, and those who accept complexity and heterogeneity and favour description and explanation.

Subjectivity refers to the self-conscious awareness of the person or 'subject', a person's own consciousness of who and how they are, feel, and so on.

How does personality fit into all this? We all have personalities, just like we all have star signs. We are introvert or extrovert, aggressive or passive, reliable or unreliable and so on. We can also be entrepreneurial or un-entrepreneurial. Given the importance of entrepreneurship to many people, it is unsurprising that under-standing *the* entrepreneurial personality has fixated scholars for so long.

In the canon of entrepreneurship studies you will find a large goodie bag of theories old, borrowed, and stolen based on this or that personality characteristic. Common to all is an interest and commitment to a concept of psychology and the human individual concerned with fixed traits and characteristics that are held *within* people. Who we are rests on the particular combination of traits and characteristics we exhibit. In order to find out which characteristics are exhibited by entrepreneurs, and what the most important and relevant traits are for being a successful entrepreneur, you need to ask a lot of people – so you can say something sensible about the whole population – via questionnaires about their traits and characteristics. This approach is called methodological individualism or reductionism: reality is the aggregation of the universal attributes of the individuals. Complex and messy big pictures are reduced to smaller ones on the assumption that a trait or characteristic is relevant to everyone. Researchers are attempting to find out how a given population relates to the successful entrepreneur category, or vice versa, to discover what the most important or optimum collection of traits is by studying populations of actual successful 'entrepreneurs'.

Brockhaus and Horwitz (1986) summarised the contribution of a number of these approaches which have found themselves on an ever growing and changing list of entrepreneurial characteristics. This textbook makes a break with this tradition. This is because contemporary theories and concepts explaining entrepreneurial behaviour have shown a lot of these ideas to be wrong. As with the famous economists of the previous chapter, the interests of these psychologists were not always aimed at identifying the characteristics and behaviour of entrepreneurs. They had different objectives, and to an extent their ideas were misapplied by entrepreneurship scholars. To see this, it is worth looking briefly at the most famous of the psychologists who influenced this tradition in entrepreneurship, David McClelland and his (1961) book *The Achieving Society*. This will help us further understand the limitations of the overall approach, whilst at the same time recognising the contribution to knowledge and understanding that was made.

McClelland was interested in the psychological aspects of the wealth of nations. Why were capitalist nations – he was American – more successful at economic development than communist and colonially dominated ones (1961: 3)? At heart his theory sought to explain what he felt was the superiority of US and Western values, specifically individualism and economic rationality. His book was not simply an academic exercise, McClelland had ideological objectives too. America and the Western world were engaged in a not so cold Cold War with Russia and China and McClelland wanted to argue that liberal democratic capitalism was best.

His key idea, following Schumpeter, was that entrepreneurs were extremely important in driving the economy and it was the Western cultural value of a need for achievement (nAch) which motivated people to become entrepreneurs. Need for achievement was central to economic growth. His other concepts – need for power and need for affiliation – were more prevalent organisational and motivational principles in less economically successful societies. The higher the level of nAch – a questionnaire could determine how much of this need you had, and by aggregation and inference, your society – the more likely it was that you would be an entrepreneur. Put this way, it seems obvious that it is too simplistic, and that lots of other successful dynamic people would also score highly, including politicians, executives and the like. But McClelland should not necessarily take the blame. It's the fault of those that followed and tried to use one or several measures such as this to isolate and predict who would be *the* entrepreneur: remember today we see entrepreneurship is a process not a feature of character.

There have been many others that have sought to solve McClelland's conundrum. Adam Smith (1776) who favoured the market as an explanation; Max Weber (1995/1930) who thought it was the early modern rise of aesthetic Protestantism; David Landes (1998) who thinks that technological development and European liberal values were the key; and Jared Diamond (1997) who thinks its our relationship with the environment. Whether the explanation is sought in psychology, society, religion, morality or the economy, authors of every generation attempt to understand and promote the underlying reasons for the success or failure of certain societies or behaviours. They are all bound to be influenced by the prevailing ideas and concerns of their own time. How best to accelerate economic growth was McClelland's project. He was not really trying to *explain* entrepreneurship, but why the entrepreneurial spirit leads to economic success. He thought that the achievement motive was better at explaining this than the profit motive (1961: 391).

Paradoxically for someone so closely linked to psychological explanations of entrepreneurship, his impressive array of investigations and arguments presented in the book are an assemblage of a variety of methods and social science approaches around a theme of nAch, not a narrow personality testing approach. Nevertheless he can be criticised for putting too much faith in nAch as special magic social-psychological stuff. And this **essentialist** – over reliance on analytical categories – view of the world is a fundamental problem with McClelland and those others who favour reductionism and aggregating methodologies. In other words personality traits are analytical and statistical generalisations, they are not *real* things. All the arguments about whether we have five, three or 16 essential personality trait categories don't really matter, as they don't offer real explanations, just an analytic description.

Personality characteristics as an approach and a method also rely too much on dualism: placing people on a scale from entrepreneurial to un-entrepreneurial, and so on. Is who we are and how we behave really like this? Can questionnaires really tell us much about subjective states or intentions? Can we be sure that reported behaviour is the same as actual behaviour? The other key problem with this approach is less

Essentialism is a word used to criticise arguments that boil complex social phenomena down to a single factor or dimension (an essence). Thus personality theory as applied to entrepreneurship is essentialist because it suggests that differences between entrepreneurs and non-entrepreneurs are due to traits, and not traits and environmental factors, for instance.

about the methodology and more conceptual. What is underplayed is the meaning and context of particular times and places, both culturally, and also in the life course of individuals. Can we be sure that the cultural meanings of characteristics such as extroversion and introversion are consistent throughout the world and history? Do personalities change as a result of experience or events? How can we be sure that our snapshot is the right one? Is there a 'right one'? The world in which entrepreneurship behaviours takes place, in which some people describe themselves or are described by others as entrepreneurs, is ever-changing and complex. Personality isn't like a piece of Ikea furniture that can be put together using an allen key and a few essential components.

People used these ideas about entrepreneurial personality traits – such as locus of control, tolerance for ambiguity, moderate risk taker, growth-orientation, intuitive, nAch, autonomy, independence (there you go; I *did* make a list!) – partly in the hope to better identify entrepreneurs and predict their likely success. Who can blame them for depicting the social world as if it worked in the same way as natural science with its certainties and laws? Increasingly complex quantifications of socio-economic entities and variables and personal 'factors' can yield insights, but at root the depiction of the process and the individual is lacking. Imagine yourself wearing an ice-hockey goalie's kit and mask whilst going on a walking tour. It will give the wearer a sense of order and security in that they won't be hurt or dented very much, but equally they will get an unnecessarily muffled and reduced sense of the world. It's the wrong kit, so go get some walking boots! (See Figure 4.3.)

Entrepreneurial cognition

Something had to be done. Personality theory was dead (Baron 1998: 275; Krueger 2003: 109; Mitchell et al. 2002: 95; Steyaert 2004). Many entrepreneurship scholars turned to cognitive science (the investigation of the mental processes of knowing) to provide answers to questions about the people side of entrepreneurship. Entrepreneurial cognition research is the result, and it currently dominates the scene (Steyaert 2004). Mitchell and colleagues have defined it in the following way: 'entrepreneurial cognitions are the knowledge structures that people use to make assessment, judgements or decisions involving opportunity evaluation, venture creation, and growth' (Mitchell et al. 2002: 97). The basic idea is that whilst entrepreneurs might not have exclusive common personality characteristics, they might or do share common thinking processes such as perception, decision-making, knowledge representation and learning (Krueger 2003: 107). Krueger argues that entrepreneurs share an 'intentional pursuit of opportunity' and the associated cognitions, or ways of thinking (2003: 106). The model of human beings in this perspective is that we are information processing decision-making machines who build up particular habits and routines of thought in order to structure and guide our organising activity. There is a range of terms used to describe different aspects of this process: cognitive mechanisms, cognitive biases (irrational decision-making errors), mental models (shortcut

Figure 4.3 The wrong kit for an enterprise researcher

© iStockPhoto

pictures of how individuals think the world works), and cognitive styles (consistent approaches to thinking and decision-making), are just a few.

A couple of examples demonstrate how the cognitive approach works. Firstly, Baron in a speculative (1998) article which helped set the agenda for this stream of research, emphasises the way in which entrepreneurs are particularly susceptible to the irrational cognitive biases and errors which provide short cuts to arriving at decisions in situations of information uncertainty and emotional stress. He suggests that counterfactual thinking – 'the tendency to imagine what might have been in a given situation' – is more likely in entrepreneurs (Baron 1998: 289). The propensity to think this way leads them to be regretful and dissatisfied about what might have been, which in turn leads entrepreneurs to 'search for, identify, and act upon perceived opportunities' (1998: 289): their regret about past failure and commitment to their ideas spur them on to act on opportunities (1998: 281). The cognitive structure or mechanism – in this case counterfactual thinking – is a way of thinking that is typical of entrepreneurs. It follows that various predictions about behaviour can be made if effective tests can be applied to an identifiable group.

A second example of how this approach is used can be seen in how Sadler-Smith has applied and tested cognitive styles in the context of the management of small and medium-sized enterprises. He found via a questionnaire survey that cognitive style ('the managers' styles of thinking and decision-making') has an influence on the performance of the firm (2004: 155). He contrasted the processing of information in a rational or intuitive style, with the way in which memory serves to organise this thinking. Specifically his research showed that 'intuitive style showed a positive relationship with financial and non-financial performance, suggesting that an intuitive style is associated positively with performance' (2004: 174). What this means is that the managers of growth firms 'are more intuitive in their cognitive styles than are their lower growth counterparts' (2004: 176). They operate successfully on the basis of gut feeling. To be sure of this conclusion there would have to be some certainty that the influence of environmental factors was weak or non-existent. Sadler-Smith argues exactly this. Cognitive styles are 'context independent' (2004: 174) and represent 'in-built modes of processing and organising information' which are not influenced by the environment or strategic choice of the individual (2004: 163).

From these studies, it is not difficult to see why the cognitions approach is popular. It dispenses with the problematic personality characteristics approach whilst maintaining a commitment to, and dovetailing closely with, the assumptions of individualism and rationalism we found in economics (Chapter 3). For example, how individuals process information is clearly relevant to their differential alertness to opportunity (Kirzner 1973: 74). Indeed the underlying focus on individualism and rationality is dominant in mainstream entrepreneurship, and the alternatives which we will explore in the next section are conspicuously absent (there is for instance no mention of discursive or narrative psychology in either Shaver or Krueger's chapters in Acs and Audretsch 2003). The approach sees human beings as essentially rational and calculating. We are fundamentally information-processing machines.

As with all theories there are fundamental assumptions and limitations. The cognitive approach to entrepreneurship is resolutely focused at the individual level. The individual possesses mental stuff which then processes information which guides or structures individual and social action. Unlike personality theory the contexts in which individuals do their mental stuff are taken into account. However, given the inherent primacy of thinking, the social, historical and cultural meanings and context of social interaction tend to be treated simply as factors. It's the individual *plus* the context, not relational engagement and action in the world taken as a processual whole. The thinking, rationalising person is still crucially detached from the world: he or she is passive and self-contained, and becomes 'the disembodied ghost of disengaged reason' (Taylor 1991: 106). The cognition approach still wants to answer the question 'why are some people and not others able to discover and exploit particular entrepreneurial opportunities?' (Mitchell et al. 2002: 94). Cognition resolutely attempts to answer this in terms of the differences in the mental stuff, the processing abilities, of the individual. 'Who is an entrepreneur?' is still the key question, rather than a strong processual approach which might ask, 'which social (cultural, economic, personal, historical, etc.) circumstances are conducive to entrepreneuring?'

To really understand the problem underlying a strong cognitivist approach we need to briefly understand its place within a broader set of positions related to science and 'disengaged reason'. Philosophers such as Charles Taylor argue that when the seventeenth-century philosopher Descartes separated the 'machine' of the body from the soul or mind, he helped create a notion of the human being as a creature of pure logical reason: 'it is all too easy for us in our culture to think of ourselves as essentially disengaged reason. This explains why so many people find it quite unproblematic that we should conceive human thinking on the model of the digital computer' (1991: 103). The alternative, one which sees human agency as socially embedded, embodied, emotive *and* rational, is something that cognitivism doesn't deal with so well. Both economics and mainstream psychology rely on this cropped conception of the human being and the metaphor of the information processor – the mind as a computer – with its inherent rationalism and mechanical rule-following process (Figure 4.4).

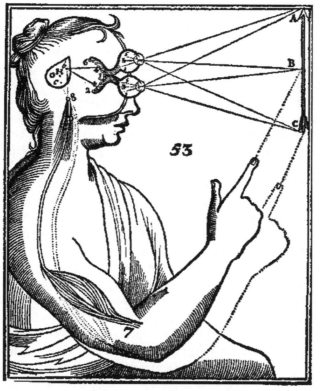

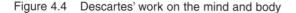

VISION Rene Descartes 1644

Figure 4.4   Descartes' work on the mind and body

This stance to the human being also has implications for how research is done. Indeed, it is possible that the stance is actually defined by the prior commitment to 'normal' science. (Remember the boy with his hammer in Chapter 2, pounding everything in sight.) That's how paradigms work: they structure the questions that are asked and how problems are researched. The cognitive approach relies on the model of testable propositions and quantifiable phenomena: if it can't be counted it don't count as knowledge. Subjective experience is objectified into numeric and quantified responses, and then aggregated and statistically prodded. It is not explored and analysed in its particular social setting or in any specific situational depth. Researchers in this tradition normally seek to purposively argue away or prove (see Sadler-Smith 2004, above) the irrelevance or controllability of environmental factors. To this extent it is similar to the 'scientific' approach adopted by exponents of personality characteristics, and despite a commitment to the *processes* of individual thinking the supporters of entrepreneurial cognition do seem – in my view – to be replicating the errors of the personality approach, rather than fully realising the philosophical implications of a process view. You can decide for yourself at the end of the chapter.

The next section shows a process view that deals with human beings and entrepreneurs as they behave, talk and think *in* society, not in their heads. But it is important to remember that as with personality theory, cognition isn't all wrong. When the problems regarding entrepreneurship are about 'thinking, reasoning, problem solving, imagining, decision making and remembering' (Osbeck et al. 2007: 250) then empirical research in this area is legitimate and welcome. Sadler-Smith's article may be flawed in terms of its methodological individualism and conception of human agency, but it does nevertheless show the importance of 'irrational' intuition in growth-oriented entrepreneurial success. Thus as far as one can reliably identify and categorise a group of people called entrepreneurs, entrepreneurial cognition research can 'help us to understand how entrepreneurs think and "why" they do some of the things they do' (Mitchell et al. 2002: 96).

This issue of the *category* – a question of making a boundary judgement, who is in, who is out – of entrepreneurship is crucial for the whole entrepreneurial cognition idea. It relies on a strongly defined boundary. The creative process view tends to accept a more emergent category of enterprise or entrepreneuring, that there is not in fact a robust category of *entrepreneurs*. Instead, it's a far more fluid and emergent process combining different behaviours, thinking and identity constructions in a social process. Thus cognitive scholars have a prior commitment to the existence of this group and the sort of characteristics they exhibit: they then try to look for the sort of thinking that goes with the characteristics. Strong and definite categories are conveniences which obscure the fact that some elements (people, in this case) will be deciding on the category that suits them, others not, and other elements will have their relationship to the category decided for them (by government agencies), and so on. Over time who is in, out and the characteristics that qualify will all change.

For these reasons to see the processes of entrepreneurial agency as *solely* a property of cognitive processes is a mistake, and the legacy of a rather stunted engagement with developments in psychology (Harré and Gillett 1994; Osbeck et al. 2007; Steyaert 2004). In other words, not all individual behaviour and action, or entrepreneurship, can be explained by cognitive processes. But some can. Even if you are wearing an ice-hockey goalie's kit you will see *something*. Having the right walking boots won't necessarily mean you'll see, find or say anything insightful if you don't look carefully.

The 'creative process' or social construction approach: entrepreneurial identity

Part of the strength of the cognition approach is that there is an agreement about fundamental assumptions. The creative process or social construction approach – which we discussed briefly in Chapter 2 – is less consensual, and a variety of quite disparate ideas shelter under this umbrella. It was only in 2007 and Chris Steyaert's article on 'entrepreneuring', where he reviews the different contributions to this way of looking at entrepreneurship, that some sense of 'an approach' came to the fore. But it builds on the strong social science traditions of narrative/discursive psychology and sociology. In the entrepreneurship field social constructionism is very much the new kid on the block and like most approaches it combines things that are old, borrowed, and stolen. I will emphasise, for reasons of brevity and coherence, the similarities in what could be called the middle ground of what I think is a coherent and persuasive alternative to understanding the individual entrepreneur.

The key relevant concept for the creative process view is the social construction of self-identity. The approach does not argue that individuals are totally *determined* by the social context. Of course we can act and create in the world. What the approach does say is that we construct who we are, a sense that we are a self, via our engagement with our social environment and language, our chief way of realising meaning.

The notion that social context is an important part of the story of entrepreneurship is of course not new. In the early days of entrepreneurship research social contexts such as the past experiences of education, family and role models were all recognised. I have already explained that the cognitive mainstream also sees social contexts as factors influencing role identity. But entrepreneurial role identity – how 'we learn to perceive ourselves as entrepreneurs' (Krueger 2003: 113) – presumes that the category of entrepreneur is relatively fixed and static, which as I suggested above is a simplification. Social constructionism would suggest that the role and category of entrepreneur itself is always in the process of being made out of the chaos of the world. What you and I understand by 'the entrepreneur' differs. The entrepreneurs of 1950s Britain, twenty-first-century Indonesia and early twentieth-century America differ greatly in many important respects. Equally in a few parts of the world today, and in the more distant past, the word 'entrepreneur' would have no meaning at all.

Social constructionist ideas applied to the individual entrepreneur began in the early 1990s (Chell et al. 1991). This contribution was understandably but crucially limited because at that time personality theory was still very dominant. Despite the alternative they offered to the personality approach it was not adopted with the same amount of enthusiasm as the cognitive approach. However, throughout the 1990s various studies started to emerge using this perspective (see Steyaert 2007 for a full review).

The implications of a social constructionist theory of self are far deeper than simply acknowledging the influence of language, cultural and other environmental factors on the way the mind works. At its heart the approach challenges the very existence of the self *as* mind. It claims to end the separation of mind and body that has typified mainstream psychology: the emergence of discursive/narrative psychology is therefore revolutionary in that it argues that selves and the mind itself are socially constructed (Harré and Gillet 1994; Steyaert 2004).

There is a difference between the terms narrative and discourse. Discourse/discursive is the broad ways of talking and writing and thinking about things that share common assumptions and provide a 'structured framework within which people see their world' (Abercrombie et al. 2000: 99). The discourse of enterprise, for instance, is all the ways of talking about enterprise; the character of the entrepreneur and the moral expectations we have of enterprising acts, and so on. We would also find discourses of motherhood, contemporary art and madness, and many other things besides. The discourse of enterprise will tend to prescribe what are legitimate acts and narratives for people who define themselves as entrepreneurs. We would want a very convincing narrative to be persuaded that an actuary, vicar or soldier was an entrepreneur: the discourse frames what is possible.

Narrative relates to specific ways of talking (writing, and so on) that individuals use to construct who and what they are. Narratives and stories are the language resources we use to tell about ourselves: the connected details which add spatial and temporal dimensions to the self-presentations we make to others and to ourselves. People who want to be seen as entrepreneurs would be expected to make up stories about themselves which include narratives and discourses we would commonly associate with enterprise. Social constructionist scholars argue about the extent to which the individual actor has control over the discourses and narratives he or she uses, but for the purposes of this chapter, and to create a distinct alternative to personality and cognition (and because it gets pretty complicated), we will under-emphasise these theoretical disputes, and assume that individuals have a choice in their use of narrative and discursive resources.

The most relevant application of narratives and discourse to entrepreneurial agency is in how we create an entrepreneurial self-identity. So what is a self-identity? According to Anthony Giddens:

> **Self-identity is not a distinctive trait, or even a collection of traits, possessed by the individual. It is *the self as reflexively understood by the person in terms of her or his biography*. […]. A person's identity is not to be found in behaviour, nor – important though this is – in the reactions of others, but in the capacity *to keep a particular narrative going*. (1991: 53–5)**

Giddens is saying that the self is not made up of personality traits or cognitions that people possess, but rather it is how we make and keep our biographical story going over time and in the different contexts where we live our everyday lives. Our ability to construct a convincing self is a bit like our CV: in our attempt to convince employers of our worth we under-play things we view as gaps or mistakes, things that tell the wrong story for the sort of identity (in this case the eminently employable graduate self-identity) we want to project. As we go through life we collect material from our interactions with others, but also with the discourses we confront on a daily basis, and select, emphasise and present the material to construct our biography, our narrative self-identity. Though not infinitely flexible, we are able to shuffle and reorganise the material sufficiently to be different things to different people, without necessarily undermining our sense of ourselves as someone with a coherent biography. Discourse is important in this because we can't avoid its influence. You can't decide what an entrepreneur is, any more than you can decide what a father or mother is. These discourses and the identities they prescribe are commonly assumed. How to 'be' an entrepreneur for instance is in large part communicated to us via education, news media, films, television shows (see Chapter 10) and other more widely known common characters and discourse, as much as it is through our personal interactions. Experience in other words is mediated through an engagement with language and social interaction. We gather and assemble identity material and construct the person; this then provides a sense of security in that it structures our activity. We know who we are.

Activity

A CV is a form of narrative identity: it's aimed at telling a certain type of story about you to a prospective employer. As a way of exploring your own self-identity narrative make up two CVs – either in class or at home – one that stresses an entrepreneurial you and another that stresses a non-entrepreneurial you. Draw on your own life experiences, emphasising different aspects of the same events. Bring the two CVs to class and discuss in pairs. Which do you and your exercise partner find more convincing? Why?

Okay, that's the theory; how does this way of looking at entrepreneurial agency change how we do research in entrepreneurship? There have been a number of studies that have adopted this approach to entrepreneurial identity (Downing 2005; Hjorth and Steyaert 2004) and the contribution is summarised by Chris Steyaert (2007). There are of course a number of different dimensions to this approach. Some have concentrated on the forms of language that make up narrative and discourse such as metaphors (Drakopoulou Dodd 2002; Nicholson and Anderson 2005) and clichés (Down and Warren 2008), and others have concentrated on the identity making process itself (Cohen and Musson 2000; Down 2006). We will look only at the latter, an example from my own research.

Reveley and Down (2009) have looked at how Indigenous entrepreneurs in Australia have dealt with the stigma of racism and disadvantage in their journey to becoming, in their own words, entrepreneurs. There is a great deal of interest from governments around the world which have Indigenous minorities, in the potential of enterprise to help alleviate the cycles of discrimination and poverty that these people often face. Unlike the majority of studies in this area which simply assume that enterprise and entrepreneurship are good for economic development in all contexts, we wanted to see what it meant to be an Indigenous entrepreneur. We adopted a narrative self-identity approach looking into the life histories of particular individuals and explored how those individuals used narratives of enterprise in 'coping' with the stigma of racism and disadvantage they reported having experienced growing up and living in Australia. Our analysis of the individuals was not based on what they were thinking or on some inferred inner characteristic, but focused on the enabling and constraining properties of the social contexts (i.e. discourses) in which they presented themselves. The identities available to Indigenous people until recently have invariably been very negative, which has meant it has been difficult for them to develop socially positive self-narratives. Does enterprise offer positive self-narratives for Indigenous entrepreneurs? What we found was that rather than simply fitting themselves into an artificial category of entrepreneurs these individuals were very conscious of the need to fit their desire for life success through entrepreneurship into their more traditional communally-oriented narratives. Entrepreneurship wasn't simply a way to make a fast buck, but an explicitly politically motivated means by which to overcome the stigma of discrimination. As an explanation of enterprising behaviour we feel that the approach is more successful than entrepreneurial cognition which would need to add specific Indigenous thinking mental models or cognitive styles, or personality characteristics which would need to argue specific Indigenous traits to reach these conclusions. Our research and the approach more generally provide a more culturally-nuanced way of thinking about enterprise which places the individual within their context.

Fenderco case study

Paul reflecting on now not being an entrepreneur

Fenderco did really well after the struggle of the first years. John and I were fairly happy with things, but I was getting a bit bored. I didn't really know whether I wanted to sell it off and go buy some new business, or go on some big adventure somewhere (I had the money that's for sure, but it wasn't really me, and I still had family commitments). In the end Europort made an offer to buy Fenderco. Would you believe it! The company we originally left – acrimoniously at that – to set Fenderco up wanted to buy us out and employ us both as executive directors. I was really suspicious to start with, but it was the real deal. Europort had totally transformed itself and it was now run by a younger generation of managers, who had been just as frustrated as we had been. So there was no reason to worry. Europort wanted to take us on board, to get rid of the competition by bringing us in. We had obviously hurt them over the years.

Initially I was worried about whether I wanted to be an employee again. I was my own boss. No one could tell me what to do. My deadlines were my own. It was a great feeling to know John and I had created Fenderco out of nothing. We didn't have to put up with corporate bollocks, all those systems and controls. But after thinking it through a bit more, and working out the terms of the deal, I realised that I was more bored with the everyday running of Fenderco than I was worried about the prospect of being an employee again. I realised that we were running a small firm, not playing at being Richard Branston. And anyway, it's not like you don't have the autonomy at director level. The deal we cut effectively meant we were independent anyway. Then there was the money of course. It was nice to see the rewards of our entrepreneurial effort.

I never went in for all that self-made man, wheeler dealer bullshit anyway. I was always more designer-engineer than entrepreneur: creating port infrastructure was more what I did than creating new business. I suppose in the beginning we did enjoy the fluff and pomp of calling ourselves entrepreneurs. We were a lot younger, and everybody loved an entrepreneur in the mid-1990s. I miss the sense of running my own business a bit, but honestly it's not much different. In the early days of Fenderco it meant a lot to me that John and I were the ones taking the risks; that we were being entrepreneurial. It didn't have to be a success; we made it one. But I've been an employee before and I'm one now. Who knows if I'll be an entrepreneur again? It's obviously something I'm prepared to do. I'm ready again if Europort start pissing us off. But it's just business. As things are though, working for Europort at a senior level suits me well.

Activity

In what ways are the identity categories 'entrepreneur' and 'engineer-designer' insufficient to explain who Paul is?

What are the key features of Paul's orientation to work, common to both the entrepreneur and the employee?

In what ways is Paul implying that the entrepreneurial character is perhaps somewhat clichéd?

Think about business people that you know. Are they entrepreneurs? Do they present themselves as such, or do they emphasise the content or skill (design, engineering, sales, etc.) of the business they run?

Do you know anyone who talks about themselves in an unconvincing way? What is it that makes people's self-narrative convincing or unconvincing?

Despite my general preference for this approach we should nevertheless look at it critically. There are three key criticisms generally levelled at the creative process or social construction view, though the published critique is somewhat thin on the ground as mainstream cognition entrepreneurship tends to ignore the approach.

The first area of criticism levelled at social constructionism is at the scientific methods used. In the narrative self-identity approach there is an explicit interest in the details of particular people rather than the universal aspects of all people.

Researchers tend to use forms of semi-structured and unstructured interviews, observation and ethnography (spending a long time embedded in a particular place) to generate thick descriptions of the particular culture or person/s they are studying. Cognitivism and personality theory sacrifice this detail in order to say something abstract and certain about the category of all entrepreneurs, arguing that particular examples won't be able to count for all entrepreneurs. The creative process or social constructionist approach is not really interested in all entrepreneurs in this sense as it doesn't accept that all interesting and important aspects of the study of entrepreneurship require this type of knowledge, as we saw in Chapter 2 when we discussed these issues (see also Cope 2005; Grant and Perren 2002; Ogbor 2000). It serves no purpose to repeat the arguments. Both the categorisers and universalists and characterisers and particularists offer insights and knowledge about enterprise (Down 2006: 29).

Another common criticism is the inverse of the criticism of excessive individualism in psychology and economics. Some social construction approaches arguably engage in excessive structural determinism. This means that too much explanatory power is given to the social context in producing entrepreneurship and not enough to the agency of individuals. The balance between structure (society, the economy, discourse, the family, and so on) and agency (individual behaviour) and how they relate to each other is a major problem within all social sciences, and all theories need to address both. In the context of this chapter, mainstream cognitive psychology doesn't really deal with social structure and context adequately, and whilst some social constructionist ideas might cede too much to it, the part is not the whole and most social constructionists accept a dynamic relationship between agency and structure.

But as with the cognitive limitation to thinking processes, there is a limit to narrative research into entrepreneurship: that limit is clearly the extent to which language is relevant. This ultimately prescribes the boundary of relevant research for this approach: if the question does not relate to how people use language, then the approach will not be particularly helpful. There is also a great deal of ambiguity and divergence of views about how language actually constructs the person. We won't resolve these debates here.

There are also those that claim that social constructionism denies the biological and genetic basis of identity formation. This is a fallacy. The mainstream social constructionist approaches assume that we create self-identities 'on top' of certain basic psycho-physiological drives which tell us to try to survive, seek security, procreate, look for food and so on. Thus, we recognise certain danger signs such as fast approaching objects, and these aspects of our physiology are as useful to entrepreneurs as anyone else, and just as useless in explaining their social and economic significance. There is an implicit separation between these more mechanical aspects of human life, which no doubt have important influences on all our behaviour, and the more reflexive socially constructed domain of intention, meaning and value relating, in our case, to the running of small businesses and entrepreneurial ventures. In short, to look for explanations of behaviour for such socially and culturally rich activity as entrepreneurship in these inner drives, genes or instincts is silly, and very few academics would argue this. If cognition or personality approaches are akin to wearing an ice-hockey goalie's kit, trying to explain entrepreneurship biologically is like driving around in a tank.

Conclusion

These criticisms all have greater or lesser salience, and will no doubt keep the social construction perspective on its toes. Before we bring this chapter to a close I want to introduce further evidence supporting a social constructionist position on entrepreneurial agency, one that shows how narrowly the mainstream entrepreneurial cognitive approach draws upon current scientific knowledge. There is increasing evidence from natural science which is beginning to support a more thorough-going creative process view of self-identity and entrepreneurship. It comes from a surprising source; the neuroscientist and philosopher of the mind Daniel Dennett (1993; 2003). Compare what we saw with Giddens above with this:

> **the strangest and most wonderful constructions in the whole animal world are the amazing, intricate constructions made by the primate, *Homo sapiens*. Each normal individual of this species makes a *self*. Out of its brain it spins a web of words and deeds, and [...] it doesn't have to know what it's doing; it just does it. [...] it works hard to gather the materials out of which it builds its protective fortress. [...] words are potent elements of our environment that we readily incorporate, ingesting and extruding them, weaving them like spiderswebs into self-protective strings of *narrative*. (1993: 416–417)**

> **We [...] are almost constantly engaged in presenting ourselves to others, and to ourselves, and hence *representing* ourselves – in language and gesture. [...] *Our fundamental tactic of self-protection, self-control, and self-definition is [...] telling stories, and more particularly concocting and controlling the story we tell others – and ourselves – about who we are. [...] Our tales are spun, but for the most part we don't spin them; they spin us. Our human consciousness, and our narrative selfhood, is their product, not their source. (1993: 417–418)***

Dennett argues that the individual self as a unified entity or thing located in the brain does not exist. He is saying that the self is an abstraction, something made up from what is around us: 'selves are not independently existing soul-pearls, but artefacts of the social processes that create us' (1993: 423). I quote Dennett at length like this to show that a narrow cognitive approach wrongly sees self-making as an aspect of brain-processing. Both the natural science of Dennett and the social science I describe above show that a constructionist view which emphasises the power of narratives and discourses in creating selves is more persuasive (though Giddens and Dennett would nevertheless disagree on much).

In terms of entrepreneurship, rather than seeing entrepreneurs as having special inner drives (particular personality traits) or particular brain processing mechanisms (cognitions) within them, Dennett *and* Giddens, despite their differences, would see entrepreneurship as a particular individual discursive and doing strategy ('words and deeds') for constructing a self, pulling together components from discourses and narratives to make themselves *as* entrepreneurs. My broader point here is that whilst it is acceptable that those entrepreneurship scholars singing the praises of cognitive science and its applicability to entrepreneurship tend to ignore developments in discursive psychology and sociology, it is short-sighted of them to ignore the natural science evidence of a social constructionist perspective.

Part of the problem here is an arguably deeper difference in the strategies of scholars. There are those people who favour sharp lines, definite boundaries and distinct entities and others who see permeated, flowing, transitional processes of change and becoming. I am obviously of the latter persuasion. For me this reflects the reality around me. However, whether entrepreneurship is a flow of social and economic processes in different states of becoming, or entities in fixed states, both may be useful ways of understanding the world. Thus extremes of argument and the consistency of logic shouldn't be too dogmatically held on to. If cognitive approaches should avoid over-extending their field of enquiry, the same should be said of social constructionists. It is the assumption of absolutism and winner takes all exclusivity and incommensurability that is the bigger problem. Incommensurability refers to the incompatibility of theories; that they can't logically fit. The problem with a strong view of this is that it over-concretises the purposes of theorising. Theories are guides to action and they are just that, guides. The real world is messy and if folk can take or make meaning from theories then this is fine. It is not the whole world. The polarisation of positions is the problem. There can be different ways to travel around the world.

Summary

The breadth of psychological approaches is explained. The chapter lays to rest the personality traits approach to understanding the entrepreneurial self and highlights the need for a more contextualised, processual understanding of entrepreneurial behaviour. The historical context and original objectives of early 'entrepreneurship' (McClelland) research are discussed. Though cognitivist approaches are an advance on traits the adherence to a dualistic separation of mind and body/environment is critiqued and the creative process approach is offered as an alternative. The concepts of narrative, social constructionism and entrepreneurial identity are explained.

■ ■ Further reading ■

Baron, R.A. (1998) 'Cognitive mechanisms in entrepreneurship: Why and when entrepreneurs think differently than other people', *Journal of Business Venturing* 13(4): 275–294.

Down, S. (2006) *Narratives of Enterprise: Crafting Entrepreneurial Self-identity in a Small Firm*, Cheltenham: Edward Elgar.

Gartner, W. (1988) '"Who is an entrepreneur?" is the wrong question', *American Journal of Small Business* 12(4): 11–32.

Hjorth, D. and Steyaert, C. (eds) (2004) *Narrative and Discursive Approaches in Entrepreneurship*, Cheltenham: Edward Elgar.

Mitchell, R.K., Busenitz, L., Lant, T., McDougall, P.P., Morse, E.A. and Brock Smith, J. (2002) 'Towards a theory of entrepreneurial cognition: Rethinking the people side of entrepreneurship research', *Entrepreneurship, Theory and Practice* 27(2): 93–104.

Sadler-Smith, E. (2004) 'Cognitive style and the management of small and medium-sized enterprises', *Organization Studies* 25(2): 155–181.

Steyaert, C. (2007) '"Entrepreneuring" as a conceptual attractor? A review of process theories in 20 years if entrepreneurship studies', *Entrepreneurship and Regional Development* 19(6): 453–477.

5

Managing Smaller/ Entrepreneurial Enterprises

Overview

This chapter has the following objectives:

- To introduce a theoretical framework for understanding the relationships between employers and employees, and to explain the historical development of theory on this topic.
- To develop an appreciation of the difficulties in understanding how control and consent are achieved in small and entrepreneurial firms.
- To understand the importance of product and labour markets, resources, strategic choice, rules and routines, and management styles in the organisation of the employment relationship.

Introduction

The next two chapters should be seen as a pair, linked and interdependent, bound together in describing employment *relationships* found in smaller enterprises. Apart from the self-employed, managers of smaller enterprises can't readily realise their dreams without workers. The relationship between managers/bosses/owner-mangers/entrepreneurs/CEOs/founders and employees/workers/staff is symbiotic, one of mutual benefit or dependence. 'Or' is such a little word, but the canyon of debate that it symbolises – from those that see only the dynamism and wealth creation of beleaguered bosses, against those that see only the exploitation of down-trodden workers – has arguably been the major driving force behind much of modern history. Even those not familiar with the history of capitalism will know what the famous philosopher Bertrand Russell once wrote is right:

> **What is work? Work is of two kinds: first, altering the position of matter at or near the earth's surface relatively to other such matter; second, telling other people to do so. The first kind is unpleasant and ill paid; the second is pleasant and highly paid. The second kind is capable of indefinite extension: there are not only those who give orders, but those who give advice as to what orders should be given. (1935/2004: 3)**

Whilst today we might stress knowledge, information and services more than 'matter', Russell gets to the nub of the employment relationship, and crucially suggests that being a manager is not an isolated endeavour. There will always be someone else wanting to give or have an influence on requests made or orders given. The same is true of smaller enterprise managers, whether they are owners or not. Despite the central nature of autonomy and independence that motivates many small business owners and entrepreneurs, they themselves are connected to and dependent on a wide range of other authority structures, hierarchical relationships and norm-driven social expectations, that control their behaviour, both within and outside the firm (contract and employment laws, expectations of fairness and the quality demands of customers and corporate purchasers are just a few). As the phrase goes, no man is an island.

Managers of smaller enterprises do however have specific and particular relationships to their employees. Somehow owner-managers or entrepreneurs of small firms have to convince workers to share the dreams they have for their business despite the workers often knowing that they will not necessarily reap the rewards of success or suffer the consequence of failure in quite the same way that the owners will do. Managers have to ensure that workers and other aspects of the business are controlled, and that workers consent to the activities and tasks demanded of them. It is not easy to control people and organisational processes. Managerial control is an unstable process which needs to 'remain dynamic and versatile enough to change and to reconstitute itself' (Storey, J. 1985: 207). This is especially the case in the uncertain environment of small and entrepreneurial firms (Storey 1994). These two concepts – control and consent – are central to understanding the relationship between managers and workers in smaller enterprises and are central to this chapter.

This chapter clearly focuses on managing and Chapter 6 on working, but the boundaries between these activities are smudged. We need therefore to build our theoretical understanding of the employment relationship here, such that it will serve both chapters. Nevertheless, the experience of managing and working will be described and explained separately. As will already be apparent the emphasis is definitely on the people side of things in both chapters, and this reflects the increasing importance of 'human resources' and their management in contemporary economies. In Chapter 8 – Reflecting on Practice: Finance, Marketing and Networking, Strategy and Growth – we look at the supposedly non-people, more 'technical' aspects of managing smaller enterprises. The aim of this chapter is to provide a means to understand how all smaller organisations manage, rather than imagine that all small firms are highly entrepreneurial and innovative. In Chapter 7 when we look at *Entrepreneuring in the corporate environment* the broader implications of specifically entrepreneurial management practices are dealt with more explicitly.

The next section explains more about the complexity and heterogeneity of the small firm environment, and asks the question, 'Just how special are smaller enterprise employment relationships?' (Barrett and Rainnie 2002; Ram and Edwards 2003). We then explore in some detail the different ways academics have sought to characterise the management of that relationship, before going on to use a framework (Edwards and Ram 2006; Edwards et al. 2006) to explain and describe different aspects and experiences of managing the employment relationship in smaller enterprises.

Development of theory about control and consent in smaller enterprises

Complicating factors

There are a number of issues that make characterising employment relationships in smaller enterprises especially difficult. Firstly and top of the list is obviously the heterogeneity of small enterprises. There are many different types of business out there, with different forms of ownership structures and sizes that operate in varying sectors, product and labour markets. To speak of a small hairdressing salon with maybe five staff as having similar management issues as a public relations consultancy with 40 staff, or a manufacturing firm with 150 employees, illustrates the problem.

Nevertheless, despite doubts about lumping together such a diverse constituency, and the need to situate small firms continually within their specific contexts, smaller enterprise scholars tend to conclude that along with this variety and complexity, there is something distinctive that sets these enterprises apart from larger organisations (Cardon and Stevens 2004: 295; Goffee and Scase 1995). Theories used to manage or explain what was happening between managers and workers in larger organisations don't seem to work: 'A small business is not a little big business' (Welsh and White 1981). Factors that differentiate smaller organisations and influence the employment relationship include: personalised ownership, which tends to place a great deal of emphasis on the prerogatives (or rights) of the owner-manager; the extent to which personalised face-to-face manager/worker interaction takes place; the prevalence of informality pervading relationships within firms (Ram et al. 2001); and the lack of bureaucratic and procedural control mechanisms.

It is worth noting though that many larger enterprises can also be seen as collections of smaller, linked, disaggregated units, which might also rely on a high degree of personal interaction between managers and staff. Moreover, for many independent small firms reliant on large firm contracts, whilst nominally independent of corporate bureaucratic controls, in practice the nature of the relationship with staff might be extensively determined by demands from the larger firm over quality control, for instance.

Secondly, it is important to understand that the research questions and topics social scientists are interested in have political dimensions. Research into the employment relationship roots itself firmly onto socio-economic philosophical positions regarding the way capitalism works in relation to labour, and has consequent political/moral implications. We saw in Chapter 3 that economists argue about where surplus and value are produced. On the one hand many economists see added value produced by the innovative thinking and actions of entrepreneurs. On the other there are those that see the surplus produced by workers as driving the capitalist economy. This latter perspective isn't especially fashionable today, with policy-makers across the world falling over themselves to make impossible heroes out of the entrepreneurial class. Supporters of the former perspective also tend to see employment relationships as a matter of market forces and essentially unproblematic. Workers contract for wages and are rewarded for their labour, and willingly acquiesce to management control for pragmatic and self-interested reasons. If the markets are operating effectively everyone is a winner. The latter perspective emphasises the way in which labour is exploited due to inherent inequalities within employment relationships and capitalist economies. Historically speaking the former sees capitalist economies and the relationships between managers/owners (capital) and workers as akin to the natural order of things, the latter as the product of specific historical circumstances. If you accept the former, there is not really much to discuss and there wouldn't be much need for chapters on managing and working in small firms. Or, rather, it would be narrowly focused on how best (efficiently) to use the labour 'resource', and see the relations within smaller firms as essentially harmonious and unproblematic.

This leads on to our third complicating issue. I suggested in Chapter 2 that the study of, and knowledge about, smaller and entrepreneurial enterprises were geographically specific. Nowhere is this more apparent than in the study of employment relationships in small firms. The majority of US research on the employment relationship focuses on entrepreneurial growth-oriented high-tech and/or innovative knowledge intensive firms and adopts a Human Resource Management (HRM) orientation, which reflects an interest in how best to manage and utilise labour as a commodity resource and the performance of the business: what firms 'should' be doing (Cardon and Stevens 2004: 295). Workers by and large are seen simply as factors of production – human *resources* – which can enhance or undermine performance (profit) depending on whether the resource is managed correctly according to best practice (Edwards et al. 2006: 704). You will struggle to find articles about the employment relationship in American small business and entrepreneurship journals.

Thus, there is no doubt that much of the discussion below focuses on the nature of *relationships* found in smaller organisations, rather than on how best to make more money. How we manage and work in smaller enterprises is simply far too important an aspect of our societies to reduce our interest to technical debates about how best to enhance performance. But a range of current perspectives, including HRM, is surveyed and unnecessarily polarised discussion is avoided. Later I apply a framework which explicitly recognises the interaction between capitalist context and the agency of employees and managers (Edwards et al. 2006): the framework accepts the underlying structural nature of the exploitative and unequal basis of the relationship, without denying the ability of managers and workers to build up cooperative, productive, enjoyable and satisfying business and working environments. The HRM approach simply assumes that there is no underlying structural inequity to the relationship between workers and managers. I think this is unrealistic.

Finally, there is a need to acknowledge the limitations of a textbook chapter. There is a great deal of national variety in the contexts in which the employment relationship takes place that will not be delved into. The differing national rules, laws, extent of unionisation, prevailing cultural and economic norms have a profound influence on the manner in which manager and workers interact. The differences, for instance, between the prerogatives of managers in Sweden, the United States and Nigeria are instructive. Swedish businesses generally operate in a high-skills, highly technologically developed and socially regulated environment which emphasises responsible practices and the protection of workers' rights. The US business environment is more differentiated in terms of skills and technology, emphasises the rights of entrepreneurs to run their businesses as they see fit, and exempts smaller enterprises from some regulation. In countries like Nigeria businesses are likely to be operating in the informal market far more, and even where the employment relationship is officially subject to legal protection, there will likely be a great deal of non-compliance (Fadahunsi and Rosa 2002). Each employment relationship reflects and reproduces different cultural, social, political and economic norms. Nevertheless, because of the increased internationalisation of business ownership, finance and management practices (we could call this globalisation), those economic norms are perhaps more homogeneous than they once were. Thus for the purposes of achieving a holistic overview of the issues in managing people in smaller enterprises we will downplay the differences.

Two models of people management in small firms

Effort bargain refers to the negotiation between employees and managers about what constitutes a reasonable amount of work and the level of pay deemed fair for the contribution.

Psychological contract refers to the perceptions of employees and mangers of what their mutual obligations are to each other.

In Chapter 1, I introduced the widely held notion that small firms are often thought to have more harmonious employment relations than large firms. This is of course a simplification that conflates the undoubtedly more personal and informal aspects of small firm organisation with the rather obscure notions of 'harmony' and 'happiness'. Small firms do have less formally recorded incidents of industrial conflict, but this is hardly surprising as many are not unionised and informality pervades management practices more generally. In smaller firms, everyday *and* more serious work problems, conflict and arguments are smoothed-over, not by recourse to formally recorded means, but by the norms of behaviour found in society more generally. That conflict doesn't rise to the surface in the form of strikes doesn't mean it doesn't exist in the form of high turnover and absence, loafing and a variety of other means by which workers give less in terms of their side of the **effort bargain** or **psychological contract** than might be expected if workers were 'happy' and fully committed (Moule 1998).

Empirical research has shown that managing small firms is as fraught with 'people' problems as any other form of organisation. One significant study which offered a theoretical explanation of the reasons underlying the different forms of management of control and consent in small firms is Al Rainnie's (1989) UK research into clothing firms. Rainnie argued (1989; Barrett and Rainnie 2002) that it was the degree of independence in the market that the firm operated within that determined the management style of particular firms. Table 5.1 shows how different types of firms are influenced by their position in the market.

Table 5.1 Economic dependence of small firms

Type	Characteristics
Dependent	Suppliers to large customers, internal organisation often regulated by customers, subject to strong pressures on prices
Dominated	Compete against large firms on basis of low price
Isolated	Operate in niches ignored by large firms
Innovative	Operate in high-risk, often new, sectors

Source: Rainnie (1989)

As Edwards et al. suggest 'In the dependent and dominated cases [...] employment relations are likely to be largely autocratic in nature, whereas the other two situations leave more space for choice within the firm' (2006: 706). A key strength of the approach is that it acknowledges the heterogeneity of small firms and the degree to which they interact in an economy, not as isolated units. Barrett and Rainnie (2002) argue that the features of capitalism are the same for all businesses. The logic of capitalism serves to control the **labour process**. Smaller enterprises are different, but only because they are at the bottom of the feeding chain, forced into exploitative relationships with larger more powerful organisations. Even innovative professional firms can't get away from this market dynamic, despite the greater degree of choice they have about how to organise internally. Even the most progressive of small entrepreneurial firms will from time to time face pressures from larger organisations seeking to cherry pick worthy investments by buying the firm out, 'poaching' key staff, or otherwise influencing the internal organisation of the firm; management processes in small firms are therefore 'highly unstable' (Dundon et al. 2001: 438) and subject to a great deal of uncertainty (Storey 1994).

Another influential typology is provided by David Goss (1991). In earlier research Goss (1988), seeking to empirically discredit the social harmony thesis, demonstrated that although small firm employees are often easy to control and comparatively compliant, this was the result of a sense of powerlessness, not any great sense of employee identification with the aspirations of the entrepreneur. In a study of UK printing firms he showed how managers controlled workers and work processes, and in what circumstances and types of firms workers could negotiate and protect themselves. The different types of employee control are shown in Figure 5.1.

Fraternalism – derived from fraternal, meaning friendship – exists in such businesses as the building trade where the business owner relies on the skill and compliance of employees to a significant extent and often works alongside employees. *Paternalism* – derived from paternal, meaning father-like – is typical of work relationship on farms, where employees are tied to their employers in bonds of mutual obligation, and are somewhat reliant on the flexibility and level of engagement of their workers. *Benevolent autocracy* – autocracy meaning unlimited power

Labour process is synonymous with 'production process' except that it denotes a view of economic activity that highlights the inputs of employees or 'labour' as the creators of surplus value, rather than raw materials and machinery.

Poaching refers to the practice of hiring employees from other companies whose training the other company has paid for.

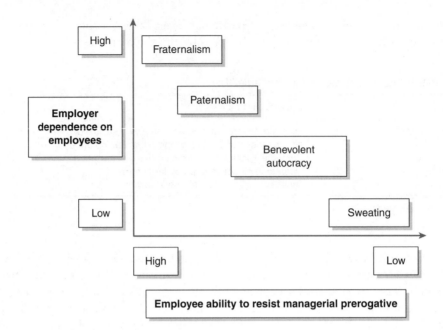

Figure 5.1   Types of employer control in small firms (Goss 1991: 73)

with a single person – describes to a greater or lesser extent the majority of smaller firms, and suggests that owner-managers are less dependent on the skills or commitment of employees and can run the firm as they see fit. Unlike paternalism however, where control might spread outside the confines of the business itself into social relations more generally, the control is limited to the business itself. Relationships are *benevolent* because there is an informality and 'closeness' (Goss 1991: 79) between employees and employer. *Sweating* – where exploited workers are literally worked so hard they sweat – refers to a situation where employees have little or no skill scarcity or ability to resist and negotiate, and are literally a human resource; a commodity (Figure 5.2). The employer doesn't feel the need to 'cultivate employee identification and there is a critical focus on cost containment' (Marlow 2000: 312).

More important than the specific types is the overall recognition of the interrelationship of mutual dependence, market conditions (i.e. labour market skill scarcity) and the ability of employees to shape their environments. As Goss states: 'the key to understanding the exercise of control lies in two related concepts: the dependence of the employer upon particular employees and vice versa; and the power of workers individually or collectively to resist the exercise of proprietorial prerogative' (1991: 73).

Both of these models have their problems. All typologies tend to over-specify their types. Real firms don't always fit the boxes very snugly and often exhibit behaviours commensurate with different types simultaneously. Moreover, the clothing and printing industries are perhaps untypical. Both these industries have

© iStockPhoto

Figure 5.2   Images typical of sweatshops

Courtesy of the Chicago Historical Society

since suffered a significant decline in the developed nations' stock of small firms, and even at the time, Goss and Rainnie's studies typified an 'old economy' bias in UK small business studies, which didn't reflect some of the more progressive managing practices others found (Bacon et al. 1996).

Theoretically too there is a problem. Goss and Rainnie over-emphasise the primacy of the market position of the firm in determining the way control and consent are achieved. This is inadequate, as smaller enterprises are embedded in particular environments and are able to mobilise internal resources and react to external contexts and pressures in different ways. They fail to allow enough agency to people to organise the relationships within the firm as they see fit. Small firms, their managers and workers, are not flotsam and jetsam on the tides of market forces, but active actors shaping their own destinies. There are also contexts other than economics that help shape the management of smaller firms: religious affinity, ethnicity, family, gender, national and international cultural norms, and industrial and sectoral behavioural norms all shape relations within small firms.

Goss and Rainnie's typologies are interested in a broad range of relationships and are not narrowly focused on how best to improve the profitability of the business. This is not to imply that a performance-oriented approach has nothing to offer. Thus, although US scholars Cardon and Stevens (2004; Heneman et al. 2000) seem unaware of the long history of interest in HRM, employment relations and management issues in small firms in European scholarship (for example, Marlow and Patton 1993), they have usefully summarised the contribution of US research. Their emphasis is on understanding the management of human resources rather than an understanding of the relationships, and they tend to emphasise high-growth entrepreneurial firms. As a consequence there is a focus on the entrepreneurial and performance perspective; what the entrepreneur or founder needs to do in terms of HR to make a successful business. They acknowledge the need to understand HR practices in emerging small firm contexts, stress the need to look at both formal and informal 'mechanisms through which very small and small firms manage their employees' (Cardon and Stevens 2004: 319), and acknowledge that not all smaller firms grow into larger ones. Overall though, their ignorance of theoretical and empirical developments (in understanding the informal aspects of small firms for instance, Ram et al. 2001) in Europe means that their understanding is unnecessarily limited.

Regardless of whether a broad relational or narrow performative approach is the correct one, we are still left with a sense of not really understanding what it's like to manage or be managed in a small firm in the everyday sense and none of the above theories, typologies and approaches really gives us a sense of this. My own view is that a relational approach is more inclusive of a broader range of relevant contextual factors. In the next section I introduce a recent theoretical synthesis and at the same time give some examples that show some of the reality of small firm management.

Fenderco case study

Paul's story (company director and entrepreneur) about how he deals with staff

Every year you obviously get round to pay rises and bonuses. Will and Mark are forever thinking it's about time they got a raise. Last year was a really good year and John and I bought a nice car each. John got a TVR which I think is a bit naff, but each to their own. I just went with a Merc. This sort of thing sets them thinking of course, but ultimately it's us that takes the risks and reaps the rewards. I try to deal with all that HR stuff professionally. But we work very closely together, so it can be difficult if we need to set them right about something, when they've buggered up I mean. Mark and Will both think the company would collapse if they weren't around. That certainly isn't the case. Both could be replaced if necessary; they don't have that much knowledge when it comes down to it. So I don't think it's a bad idea – if it was really necessary (I don't mean Mark and Will, they are fine, great employees) – to get rid of somebody very swiftly. It's surprising I guess that when it comes down to it, despite the time we spend with Mark and Will down the pub having a laugh and all that, no matter how friendly you are, when it comes down to it, business is business and the business is ours, if you know what I mean. So when it comes to them asking for money, a pay rise like, it's … not easy – I mean I feel I'm being a bit of a hard arse, but you just do it. We pay them the market rate. I've been an employee before, on the other side of the table, and I know how nervous and uncomfortable it feels to ask your boss for money. So basically I have all the answers to their questions. I'm ready for them. I also like to do it with an element of surprise. Call them in when they are busy and say, bang, that's what you're getting, no discussion! You should see their faces! But it's important that John and I don't let our emotions – they're good lads after all, and they have both done extremely well – get in the way of sound business practices.

Activity

1 Have you ever asked for a wage rise or had a performance review? How did it feel?
2 How can Paul's attitude be justified?
3 Thinking about Goss's typology – fraternalism, paternalism, benevolent autocracy and sweating – what best describes Paul's approach and why?

Understanding management of the employment relationship

Any theory or framework has to be able to incorporate and explain the 'linkages' between broad structural contexts, such as labour and product markets and 'actual concrete practices of control at work' (Storey, J. 1985: 194) that take place over time and in different places and cultures. The framework of Edwards et al. (2006)

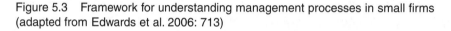

Structural variables		or	
a. Product market	Under a degree of *control*		Highly *competitive*
b. Labour market	Recruits in *open* market		Recruits from *restricted* pool
c. Resources	Human and social capital *positive* aid in responding to market pressures		Human and social capital a *negative* constraint on flexibility
d. Strategic choice	Has clear *strategy*		Largely *reactive* to events
e. Rules and routines	*Universalistic* and formalised		*Particularistic*, unwritten and informal
f. Management style	*Participative*		*Authoritarian*

Figure 5.3   Framework for understanding management processes in small firms (adapted from Edwards et al. 2006: 713)

stresses both the external context (structure) and internal resources of firms (agency). Their approach avoids the narrow performance orientation of most US scholars and the overly structurally deterministic typologies of Goss and Rainnie.

We need such a theory to deal with the heterogeneity of the smaller organisational environment, and to deal with the linkages between structure and agency: between the environment and concrete practice. Edwards and his colleagues' framework also highlights the foundational need for management to gain control and consent in order to be able to apply a range of more functional management practices which include recruitment and selection, compensation, training and development, discipline and exit (redundancy, dismissal and so on), employee relations (union management), and other newer management techniques such as managing change and employee involvement schemes. Figure 5.3 outlines the approach. I then use the framework to describe specific management processes found in small firms.

The point of this framework is that it can explain the different variables within *any* small firm, and stresses the 'interaction between structural factors and choices within the firm' (Edwards et al. 2006: 707). The two columns do not necessarily represent real small businesses, but a dichotomy of idealised types: every real firm is unique. Thus, for example, a 'modern firm' might be expected to have a degree of *control* over the product market, recruit staff from the *open* market, use its people as a *positive* aid to the business, work to a clear *strategic* plan, have formal and *universal* rules and routines, and manage with a *participative* style. A classic sweatshop business on the other hand would operate in a competitive market, recruit from a restrictive pool of labour, perhaps connected to family or ethnic networks, see its employees as a negative constraint, be unwilling or unable to plan and have to fire-fight all the time, work to informal and idiosyncratic rules and routines, avoiding legal compliance where possible, and be run by an dictatorial manager (Edwards et al. 2006: 713). We now look at each variable in turn, showing real life examples taken from ethnographic research accounts.

Product markets: control/competitive

The type of product market a firm operates within obviously has a profound effect on the way the business is managed and the sorts of business strategies that can be adopted. A small London-based fine art auction house and gallery will require very different management skills in producing control and consent of its highly educated, professional and independently-minded staff, than that of a labour intensive Vietnamese clothing manufacturer. The scarcity and desirability of the products – fine art versus mass produced bargain clothing – and the structuring of the markets that produce the goods will influence the internal organisation too. In firms that operate in highly competitive markets with lots of other firms producing similar products or services they will often be faced with little control over such things as price setting. Firms that have specialised or novel products will conversely have a degree of control on price. What this means for internal management of the firm is clear from Rainnie's (1989) model: the more dominated or dependent a firm is, the more likely it will have autocratic and particularistic management styles.

A study of a manufacturer producing buttons (someone had to do it!) shows this dynamic well (Moule 1998: 651–652). Moule explains that the firm 'operated in a niche market and was sheltered from the intensity of competition found more generally in the clothing sector. Its diverse customer base meant that Button Co.'s profitability was only partly linked to its relationship with large retailers'. This meant that control was fluidly negotiated rather than managerially imposed. This negotiated aspect of management control was most apparent in the way that workers would vary the quality and consistency of the colour required depending on the importance of the customer. For large corporate customers such as the retailer Marks and Spencer, because of a greater degree of the scrutiny from the managers there was little room for negotiation, but on other less vital customers' orders there was space to work at a more relaxed pace.

Labour markets: open/restrictive

Interaction with the labour market is also an important aspect of how small businesses operate. A firm's ability to recruit staff can be pivotal to its chances of survival and growth. Founders often believe that prospective employees are falling over themselves to work in their dynamic entrepreneurial ventures. Whilst this is no doubt true of some people looking for work, the reality is that small firms often struggle to appear 'legitimate' (Cardon and Stevens 2004), attractive, or even visible to prospective employees. In contrast, larger organisations are often seen as legitimate and attractive by applicants because, even where pay is the same (which it often isn't; small firms generally pay less), they are perceived to guarantee more security, established training programmes and career progression.

A small firm therefore operates in a labour market dynamic where it 'recruits *openly* for labour of a given kind, or it fishes in a *restricted* pool defined by ethnicity or other factors' (Edwards et al. 2006: 710) such as family connections and friendship, rather than on objective and strictly rational factors. A small firm adopts restricted, informal, particularistic and 'irrational' recruitment practices in order to minimise the perceived risk of the unknown and untried recruit. The employee recruited through a restricted pool may not be the 'best' person for the job, but they will likely be willing to accommodate the values of the owner-manager and work in the desired manner.

An example of a relatively restricted firm can be seen in Holliday's (1995) ethnographic account of the employment relationship in three UK small firms. One of the firms, 'Wellmaid Clothing', which makes waxed jackets, occasionally uses more formal means of recruitment but normally it is by word of mouth. The labour market in which Wellmaid operates is tight and restricted because of the number of similar firms looking for a relatively small pool of skilled workers. As one of the managers Rita says 'All the surrounding area's got factories. It seems to be a machinist's paradise around here. You can go from one job to the next' (1995: 43). In this case the market for labour is very localised and the firms have to compete for workers.

At the more *open* end some small firms have begun to ape the more contingent recruitment practices of larger businesses and will outsource recruitment and other personnel functions such as payroll management to firms that specialise in providing HR services (Cardon and Stevens 2004: 303). From the small firm manager's point of view, outsourcing HR – paying another firm to deal with the legally and socially important, but bureaucratic and time consuming aspects of recruiting and managing staff – can provide the benefits of a rational approach (getting the best technically qualified employees, expertise on HR practices and regulatory compliance) without the requisite and ongoing investment in personnel/HR knowledge.

Resources: positive/negative

With this variable people, and the skills, attributes and attitudes that they bring into the business (resources: 'human and social capital'), are 'either a *positive* aid in responding to market pressures or a *negative* constraint on flexibility' (Edwards et al. 2006: 710). In reality of course people at work bring their *resources* to bear on the activities of the business in many different ways. Individuals can act in both positive and negative ways within a single day or hour, or indeed have qualities that are both negative and positive at the same time. But the variables do help us to characterise the human resources within firms, and the manner in which they are engaged and perceived by the firm.

These resources can be illustrated if we look at the family firm or small firms run as if they were family firms. In both types of business the rhetoric of 'family' is understood by both managers and employees as a valued resource. Something that helps the business work. As Rosanna, an employee at Wellmaid, said, 'We're like a family. A little family. If there's anything wrong they know, they can tell. Everyone knows everybody. Like when I'm bad or anybody else is bad then you come back then they've found out anyway what's wrong with you. Little things like that. It's nice' (Holliday and Letherby 1993: 55). To Edwards et al. family labour 'is certainly a positive resource, but it can also impose problems for firms for example where a family member who lacks skills is employed in the firm to meet familial obligations. There is thus a tension between different elements of the same resource, and firms will need to find ways to manage this tension' (2006: 707). In other words the informality and obligations found in family firms work both ways; management is both facilitated and constrained by the family organisation. The manager (often the family head) will tend to get stability and discipline from employing family members and other core employees but these staff will often have relative autonomy and can act in idiosyncratic and negative ways which might be counter-productive to the business. As Holliday notes, in the family firm 'everything is negotiated through networks of affinity and antagonism' (1995: 153).

Many growth-oriented entrepreneurial firms and their CEOs will clearly see staff as positive resources. We would expect that in a culture of enterprising candoism staff would have both the adaptable skills and flexible attitudes required to progress the aims of the founder/entrepreneur. A study by Heneman et al. (2000: 13) focused on entrepreneurial growth-oriented firms and found that HRM practices of staffing (recruitment, selection and retention) and reward and compensation were perceived by the CEO/founders to be of vital importance to the development of their ventures. As one of the CEO/founders they interviewed commented: 'I have to assure myself that people know what they are committing to and that they are committing because it is aligned with their own value and philosophy not because they need a job. By the time I talk to a person they are technically qualified so I am interested in the passion' (2000: 17). 'Awesome' and enterprising people were perceived as vital to the success of this type of business. Formal HRM techniques were perceived as unimportant. 'Concern was instead expressed about matching characteristics of the person other than knowledge, skills, and abilities to the values and culture of the organisation' (2000: 18).

Strategic choice: strategic/reactive

Having resources is one thing. Knowing what resources will be needed in the future as the business grows and changes is another. Most small businesses exhibit very little strategic behaviour. This is not surprising given that autonomy and independence are often the key goals of founders (Curran and Burrows 1986: 270), and that 'For many small firms, management decisions are made in the context of survival and operational necessity, rather than growth and business development' (Beaver 2003: 65). Thus a distinction can be made between businesses that have a clear *strategy* and those that are 'passive and largely *reactive* to events' (Edwards et al. 2006: 710). Even in the context of entrepreneurially oriented growth firms which might be expected to exhibit a clear strategy overall, human resource strategy is not seen as especially important by founders (Heneman et al. 2000: 20).

In the case of Wellmaid there was very little strategy in evidence, and the business was generally 'confused and short term' in its outlook (Holliday 1995: 55). As one of the other partners said to the researcher expressing her dissatisfaction with the way the firm is managed: 'Decisions are made without being talked about ... decisions are made without you knowing. [...] Communication isn't as good as I thought it'd be, and I hope it gets better. It's got to get better' (1995: 51). In my own research at 'Fenderco' there was at least a tacit and informal understanding and articulation of the strategic direction of the business. Discussions of a strategic nature where very much bound up in the relationship between the two owner-managers, Paul and John, and 'strategic planning' discussions were often held at the pub early on Friday nights before the beer flowed, minds were muddied and conversation slurred: 'we maybe go down the pub rather too much but really that's really just to catch up, because he [Paul] is busy during the day and I am busy during the day. How do you get the chance to share ideas and talk about strategy and so on? It's best to do it outside the office' (Down 2006: 77).

For many managers their approach to strategic aspects of running their business is undermined by their lack of awareness of the skills that are needed. As Watson has argued: 'However strong the need for entrepreneurialism, innovation, creative flair and the devising of new businesses may be, there is going to be no less a need for the skills of competent management' (1995: 44). Quality 'professional' management is still required. As one former employer of more than 70 employees quoted in Scase and Goffee (1980: 56) noted, reflecting on the mistakes and limitations he had seen in others: 'The guys I've spoken to don't seem to think they've got to keep books. This is where a lot come unstuck – they haven't got a clue. Just hard work doesn't make a successful business, you've got to have a good business mind. You've got to know how to negotiate, how to talk to people and how to do paper-work. So many fail because they haven't got a clue of how to control or run a business'.

Though not all strategy need be growth oriented – a founder for instance might have a clear 'endgame' strategy for the progressive reduction of business activity and asset/capital realisation – reactive firms are often content to bumble along fairly successfully without aiming for growth (though as a strategy for survival Storey feels growth is necessary, 1994: 310). The main reason for this is the reluctance of CEO/founders to give up the autonomy, independence and direct control over business operations that the employment of more staff, and the increased formality and professionalism it implies, would entail.

With growing entrepreneurially-oriented businesses the picture is different, and one would expect a degree of strategic behaviour. It should be noted however, that having a clear strategy shouldn't be seen as simply a better, more professional approach, and reactive more negative. Strategic choice is contingent on the configuration of other more structural factors. This reflects a broader theoretical problem with strategising in all businesses: whilst businesses have some room for strategic choice, the structural constraints of capitalist economies (labour and product markets, boom and bust, credit crunches, interest rates, fluctuating prices, and so on) mean that ultimately 'no strategy will prove successful' (Hyman 1987: 25). In other words, strategic choice can only ever result in better or worse rates of water loss in an inherently leaky bucket: strategic behaviour equals topping the bucket up with fresh water every now and again. It is no surprise that smaller organisations tend to spend more time and effort on reactive management than strategising.

Rules and routines: universal/particularistic

All organisations function on the basis of rules and routines. Some are provided by the environment, locally interpreted and enacted, others are generated internally. Small firms will have rules and routines that are 'either *universalistic* and formalized, or *particularistic*, unwritten and informal. [...] The closer a firm is towards the latter category, the more will it allow privileges to some workers, based on kinship or length of service, that it does not permit to others' (Edwards et al. 2006: 710–711). The informal nature of employment relationship management in small firm is well known, but it is only recently that the nature of that informality, often simply assumed to be an unalloyed benefit to all, has been seriously examined: '"Informal" employment relations may be defined as a process of workforce engagement, collective and/or individual, based mainly on unwritten customs and the tacit understandings that arise out of the interaction of the parties at work' (Ram et al. 2001: 846). The effective management of control and consent within small firms is thus achieved via the informal interactions found in everyday work life.

Informality is an oft noted feature of small firms. Vera, a worker at Wellmaid, explains, 'you can do what you want more or less, up to a point. I mean we do have rules but not like what the big places have' (Holliday 1995: 49). Similarly, in an exception that proves the rule, a manager in Wellmaid also explained on one occasion where she did resort to the more formal means of a disciplinary letter,

> **You can only stand so much from people. And some of them tend to treat you … they get away with a lot more here than they do at a big company, you know, they come in late, if they want time off they can have time off, if they have to go at three o'clock or two o'clock to the dentist, there's never any question, they go. [...] We're very lenient with them here to the point where you just have to draw that fine line between management and employee. And some of them tend to cross that line, and this particular girl did and so I wrote to her. (Holliday 1995: 49–50)**

Although one would expect to find more formalised rules and routines the bigger and more growth-oriented a small firm became, even quite large small firms can operate successfully with an informal approach. Scase and Goffee (1980: 66) cite a senior manager of a substantial small firm: 'The management plan we've got here is pretty rickety. It seems to work but there's no rigidly-defined management plan or structure. It sort of happens. Whether that's good or bad, I wouldn't know. If you read a textbook I'm sure it would say it was bad. But, believe me, it definitely seems to work here'.

But the type of approach to rules and routines is not simply a matter of choice. As Ram et al. note,

> **Too often [informality] is accepted as an inevitable product of entrepreneurialism and close interpersonal relations in the workplace, promoting individualised and *ad hoc* patterns of decision-making and behaviour. In fact, it is structured by external influences relating to the nature of the product market and the characteristics of the available and existing labour force. It is also shaped by the demands and constraints imposed by existing modes of work organisation and technology. (2001: 859)**

These demands and constraints on the application of rules and routines often include an approach to business rationality which focuses on the practical facts as they are and specific and immediate outcomes, rather than any prescribed set of business best practices.

Management style: participation/authoritarian

The final factor in the Edwards et al. framework addresses the influence of the manager or managers of the firm. The dichotomy here swings from managers who act in an *authoritarian* autocratic and domineering manner, to those who are more *participative*. 'The former is based on the power of the manager and it can entail the arbitrary use of sanctions. The participative label is used here to index the degree to which there is a degree of discussion and the flow of opinions up as well as down the hierarchy' (Edwards et al. 2006: 711).

Much research into small businesses has shown that the management style found in small firms is 'autocratic, egocentric, impulsive and often unpredictable' (Beaver 2003: 65). Owning the business can also have a profound impact on how the manager sees his or her right to manage the business in the way they see fit. It is quite common for owner-managers to see their business as a domain of absolute authority. However, even in this type of authoritarian small firm a manager cannot be all powerful or all seeing. Some degree of delegation and consent is always necessary, and time and time again small business research has shown that employee self-management of business processes is an important aspect of how businesses really function (Holliday 1995; Moule 1998). In a firm with 20 employees a small firm manager explains that 'most of our chaps have got to be able to work with a minimum of supervision – use their loaf [brains]. I mean that they are fantastically good, they are very responsible. You see, with us, we haven't got a big enough labour force to employ supervisors' (Scase and Goffee 1980: 59).

Small firm managers are not 'marionettes' of the market. Nor are they slaves to the informality of the interactions within their firm (Storey, J. 1985: 195). They obviously have a real effect on the course of their business. The 'style' a manager develops is specific to the particular identities and forms of interaction within the firm as well as the influences of the external environment. As ever, the heterogeneity of small firms should be borne in mind here. Small firm managers are not all of a type. They are real men and women, Swedish, American and Nigerian; young and old; educated and uneducated; poor and rich; black or white; law-abiding or criminal; and can be pleasant and easy-going or total money-grabbing bastards.

Summary

This chapter has sought to introduce a theoretical framework for understanding how control and consent are achieved within smaller enterprises, building on earlier attempts to understand this topic. An appreciation of the difficulties in understanding how control and consent are achieved in small and entrepreneurial firms was developed. The specific, more technical aspects of managing have not been a focus (see Chapter 8). More stress has been placed on the theoretical importance of explaining how managers run businesses in the structural context they work within, but also the realities of the concrete practices and relationships found within the firm. This has involved a discussion of the importance of product and labour markets, resources, strategic choice, rules and routines, and management styles in the organisation of the employment relationship. The next chapter – *Working in Smaller/Entrepreneurial Enterprises* – focuses on the world of work within small and entrepreneurial firms.

Further reading

Bacon, N., Ackers, P., Storey, J. and Coates, D. (1996) 'It's a small world: Managing human resources in small businesses', *International Journal of Human Resource Management* 7(1): 82–100.

Barrett, R. and Rainnie, A. (2002) 'What's so special about small firms? Developing an integrated approach to analyzing small firm industrial relations', *Work, Employment and Society* 16(3): 415–431.

Cardon, M.S. and Stevens, C.E. (2004) 'Managing human resources in small organisations: What do we know?', *Human Resource Management Review* 14: 295–323.

Edwards, P., Ram, M., Gupta, S.S. and Tsai, C. (2006) 'The structure of working relationships in small firms: Towards a formal framework', *Organization* 13(5): 701–724.

Heneman, R.L., Tansky, J.W. and Camp, S.M. (2000) 'Human resource management practices in small and medium-sized enterprises: Unanswered questions and future research perspectives', *Entrepreneurship, Theory and Practice* 25(1): 11–26.

Marlow, S. and Patton, D. (1993) 'Managing the employment relationship in the smaller firm: Possibilities for Human Resource Management', *International Small Business Journal* 11(3): 57–64.

Ram, M. and Edwards, P. (2003) 'Praising Caesar not burying him: What we know about employment relations in small firms', *Work, Employment and Society* 17(4): 719–730.

6

Working in Smaller/
Entrepreneurial Enterprises

Overview

This chapter has the following objectives:

- To understand the contemporary work environment, and its increasing reflection of enterprise ideology and values.
- To show the lived experience – focusing on the university graduate – of working in and managing smaller and entrepreneurial enterprises.
- To provide an extended empirical illustration of the management processes framework introduced in Chapter 5.
- To understand the work experiences of the self-employed and franchisees, and the influence of enterprise at work more generally.

Introduction

In the last chapter we saw how unrealistic it is to expect that all small firms have an harmonious employment relationship, and that nevertheless there were distinctive attributes to how management controlled their enterprises. In Chapter 1 we also discussed the centrality of large structural, corporate and political changes to the rise of enterprise, small firms, self-employment, flexible and contingent work. The purpose of this chapter is to give some lived experience to these debates about the employment relationship and enterprise. As with other topics there are divergent arguments about what is happening in the world of work (see Beck 2000; Gallie 2007; Sennett 1998). These debates often turn on arguments between universalists and particularists: those that are interested in world trends, as opposed to specific issues for particular workers, regions or industrial sectors. Wherever you are positioned in the spectrum of available knowledge about work it *is* difficult to generalise, but in the developed nations it would be fair to say that in recent years there has been increasing 'flexibilization and individualization in contemporary work arrangements' (Fenwick 2002a: 703). Workers are expected to take on risk – and whether that risk is real or felt is a key aspect of this debate – and be

Figure 6.1   Charlie Chaplin in *Modern Times* (1936)

© Roy Export Company Establishment

'autonomous and competitive, self-reliant and continuously innovative' (Fenwick 2002a: 707). It is nevertheless worth stressing that despite the growth in these often insecure, innovative new forms of employment 'the permanent employment contract remains the dominant form' (Edwards et al. 2008: 1163).

Even within permanent employment, with words like self-reliant and innovative, it seems like workers today need to be enterprising in ways that they didn't used to be. It is important to recognise that work, how it is organised, managed, people's attitudes and expectations, is historically and geographically specific. If we think about America in the 1930s, as depicted in Charlie Chaplin's film *Modern Times* (Figure 6.1) or the nineteenth-century world of Charles Dickens and his novel *Hard Times* (Figure 6.2), we can see visions of relentless monotonous manual and factory labour where 'jobs just aren't big enough for people' (Terkel 1974: 521). These historical images have all but disappeared from the mental landscape of the West, but plenty of this work still exists. There are factories and sweatshops all over the world. In my lectures I illustrate this by asking people to find the labels on their clothes and see where they were manufactured. Fifteen years ago it would likely have been Hong Kong, Taiwan or China. Today it might be India, Indonesia or Vietnam. Have a look at where your clothes have been made. Fifteen years from now, who knows, it might be in Africa. Whether you see this as positive industrial progress or the spread of capitalist exploitation, around the world there are many geographical differences, and plenty of 'hard times' can be found if you look, even in the wealthiest nations. Call centres are often depicted as the bleak factories of the twenty-first century. And it's worth noting that for

Figure 6.2   Manchester, about 1870: mills, factories, pollution, smoke and dirt, typical of Dickens' *Hard Times*

some people in the factories of developing nations, what I suggest are hard times, are actually perceived as boom times of increasing wealth and prosperity compared to the subsistence-based lives that they left behind in the countryside.

In addition to the changing shape of work, the developed world turned another corner in the 1980s. After decades of distributionist policies that sought to maintain full employment and to reduce the gap between the rich and the poor, Western governments since have looked to emphasise economic growth, enterprise and freer markets, over managed stability and socio-economic equity. The hope had been that greater economic growth for all would ameliorate and keep one step ahead of the problems caused by greater socio-economic divisions. Notwithstanding other achievements these political and economic shifts in emphasis may have led to, inequalities have widened over the last 30 years or so. This is the case in terms of wealth generally, but more important for our discussion, the gap between earnings has grown. America leads the way in this. According to Nobel prize economist Paul Krugman executive pay is now '367 times the average worker's pay' compared to 'the 1960's and 1970's, [when] C.E.O.'s of the largest firms were paid, on average, about 40 times as much as the average worker' (Krugman 2006). Since the financial crises of 2008 'excesses' in top level pay have become a hot topic, and the voices that question the dominance of markets ideologies and casino capitalism have grown louder and more persuasive. It seems likely that with increasing social and political instability, especially the rise in unemployment, a political re-evaluation of the neo-liberal approach might ensue. Neo-liberalism – the desire to let markets organise economies and reduced state management and responsibility – has profoundly affected the nature of work. It is probable that the failure of markets and this ideology and the subsequent emergency political responses to shore up damaged economies will also have a longer-term effect on how work is organised and distributed in the world economy. The *protection*, rather than the promotion, of small business and small business jobs is once again high on the political agenda.

Regardless of the effect of large scale economic shifts and political ideologies, small firms and entrepreneurial businesses can offer good and hard times for workers, just as large businesses can. There is an awful lot of different forms of work. Exactly how the work in smaller and entrepreneurial firms is organised is dependent, not just on the values and morality of the owner-manager (though these aspects of management style will have an important impact), but also on the labour and product markets in which the firm is situated, as we saw in the previous chapter. In this chapter I concentrate on work understood quite broadly. That is, in addition to people who work as employees in small firms or in larger organisations which have been influenced by a culture of entrepreneurialism (a topic that prefigures a more specific emphasis on the world of corporate entrepreneurship in Chapter 7), we also look at forms of enterprise which straddle the domains of work and running a business; the self-employed and franchisees.

The experience of working in smaller enterprises

People have very different experiences of work. 'People' vary a fair bit too. Consider this.

Criminologist Dick Hobbs wrote a book in 1988 called *Doing the Business* where he described a world of cops and robbers in the East End of London. He also described the work and lives of petty thieves and how at this time and place these individuals would often replicate and bastardise their own version of the work values and ethos of the financial traders of the City of London, which lies just a mile or so down the road. Hobbs explained how Jack, one of the enterprising, wheeling and dealing petty criminals, made his living:

> **Flexibility and optimism are key characteristics of any successful entrepreneur and Jack is no exception. One night he attempted to rob business premises but was thwarted by security arrangements, and the one accessible article of worth was an ancient wooden ladder. The following day he became a window-cleaner, the next day he decided that he was scared of heights, and by the end of the week had sold the ladder. (1988: 155)**

Jack enjoyed taking his chances, seeing big and small opportunities to make money where he could. According to Hobbs, Jack's 'reputation as an entrepreneur provides the corner-stone of his public *persona*. He is a man to be respected' (1988: 156, emphasis in the original). Despite the ups and downs, his work provided him with a decent enough living. As Jack himself says, 'No guv'nor [employer] can afford my wages' (1988: 162).

When thinking about work in smaller and entrepreneurial enterprises it's important to realise that different people will have varying orientations to work. The difference between someone like Jack, crafting a good living out of the informal economy (Williams 2007), or an electrician working an entrepreneurial economy of favours in Soviet Russia (Rehn and Taalas 2004a), and a young graduate starting their first job in a small firm speaks for itself. That difference of experience is worth understanding. Differences of social class, geography, age, gender, ethnic origin, and so on, will all have an impact on the experience of working. However, rather than attempt to focus on the whole range of experiences, we'll focus on younger people, specifically university graduates who find themselves working for small and medium-sized enterprises. What is it like to work in a small firm?

Let's see what Mark, an employee at Fenderco, has to say.

Fenderco case study

'Mark's story' looking back at his time working at Fenderco

I'm sure that's how Paul views it (see Chapter 5, page 87), but he can say what he wants. He's the boss; back then he was, I mean. I can't say I didn't gain a lot from the experience. I learnt a great deal. Wouldn't change a thing. No point having regrets. Now it's been a while, now that I have moved on, and seen how things are elsewhere, where its more professional-like, I look back on it … well, you know, they did struggle at the beginning and you … I can see why now. I didn't know anything else you see. I didn't realise then but Paul and John didn't really know what they were doing half the time. They knew sales and design, but they knew nowt [nothing] about managing people, getting the law right and so on.

I was straight from uni. I didn't really know what I wanted to do. The money was great. At least, compared to nothing it was. I was living at home, me mam didn't really want much. I bought that Honda CBR with my first month's salary: with savings like, the pay weren't that great! Used to get up early, drive 50 miles out of me way to get to work: used to scare myself half to death. Work was fun most of the time. Will and me – he was the other junior bloke, doing the bread and butter stuff – we called John and Paul 'the lads'. We were all 'the lads'. Every Friday night we'd be down the pub. It was fun. They both had young kids you see. I guess they needed the space; hanging onto their youth; whatever. They used to pretend that Friday was important-for-work, but they were just having a laugh really. Have you seen them both now? Fat and bald, both of them. Hah! Happens to us all I suppose.

But there were some proper-bastard problems too. The way Paul tells it makes working at Fenderco sound a bit Christmassy; with bells on. We worked some of the shit out in the pub. It was all good banter really. Well, mostly. The office layout didn't help; it was really claustrophobic. Everyone could see and hear each other. Meant we all knew what was happening, until we didn't. Sometimes John or Paul would just assume that we knew everything, but they were out loads … Anyway, where was I? Right. Sometimes it could be the pits. If either of them were in a bad mood you just had to keep your head down and hope one or other of them, or both, pissed off somewhere on site, whatever. It could get really bad, with folk shouting and all that.

One time we had a little purchase order for somebody. The file was swinging around on top of one of the cabinets behind me and then one morning John was prating around between meetings. Will and me dreaded this; he just couldn't let things be. He had to be doing something. Workaholic. He was so suspicious of people. Anyway, he picked this file up; none of his business really. He said it was a bit of a mess and out of sequence or some rubbish and then sort of went mental at me, shouting and everything. I was gobsmacked; didn't even respond. Probably in shock! No really, I remember being quite shaken, angry-like. Later I had a look through it and it was all there, in order. So I went back and threw it on his desk and told him. We had a bit of an argument and I accused him of treating us like children and said it was about time he stopped doing it, shouting and bawling in front of everyone else like that.

Like I said, it was fun!

(An activity related to this case study follows on page 103.)

What of graduate experiences of working in SMEs more generally? In a survey of UK and Dutch graduates working in SMEs, Arnold et al. (2002: 477) showed that expectations were exceeded by experience: working in smaller firms was 'better than expected'. Although pay levels, the extent of formal training and longer-term career prospects were typically weak, the graduates reported high degrees of autonomy, opportunities to develop a wide range of skills and a good initial start towards their career goals. These findings are consistent with 'the image of small organizations as being relatively free of procedural constraints and tightly defined job descriptions' (2002: 490). Their research also suggests that when compared to graduates and younger people generally, graduates starting their careers in smaller firms tend to have a more realistic understanding of the world of work (2002: 479). This might have something to do with increasing levels of enterprise education at university, or perhaps the extent to which students entering SMEs are often themselves sons and daughters of business owners (ibid.). However Arnold et al. are careful to avoid reaching definite conclusions. They rightly stress other factors such as important changes in the structure of work, where 'delayering and outsourcing may have made working life in large organizations more similar to that in small ones' (2002: 490). They might add too that attitudes to work will also have changed. As work in larger organisations has become harder to differentiate from small ones (many large organisations have disaggregated into small units), and opportunities through the 'milk round' or corporate recruitment fairs have declined relative to the number of graduates, attitudes are bound to have changed.

We can see this in an example of research that tracked the development of a number of former graduates over time, looking at their transition into full-time employment from higher education. Joanna left university with a degree in business and got a job with Soft Furnishings, a medium-sized company producing cushions and the like for large supermarket chains. She started as a product manager, but was a 'bit confused' as to what it entailed (Holden and Hamblett 2007: 560). Joanna was thrown in at the deep end, expected to manage from the off. She was no graduate trainee.

Early on she made a pretty big mistake which meant thousands of cushions were unsaleable:

> ... yeah I mean as a company that don't have a proper induction programme I don't think they can expect much less, they throw you in and make you learn on the job. You're always going to encounter mistakes. There's not a procedure manual, there isn't anything to follow it's kind of, you know, like that. So unless they give you something, you know, strict guidelines to stick to, [...] Well as much as I hate to say it a procedure manual did come out of my mistake. [...] it's been something that everybody's found useful because, you know, there's no standardization. (ibid.: 562)

Later as Joanna grew more confident in the role she became frustrated at the nature of 'her own role vis-a-vis her boss', John:

> I was getting quite bored with the fact that, you know, you get the job title Product Manager and you're given these accounts yet all you seem to be doing is, you know, you're administration ... and things just go over your head and, you know, people go direct to John you won't be involved in the whole loop [...] he has to make a decision he'll make a snap one like that and it's out of your control already. [...] he'll get a new account and to get them on board he'll promise them the world, you can have this, you can have that yet it's us you know. He'll probably sidle up and say right sort all that out and, you know, you're like well 'How can I John, you've given me, you know, a two week lead time which is normally six weeks how can I do that?' (ibid.: 562)

She situated her frustrations at the lack of delegation and the centralised nature of operational control vested in John's management style, which was typical of SMEs. Joanna's frustrations were also mixed with admiration: 'my role model, ultimate role model in the company, is probably John because although he's absolutely horrendously rubbish at anything procedural or, you know, anything that remotely makes the system run smoothly he's probably the most knowledgeable, [and] forceful in a good way [as a] sales person' (ibid.: 567). Also typical of SMEs were the firm's management, who were 'very relaxed in the sense that, you know, everything's very ... it's quite informal. [...] nobody's in, you know, their ivory tower locked behind the door where you can't go in' (ibid.: 567). Eventually Joanne's persistence and desire to take on more responsibility led to a promotion to Senior Product Manager and bigger accounts with larger supermarket clients.

This informality also extended to how training was organised at Soft Furnishings. It is well known that training and development in many smaller and medium-sized enterprises is predominantly informal, on-the-job training: not necessarily a bad or irrational way of doing things (Holliday 1995). A lack of financial resources and time is normally cited as reasons for not investing in formal training (Cardon and Stevens 2004). A perception of the external training provision not being of an appropriate quality or specific enough to the needs of the firm is another (Westhead and Storey 1996). Joanna puts it like this:

> It's not the kind of job that they can write a text book on and say here's, you know, read this you'll know it all inside out within two days. So a lot of it is through, you know, shadowing the Sales Director just generally getting a grip. I mean there is obviously generalised information that they can give me that will help me build on my activities but I think it's not really the kind of thing that you could just throw a manual at me and say learn it. (Holden and Hamblett 2007: 566)

Later when she herself became responsible for training new Product Manager recruits she made no attempt to veer away from the learning-by-doing route towards more formality. But she also realised that the seat-of-the-pants rushing around that typified her role and the style of the business generally didn't allow for her broader longer-term formal development: 'I haven't really been given the opportunity to think, sit and think "well that [formalized training] would be useful" ... And I think a lot of that's as well because Soft Furnishings don't make it known that this is what's out there, you know, they don't' (ibid.: 568–569). As a result she concluded that ultimately she might outgrow the firm and its way of doing business: 'I'm nearing a point where there's not much further I can go. [...] I've always known that there would come a point where, you know, there is no room for natural progression really' (ibid.: 571).

Activity

1 Having read Mark and Joanna's stories, think about the consistent features of working in small and medium-sized firms in relation to:

   a) Training and development.
   b) Management style.
   c) Operational processes.

2 Drawing on Mark's story, in what way might the spatial characteristics of an office influence its employee relations? (See Reveley et al. 2004 for a further exploration of this topic.)

3 Why might working in a smaller or entrepreneurial firm be less amenable to using a 'text book' to learn how to do the job? The implication that Joanna makes here is that it is like this in large organisations. Is this a fair description of corporate employment?

4 What are your experiences of working in a smaller or entrepreneurial business?

Self-employed work

Being self-employed can mean being an employer, but for most people the individual is responsible just for themselves: they are a special form of worker, rather than a form of entrepreneur or owner-manager. Self-employment is interesting as it encompasses a spectrum of activity that ranges from those whose work is 'professional, rewarding, de-institutionalised', and centrally situated in the knowledge economy, who 'flexibly exploit' their in-demand status, to those in 'highly precarious and low quality' self-employment situated in the marginal economy who 'are sidelined and exploited by restructuring organisations' (Smeaton 2003: 379–380). These describe positions at the extremities. Some professional self-employed would no doubt prefer to have standard permanent jobs, and some less skilled self-employed workers are happy with the inherent flexibility of this form of work. Smeaton concludes that whilst more people are being pushed into self-employment by the lack of viable employment, the evidence suggests that many are not 'clamouring to return to employee status' and enjoy autonomy and initiative enabled in self-employed contexts, 'even when self-exploitation in the form of long hours exist' (2003: 389).

Self-employment of all kinds has increased *as a proportion* of those in employment in most Western countries (for the UK see Brooksbank 2006). The experience of the self-employment varies greatly. It will also be shaped by the particular national institutional and legal framework, as well as cultural attitudes. In Britain for instance the building trade has traditionally seen a preponderance of self-employed workers. Generally the 'self-employed are concentrated mainly in industries and trades where there are many producers, where entry is relatively easy and competition vigorous' (Brooksbank 2000: 13). Because they take responsibility for their own retirement arrangements and savings, some self-employed people can experience problems, though these days employees also worry about the future of their pensions and superannuation arrangements. Evidence does show that many of the self-employed work long hours for low pay and that the work can be precarious and insecure. The rise in self-employment has many causes, some of which are attributable to general rises in enterprise discussed in Chapter 1. Many of the people, especially in the US and UK, with assistance and encouragement from enterprise-keen governments, have been encouraged to borrow or use their own capital (often redundancy payments) to attempt to realise the dream of working for themselves. For many the opportunity to work for themselves has been a resounding success, especially for those with high skills. However, as we shall see in Chapter 11 when we look at government policy in more detail, encouraging people in this manner can have the effect of driving prices and incomes down if too many people become self-employed window cleaners, hairdressers and plumbers. The prospects for many such self-employed workers following the credit crisis and economic decline might show the optimism vested in this form of enterprise economy to be somewhat illusionary.

Another interesting development has been the growth of female self-employment relative to the larger proportion of self-employed men. Female entrepreneurship more generally has generated significant academic and policy interest in the last decade or so (Carter and Bennett 2006). Some of the lived experience of female self-employment can be seen in an article by Fenwick (2002a) which seeks to explain the individual desire and passion of women in starting self-employed careers. This article, based on interviews with self-employed women in Canada, is unusual in that it gets to the bottom of why some individuals find the pain and financial uncertainty often associated with self-employment so enthralling. One web-designer for instance said 'I find it hard sometimes to stop working because I'm so passionate about what I'm doing' (Fenwick 2002a: 711). Similarly a swimwear designer said 'I truly am doing what my passion is, that desire … [designing fabric] and being in control of things' (2002b: 168). Some of the women Fenwick talked with explained that a frustration with hitting a '**glass ceiling**' in the larger organisations they previously worked for had contributed to their willingness to break out on their own. Fenwick's research shows that self-employment isn't just about the resigned acceptance of employees who have to restructure their work to the tune of the neo-liberal and flexible new economy piper, but rather is a 'seize the day' response by individuals looking to explore limits and develop a sense of who they are through work. Self-employment gives the women in Fenwick's research a sense of control over and passion for life: A case of 'I take risks and control my own destiny, therefore I am'!

For others though the experience of self-employment is more negative. There is evidence that some people are increasingly being 'forced' into self-employment. This is described as reluctant entrepreneurship, false or dependent self-employment, or more recently, involuntary entrepreneurship (Kautonen et al. 2010). These terms describe a situation where a worker is offered work but only if they enter into a self-employment contract, which often means the individual has to accept less employment rights. There are not huge numbers of workers in this situation but it is at the bleeding edge of innovation in the world of work. The 'employer's motive for such arrangements is to look for flexibility by avoiding the ongoing commitments, costs, obligations and responsibilities typical of standard employment relationships. The individual, on the other hand, is 'forced' into becoming a subcontractor, or to search for other more standard work. In some situations existing work arrangements are simply restructured, forcing employees to apply for new self-employed contracts or leave the company.

Concerns about involuntary entrepreneurship have emerged in the context of increased outsourcing by large enterprises and the growth in agency and casual employment. These shifts in how organisations demand labour have created entrepreneurial opportunities for employment agencies. An 'innovative' example of these practices can be seen in the UK with some migrant workers especially prominent in more marginal forms of employment, and where a grey hinterland of illegality and lack of enforcement exists. Some migrant workers in the airline ancillary services industry, especially those with eastern European origins, are known to have been 'forced' into only dimly understood complex and self-employment contracts. The exploitative dimensions of these 'innovations' are no doubt exacerbated by competitive pressures in the low cost airline industry, with ancillary services such as baggage handling coming under severe pressure to cut costs.

Other research into involuntary entrepreneurship has concluded that it is unlikely that workers like these will develop and expand their income through self-employment (Stanworth and Stanworth 1997: 71). Whilst some groups forced into self-employment through deregulation and industry restructuring, such as

Glass ceiling refers to the situation where it seems as if promotion is meritocratic, but in fact discriminatory practices form barriers for some groups (i.e. women).

those in the entertainment industries, computing consultants, actors and other cultural workers, have benefited from certain taxation exemptions which have encouraged this form of employment, it remains fairly clear that, 'Where the choice to be self-employed is a forced or constrained one, there can be no meaningful talk of entrepreneurialism' (Harvey 2001: 15). This conclusion is backed up with other studies looking at self-employment more broadly that suggest that the 'realities of survival self-employment developed in the face of permanently high rates of local unemployment do not accord with notions of an "enterprise culture" [...], but are better understood as part of a growing culture of informal and risky work' (MacDonald 1996: 431). It seems unlikely that 'forcing' people into enterprise in this manner by redefining 'normal' work as self-employed will lead to greater entrepreneurial dynamism in the economy.

Franchising

Another area of enterprising work is franchising. Some of you will have seen *The Simpsons* episode where Marge Simpson, after attending a franchise exposition, sets up as a franchisee of the 'Pretzel Wagon' franchise. Initially Marge has her reservations: 'I'm not wild about these high-risk adventures. They sound a little risky.' But she pays her sign-up fee, buys the branded equipment and pretzel-making ingredients and is soon baking and selling away. Ultimately Marge struggles to make a profit because of all the other fast food franchise outlets that have sprung up in Springfield as a result of the success of the exposition. Homer Simpson decides to get Fat Tony, Springfield's mafia boss to help Marge out ...

This highlighting of franchising on *The Simpsons* reflects the growth of this form of business, which can be defined, according to Curran and Stanworth (1999: 540) as 'A business form essentially consisting of an organisation (the franchisor) with a market-tested business package centred on a product or service, entering into a contractual relationship with franchisees, typically self-financed and owner-managed small firms, operating under the franchisor's trade name to produce and/or market goods or services according to a format specified by the franchisor'. This form of business is typical of fast food (McDonalds) and printing (Kall-Kwik) businesses, and is 'especially well suited to service and people-intensive economic activities, particularly where these require a large number of geographically dispersed outlets serving local markets' (Stanworth and Purdy 2006: 462). As Curran and Stanworth (1999) put it: franchising is all about colas, burgers, and shakes.

So why place a form of business in a chapter predominantly concerned with working? As the previous section implied the boundary between worker and enterprise is not a clear one: Chapters 5 and 6 work together to describe different aspects of the employment relationship. Yes, franchisees are likely to be managers of their own workers, but at one extreme franchising can also be seen as a 'modern form of long-term indentured servitude' (Emerson 1998, cited in Clarkin and Rosa 2005: 319). This is because what they do and how they do it are controlled by another company in a way that independent businesses are not. Curran and Stanworth report that 'franchising attracts people who otherwise would not become business owners' or 'self-employed' (1999: 334). In part this difference is because there is a lower risk of business failure associated with franchising (Hoy 1994); the sustainability of the business idea, service or product has often been tried and tested. Neither do franchisees see themselves 'as conventional employees [they] have certain expectations of participation in the process of which they are an integral part' (Stanworth et al. 2004: 539). Franchisees span the boundary between employment and entrepreneurship.

Like many of the forms of work and enterprise I have discussed, franchising reflects changing degrees of interconnectedness in the economy, and the trend for larger organisation to divest themselves – as we saw in Chapter 1 – of centralised control and the costs associated with being directly responsible for employees. In the franchise, because the franchisee owns the business, he or she takes responsibility for this. If Marge had made a success of 'Pretzel Wagon' she would have managed the business to a set standard and process (specified in contracts, agreements and business running guides), and with the support of the franchisor. The profits, if the business is successful, are shared.

If the impression you have is of franchisees having little or no discretion about how to run their franchise, recent research has shown that this is because researchers have taken the contracts, agreements and manuals (which can be centimetres thick!) too seriously. Clarkin and Rosa (2005: 303/321) note that in practice 'restrictive franchise agreements were not always rigorously enforced unless problems occurred, allowing room for entrepreneurial activity by franchisees': the letter of the agreement was a 'last resort', not the everyday basis of how the relationship worked. One of the people they interviewed ran a coaching and consulting service franchise. Steve said when asked about the practical importance of the formal franchising agreement: 'In terms of running my business, very little. I had an attorney [solicitor] look over it. After I signed the agreements, they went into the drawer and I never saw them again' (Clarkin and Rosa 2005: 320). Another franchisee they talked with, Susan, who purchased a franchise that markets window treatments also described a more rounded and autonomous relationship: 'They [the franchisor] will spend time with you and say here's the things that we think will help you with your business. They are real people, and truly interested in us succeeding' (ibid. 2005: 323). The authors concluded that relationships between franchisee and franchisors 'tended to be much more productive where the formal rules were confined to the background in favor of positive and flexible management strategies' (ibid. 2005: 324).

Clearly the experience of being a franchisee can vary a great deal. Some franchisors are good, some bad. Some franchisors are accused of running businesses that profit from hefty sign-up fees, with little regard to, and offering even less support towards, the likely success of their franchisees. One hopes that the majority provide a great opportunity for those without the 'killer' idea or large enough capital resources to start their own entrepreneurial business. Indeed some franchisees use the experience as the starting point for running their own franchise business, often in competition to their original franchisor.

Franchising is the least employment-like form of enterprising work considered in this chapter, and the above section shows that franchisees consider themselves to be enterprising. However, even those employees or professionals who work in ostensibly 'non-enterprising' environments often have to behave in enterprising ways. Enterprise and entrepreneurialism affect far more employees than those who happen to work in small or entrepreneurial firms. If we accept that recent decades have seen enterprise become a pervasive aspect of our culture, then it is likely that most people's work has been influenced by it. I know my job as a university lecturer has. I regularly talk with colleagues about the need for, but also the dangers of, an entrepreneurial spirit in universities. This can be seen in balancing the desire to exploit the market potential of high fee paying international students, whilst at the same time not lowering qualification entry standards to achieve it. Exactly how entrepreneurial should your university (hospital, care home, energy company, bank, etc.) be?

Exactly how does the culture of enterprise affect work? This final section explores two aspects of this. Firstly, we can see how some have suggested that the culture or discourse of enterprise (which we discussed in Chapter 2) has become omnipotent, dominating large swathes of the contemporary work environment, from private companies, to much of the public and voluntary sectors. Secondly, we can look briefly at the lived experience of working in an entrepreneurial environment. Unsurprisingly, the lived experience does show some of the pervasiveness of the discourse, but also the dazzling variety of cultural, social (and so on) influences on the way people work.

Cohen and Musson (2000) looked at the way the language of business seeped into the everyday lives and organisational practices of doctors running general practices as part of the UK's National Health Service in the mid-1990s. They explain that GPs 'contract with the state to provide a primary health service to a designated list of patients' (2000: 36), and that various structural changes meant that GP practice activity became more like running a small business. Their research shows how after the institutional changes and the new business language and thinking that GPs started to use, patients came to be described as customers. Subtle and not so subtle shifts in the way that the doctors thought of themselves and the purpose of their work took place; their professional medical discourse of public service was being transformed. What Cohen and Musson suggest is that a new common sense was formed out of the changes.

Similar research in New Zealand (Doolin 2002) looking at change in medical services, in a hospital this time, describes a similar story. The study describes a restructuring process that according to one of the hospital managers was 'a mix of entrepreneurialism tempered with common sense' (2002: 378). But like the GPs in Cohen and Musson's study the clinical consultants adopted a variety of complex positions in relation to the new language and changes. One doctor said, 'I don't see this as a business, and I never would. And I wouldn't work here. I'd walk out if they said it was a business, [...] I've got a social conscience' (Doolin 2002: 383). Other clinicians were more amenable to entrepreneurialism:

> I'm a sort of socio-capitalist. I guess I'm an amalgam of the two ... . In private practice what I'm interested in is dollars. In here [the publicly funded hospital] I'm interested in patient care. In private practice dollars do equate to patient care because that determines future business. But I'm not driven by patient care in private, I'm driven by dollars ... I personally see my private practice as only business. (Doolin 2002: 384)

There has been much other research emphasising the discourses of enterprise and entrepreneurialism in shaping work. However, one problem with seeing people's engagement with their world in this way is the imprecision and inclusiveness of 'enterprise'. Can management, business and accounting (and so on) talk and texts all be subsumed under the notion of enterprise? Another problem is that often the ambiguous and complex detail of these studies show that although the languages of entrepreneurialism and enterprise have an effect on shaping the world and how people construct a sense of who they are at work, the lived experience and engagement with the discourses mean that whilst they might be pervasive and powerful, they are not omnipotent. People can and do ignore, resist and subvert the language as well as comply with it. I develop this point about the discourse of enterprise in my book *Narratives of Enterprise*:

> The lack of thinking that often goes with positive renditions of enterprise is worrying given the degree to which our institutions are restructuring themselves based on such a vague and catch-all notion. I do not however hold with those naysayers at the opposite end that denigrate the achievements of the enterprising. Those that seek to represent enterprise as the driving metaphor of civil and moral collapse are as guilty as those that promote it as an epoch defining curative. (Down 2006: 114)

Fenwick agrees and argues the naysayers are wrong to 'simplify and demonise enterprise as a slippery slope to the worst excesses of globalized corporate capitalism' (2002a: 720). The 'conditions of risk, flexibility, and the new ideal of enterprise prevalent in neo-liberal western society are, at least in part, influencing the trend of people "choosing" or being compelled to "choose" to enter various forms of self-employed enterprise' (Fenwick 2002: 718). But as Fenwick shows in her article about women becoming self-employed in Canada, the self-employed are not simply victims of the tectonic plates of capitalism. The self-expression inherent to enterprising work exhibits values that are also critical of individualism and economic motives, such as the desire to offer a better quality of product or service, or to build a community through the business (Fenwick 2002a: 719).

Looking now at the second more practical level, we should ask the question 'what's it like working in an entrepreneurial venture?' Of course this is a big question and I only intend to finish this chapter off with an illustration or two, building on what we saw earlier about how graduates get on working in smaller firms and on how the self-employed and franchisees fare. Of course the argument made throughout this book is that entrepreneurs will vary a great deal. Working for one will also vary, and despite the positive image in which they are often portrayed, the lived experience of working with entrepreneurs can be quite challenging. For one thing the relationships in the business are very much coloured by the predilections and neuroses of the entrepreneur. Work for a mad entrepreneur, and you're likely to have to do mad things yourself. We also saw in the case study that Mark would often have to deal with self-centred bad behaviour from the entrepreneurs. That fictionalised story is derived from real data collected in my own research (Down 2006; Reveley et al. 2004), where I spent a couple of years or so hanging around Fenderco. Whilst doing the research I got to know John and Paul, the two owner-managers, and staff well. In one interview Will, a younger employee tasked with 'bread and butter' sales and marketing, told me about his relationship with Paul:

> You will ask him [Paul] a question and he will just look at you. Typically he will look at you and just give you a really filthy look and turn away from you and carry on with his work. And you will say; 'Paul I have a problem and I need to ask a question', and he will start to discuss it with you and then he will just forget what you are talking about and just ignore you. In the office you will say; 'Paul, are you at work?' and he will say 'yes' and just walk off. [...] that is how this company works. (Down 2006: 47–48)

Mark, the other junior employee, said the following about John:

> John isn't that easy going. Some days you come into work and John's the nicest bloke ever: he's nice and makes you coffee; 'thanks for that, that's really nice of you mate'; 'thanks for doing a good job on a drawing'; 'great job, nice job mate'. And then he can start shouting for no apparent reason. (ibid.: 47)

Will told me about one night in the pub (Friday nights down *The Grinning Cat* were regular events which I also attended: don't think that research is without its fringe benefits!). Will was talking about his relationship with Paul:

> One night ... I think I really pissed him off [following an argument] I wrote on a piece of paper 'I resign', and he said 'I'll keep that piece of paper until Monday'. So on the way out I thought I'd get it out of his back pocket and bin it: this writing. What happened was that I went for his back pocket, unbeknownst to him, and he just turned round and grabbed me, I insisted on going back and we were going back and eventually I just fell on the floor. And er, I er ... thought, Christ! [Laughs]. And I felt really bad about what had happened, and I thought well, that's my fault what went on there, that shouldn't have happened, and on Monday morning he was in a real strop with me. So I ... have walked in [the office] and he says 'I want to talk to you about Friday night'. And I thought oh no.
>
> *Did you think here's the job gone then?*
>
> Here comes ... not a written warning, because it doesn't happen here, but here comes Mr Big Bollocking time. And he never said anything to me.
>
> *What, he didn't talk to you?*
>
> He didn't talk to me that day. And I must admit I'd actually sustained really quite a badly bruised shoulder after I had gone into the wall. I mean he did push me: it

was the way he pushed me or something. [Then later that week] Paul come up to me and said 'I'm sorry about what happened the other night [...] I'm really sorry to have hurt ya', he said ... And that was it. Nothing more was said. There's been the odd joke [at the office].

Aside from being (hopefully) an unusual example, the incident shows the very real nature of human relationships between managers and workers at work: people enjoying a drink together, straying over normal work role boundaries, the informal nature of work relations and management practices securing control and consent in small firms. This is real life everyday work. My research showed that the owner-managers' entrepreneurialism is only one aspect of the work experience, sometimes the employees Mark and Will were inspired and energised, sometimes they were angry and frustrated. Just like any other job really. From this example and the others I have shown in the chapter we have seen that there are some particular aspects of working in smaller and entrepreneurial enterprises. Equally though, there are many similarities to other forms of work. Thus there is not one single answer to the key question of this chapter – what's it like to work in a small firm? Rather, there are many answers depending on what type of organisation is being worked for.

Summary

This chapter has shown some of the variety of the lived experience of work in smaller and entrepreneurial firms, and other enterprise contexts. The influence of enterprise ideology and values of the contemporary work environment has been stressed, especially through an examination of the university graduates' experience of work in smaller firms. In this way an illustration of aspects of the management processes framework introduced in Chapter 5 is made. Other forms of work such as self-employment and franchising are explained, and examples of how work more generally has been influenced by enterprise ideology are given.

▌ ▮ Further reading ▮

Edwards, P. and Ram, M. (2006) 'Surviving on the margins of the economy: Working relationships in small, low-wage firms', *Journal of Management Studies* 43(4): 895–916.

Edwards, P., Ram, M. and Smith, V. (2008) 'Introduction to special issue: Workers, risk and the new economy', *Human Relations* 61(9): 1163–1170.

Fenwick, T. J. (2002) 'Transgressive selves: new enterprising selves in the new capitalism', *Work, Employment and Society* 16(4): 703–723.

7

Entrepreneuring in
the Corporate Environment

Overview

This chapter has the following objectives:

- To explain the historical context of corporate development and the place of contemporary ideas about corporate entrepreneurship.
- To develop an understanding of bureaucratic organisations which goes beyond everyday notions of obstructive red tape to seeing these as a tool which can both facilitate and constrain entrepreneurship.
- To introduce different ideas or schools of thought about corporate entrepreneurship, and discuss the rise of corporations in their broader socio-political context.
- To illustrate ideas about corporate entrepreneurship though an examination of the criminal failure of the Enron energy corporation.

Introduction

Small and medium-sized firms and the self-employed make up the vast majority of individual businesses and account for the largest proportion of the working population. But it is the large corporation that is the engine of the economy. It is the dynamic corporation that creates the output, wealth and prosperity of capitalism. It is not solely responsible; the corporation is part of an economic system of interpenetrating parts. But it structures the economy and is the focal point that drives change and innovation. It is obviously vital therefore for us to understand how corporations function, and in particular to understand their dynamism. This means of course understanding the entrepreneurial activities of corporations.

Corporations have a bad press. This chapter won't shy away from some of the reasons for this, and we'll see that sometimes 'capitalism is so innovative that it is forever advancing into gray legal areas, and business scandals – especially in finance – have been so frequent that they may be regarded as endemic to the system' (McCraw 2007: 148). But corporations are as morally suspect as the people that run them and set their goals. They are institutional forms geared towards achieving specific material and economic aims; which are normally rather narrowly focused on profit maximisation, but they needn't be and sometimes aren't. As well as the bad behaviour of bad people, who from time to time will steer their corporation into criminal or muddy moral waters, the plurality of interests concerned with the performance of corporations – managerial interests, shareholders, society, politicians, and so on – means that their aims are not always agreed upon. What's good for the tobacco industry might not be so good for the taxpayer.

Corporations were not so long ago described as lumbering dinosaurs which were failing to maintain the engine of capitalist prosperity. In our time we have seen a great deal of grey territory being explored and a strong belief in the benefits of innovation, entrepreneurship and enterprise has been a driving force. The last 30 years or so have seen corporations reinvent themselves. Largely this was achieved through a renewed belief by both political and economic elites in the ability of large scale capitalism to change economies and innovate, to make the world materially better. As a result corporations have become more entrepreneurial, more able to creatively destroy and innovate.

As McCraw (2007: 5) has written, this renewed belief brought with it 'the riotous prosperity of the 1990s, when entrepreneurs became folk heroes'. Yet it also brought an 'ensuing epidemic of corporate scandals, which bankrupted shareholders and employees and disgraced capitalism itself'. Capitalism is if anything even more disgraced now that we understand the extent to which the life blood of the system, credit and finance, was allowed to over-innovate. In all the enthusiasm it was forgotten that in order to work effectively the capitalist system 'requires repeated adjustments of the law, credible enforcement mechanisms, and constant vigilance. Public regulation through intricate legal frameworks – the law of contracts, competition, partnerships, corporations, and so on – is essential' (McCraw 2007: 148).

Given this background this chapter seeks to understand corporate entrepreneurship as a feature not just of corporations themselves, but also within the context of the economy and its historical development as a whole. It is organised in the following way. Firstly, we learn about what a corporation is, and from whence it came. And we learn about how it operates, entrepreneurially speaking. We consider the question of why this particular form of business organisation has come to dominate. We then address some common confusions found regarding the nature of large enterprises, namely the error in thinking that large bureaucratically organised businesses cannot be enterprising and that large enterprising organisation aren't essentially bureaucratic in nature: entrepreneurship and bureaucracy are different things, they are not opposites on a fixed scale. We then look in more detail at how corporations can and have systematically organised themselves to be entrepreneurial, before also looking at a real example of where corporate entrepreneurship can lead.

What is a corporation?

We are so used to the notion of a corporation that it is easy to overlook their real character. They seem so fundamentally part of the economy that they appear to be as natural as the oceans. But corporations as a distinct form of business organisation have an evolving history, and it is a relatively recent one.

A corporation is a type of business organisation which varies in its legal detail in different nations but whose key feature is its legal independence from the people who own it. The owners have liabilities limited to the original investment, and ownership is in the form of share holdings which can be bought and sold on stock markets. A corporation – from the Latin *corpus*, meaning body – is a separate legal body with rights and responsibilities. In effect, it is an artificial person. The purpose of creating these entities is to spread or socialise the risk and obligations involved in large scale economic activity. They are created to reduce the risk and accountability that in other business forms, a partnership for instance, remain with the owners. They also hold the advantage of permanency over other business forms in that they exist beyond the lives of their owners.

Before the modern era the corporation was a special legal form – often begun by royal charter – granted by the state on rare occasions to achieve large publicly useful projects that would not likely come to fruition through the private wealth of capitalists (see McCraw 2007: 261–266 for a short history of the development of the corporation; and Hendry 2004: 4–10). The corporation was, as economic historian William Roy notes, 'a quasi-public device used by governments to create and administer public services' (1997: 6). Throughout the nineteenth century as industry and commerce grew in size – particularly in the US where entrepreneurial 'robber barons' amassed vast sums through dubious and ruthless ways (Hobsbawn 1975: 143–146) – various liberalising legal innovations took place that gradually transformed the corporation into the dominant form of business organisation.

Activity

Read a selection from Thomas K. McCraw's *Prophet of Innovation: Joseph Schumpeter and Creative Destruction* and John Hendry *Between Enterprise and Ethics* available via books.google.com[.]

The rise of corporations was and continues to be facilitated by the availability of credit. Without credit, confidence in the achievability of large projects in the future is lost. Corporations are vehicles to draw in investment and create futures. In the US at the end of the nineteenth century a corporate revolution took place where large numbers of businesses, in the oil and steel industries for instance, merged and became large modern corporations. The key aspect of this revolution was the change in the nature of ownership; 'economic entities were [now] each owned by many individuals rather than a few, and many individuals owned pieces of many units' (Roy 1997: 6). In short, private capital was socialised. Separating ownership from control in this way also meant that a new class of professional management began to run corporations: these managers and corporate executives became corporate entrepreneurs.

Why this slow burning fuse of legal and organisational innovation during the nineteenth century suddenly reached its charge and exploded into revolution is complicated and contested. Put simply, the growth of industrial production in the US and Europe coincided with and was 'germinated' by the sophisticated financial system of 'stock markets, brokerage houses, and investment banks' (Roy 1997: 7). The entrepreneurial owners of big businesses found that in order to achieve the necessary economies of scale and to continue making profits 'that corporatization was the best option in an increasingly industrialised economy, to avoid the perceived dangers of "destructive competition"' (Down 2001: 398). That is, businesses merged and consolidated to avoid competing with each other too aggressively. To survive, and continue investing in long-term large projects, markets needed to be stable, and corporatisation helped achieve that stability. Big business has continued to be the dominant form of organisation ever since, with, especially in the late twentieth century drive to privatise and deregulate, increasingly greater aspects of society organised through this legal and organisational form.

And corporations continue to develop and innovate. This is because 'large established corporations face major challenges in innovation arising from technological and resources lock-ins, and routine and cultural rigidities' (Jones and Wadhwani 2006a: 25). This means that corporations are rather like large unwieldy oil tankers. They are **path dependent** and can find it difficult, or at least can be unwilling when there are other options available, to change course. One result from this is that the corporation has an interest in avoiding too much competition, which can force rapid change. It deals with this through innovations in one form or another.

Path dependent describes an aspect of logic regarding a particular social actor or phenomenon such that the direction already taken will have a profound influence on what will happen.

A key aspect of this process of continual innovation has been to ensure that new ways of doing things are being continually explored both organisationally and technologically. Ever since the early part of the twentieth century corporations have recognised this need. As McCraw puts it 'they made innovation itself part of their business routine' (2007: 164) by setting up permanent research and development departments. In more recent times as the readiness for change has grown more pressing, corporations have had to pay more attention to being agile. This has involved being smaller and developing new ways of controlling the economic activities of others without being linked through ownership: activities such as outsourcing and quality control typify these innovations. Similarly, another way to enhance the agility and responsiveness of their business is to chop it up into separate but related companies: 'The creation of internal venture units has provided one's means to escape the inertia of existing organizations' (Jones and Wadhwani 2006a: 26): less oil tanker than a flotilla of tugboats.

Another innovation inherent to the corporate form is simply to avoid reacting to the market and instead to influence and shape it to suit what you want to do or are already doing. Small businesses obviously do not wield a great deal of power. Corporations, many of which are larger economic entities than very substantial nations, wield quite a bit. Thus corporations both create *and* protect markets. As Schumpeter had written in the early twentieth century when large corporations themselves were new innovations: it is 'the producer who as a rule initiates economic change, and consumers are educated by him if necessary; they are, as it were, taught to want new things' (cited in McCraw 2007: 72, from Schumpeter 1934/1911: 65). To believe that consumers bend corporations to their will is naïve. Corporations invest too much in certain paths for market responsiveness to be the only tactic: the 'apparatus of persuasion and exhortation' is a key part of corporate strategy (Galbraith 1967: 15).

This need for innovations – to create new technologies, new organisational forms and new ways of responding to, and creating and controlling, markets – requires managers in corporations to be entrepreneurial. But before we look in more detail at how corporate entrepreneurship works, we need to make a short diversion to learn a bit more about some common confusions about organisation, bureaucracy and enterprise.

Common confusions about organisation, bureaucracy and enterprise

Bureaucracy gets an even worse press than corporations. The word – literally meaning rule (-cracy) by office (bureau-) – has come to mean the same as red tape: meaning that effective organisational action is hindered by over-rigid or complex procedures. Clearly this *is* the antithesis of enterprise. However, this everyday meaning obscures both a more neutral and general meaning, and the essentially bureaucratic nature of corporations, indeed of all organisations. All complex organisations behave in largely unremarkable bureaucratic ways, as well as in the very noticeable and irritating ways we are all familiar with. Most people hate red tape getting in the way of getting things done. But for the most part it's a good thing that organisations behave bureaucratically (see Du Gay 2000, for an insightful defence of the moral importance of bureaucracy, and Hendry 2004, for a similarly important exploration of enterprise and its ethical dimensions). Corporations aren't bureaucracies any longer, but they are still bureaucratic.

Bureaucracy protects people and organisations from excess and chaos. As we saw in the introduction, capitalism needs regulating and corporations need internal regulations, rules and routines. Bureaucratic mechanisms provide these. This is just as true within corporations as it is with the system as a whole. It may not be popular or fashionable, but the vilification of bureaucracy is odd given the extent to which it helps organise our world. Try to imagine working in a large or even a small organisation without any rules or guides about how to behave. All the organisations I have worked for – a petrol station, a speaker manufacturer, a supermarket, a pub, a military hospital (it's a long story), a language school, London Underground Ltd, and numerous universities – all relied on bureaucratic processes to function. Even the independent music label I ran (a limited company, but very small), whilst it didn't have much in the way of internal bureaucracy (it certainly needed more of it, especially when it came to finance!), was influenced by the bureaucratic requirements of contracts, and the rules and terms of business of a variety of other companies: manufacturing and distributing the records; graphic services designing the record sleeves; recording studios where the music was produced; and media companies who publicised the music. To achieve my goals as an entrepreneur I had to follow the rules of others.

What does bureaucracy consist of? Here are some features that exist in all complex organisations: 'a high degree of specialisation and a clearly defined division of labour'; 'a hierarchical structure of authority'; 'a formal body of rules to govern the operation of the organisation'; 'administration based on written documents'; recruitment based on 'ability' (Abercrombie et al. 2000: 33). All of these features exist in the modern corporation. The language used to describe these bureaucratic mechanisms is different and somewhat vaguer sounding today: systems, processes, control mechanisms, routines, regulation, responsibility, boundaries, etc. But they all refer to essential features of bureaucratic administration. It is very true that a slavish and unthinking attachment to rules and procedures is extremely inefficient; as in most things organisations need a balance in pursuit of their aims and objectives. There are also other features that typify the classic bureaucracy which are not so prevalent in today's organisational environment – such as a 'fixed salary'; 'impersonal relationships between organisational members and clients'; 'long-term employment, promotion on the basis of seniority or merit' (today the latter is preferred over seniority); and the 'separation of private and official income' (Abercrombie et al. 2000: 33) – but the basic forms of administration and organisation are. The decline of the classic bureaucracy – which these contemporary absences represent – and the emergence of the flexible, agile and entrepreneurial corporation is nonetheless a revolution. (The reasons for this revolution in corporate behaviour in our period are as complicated and contested as the first corporate revolution discussed above – Hendry 2004:1–36 explains this as well as anyone I have read.)

Some forms of bureaucracy – rules, the division of labour, task specialisation, hierarchical authority, written documents, recruitment based on merit and technical ability – are nevertheless absolutely vital for the efficient functioning of large organisations. If you have ever tried to deal with a large corporation as a consumer with a problem that sits outside the norm you'll know how reliant they are on standard procedures embodied in the computer screen or telephone options. Retail chains are good examples. Supermarket stores, for instance, tend to be more or less identical and are managed according to an operating manual – the corporate store 'bible'. Whilst some localised and minor discretion and initiative is encouraged, particularly at the customer interface, what goes on in stores, the dos and don'ts about people management, how they are supplied logistically, how data are fed back to head office, and so on, are all subject to exact written bureaucratic controls. Some controls are automated and do not allow for management discretion at all. Management information systems force managers to do things in certain ways or indeed, in the case of stock replacement, take the decision away entirely.

This does not mean that the super-marketing retail industry is bereft of innovation. Supermarkets and retail business generally are aggressively entrepreneurial, and their enthusiasm for introducing new technologies and innovative forms of organisation demonstrates this. Largely though, the innovations are generated through dedicated specialised staff at head offices, who will then pilot projects experimenting with new ideas in the stores. To reap the benefit of these innovations the application of bureaucratic standardised processes and procedures is invariably required. In a Schumpetarian sense, bureaucratically based routines may get rightly broken in the gales of creative destruction, as entrepreneurial managers in corporations do their innovating, but for their new innovations to succeed they will need to introduce routines and bureaucratic mechanisms to drive through their changes. Bureaucracy is not the opposite of entrepreneurship in a large corporation. They work together: the corporation can exemplify an excellent bureaucratic organization *and* outstanding entrepreneurship. Organizational bureaucracy is a tool: it can facilitate entrepreneurship just as it can constrain it.

Let's look at how the corporation behaves entrepreneurially.

Fenderco case study

John's (Fenderco director and entrepreneur) story about his corporate past

It makes me laugh now. I used to get so pissed off. After my engineering degree I was lucky enough to get a traineeship at Tyrecorp. It took a while to find my feet – the stint I had in HR was a disaster. I should have been sacked! Once I got to sales and started working with Mike Hutchinson, it was like I'd come home. I learnt so much from Mike. He was very much an entrepreneurial guy. Really unorthodox. He wasn't a natural fit in Tyrecorp, and I was pretty much the same. We were a real team for a while.

I just loved the buzz of making the deal, getting the sale. We didn't do the bread and butter stuff, you know, standard products. We interfaced with production, feeding back info about bespoke rubber products our business customers wanted – weird stuff some of it, if you know what I mean – responding to tenders and the like. If we didn't come up with the right product at the right time at the right price, you know, we were stuffed.

It was an uphill battle though, especially after we merged. Before the merger systems were pretty good; things would piss us off but looking back it was more or less right. It was pretty bureaucratic, it just didn't stop things happening; just slowed them up a bit. Nobody likes filling in forms, but things worked pretty well, before. The merger just clogged things up so much. It was just so slow and plodding and nothing happened quickly and it was just really tedious, you know. If you wanted to get anything done, whatever, it took weeks and weeks to get it through the factory. You had loads of obstacles put in your way all the time. And the new managers wondered why we didn't meet performance targets! If you wanted to circumvent the system you could never get round it or you could but it was so difficult and you really had to work hard to achieve things for the customers. Everything got all committee-ised. I look back on it now and realise that the new managers got all control freaky because they needed the authority to carry them through the changes. I couldn't be doing with it all and I got a new job in fendering with Europort. Eventually even they were too stuck in the mud for me, and Paul and I started Fenderco. Now I have to run a company and I can see that you need rules. I still get really angry sometimes about all the red tape, and boy is there a lot of it running your own business, but it protects us as well.

Anyway, getting back to Tyrecorp. Mike couldn't just up and leave, he had more to lose, so stayed and worked through it. He told me later that the new top managers pushed through much better systems eventually as everything calmed down and people started trusting each other again.

Activity

1 Speculate as to why John's time working in human resources was a disaster. Think of how a human resource department might act entrepreneurially.
2 Would a takeover or merger always necessarily lead to more bureaucratic control?
3 Why might slowing things up a bit be a good thing for a merged new business?
4 What explains Mike's decision to develop his career in Tyrecorp? Does it make him less of an entrepreneur?

Corporate entrepreneurship

This book has stressed the breadth of enterprising activity. Lots of people in different circumstances can and do behave entrepreneurially. This of course does not mean that all these people or all small firm owners or self-employed workers are classical entrepreneurs. Entrepreneurship in its classical narrow sense – one limited to dynamic and growing business environments – is a rare and special behaviour, and 'just as likely to be found in large firms as in SMEs' (Casson 2005: 340). There are also significant barriers to starting your own entrepreneurial venture, including the lack of 'financial endowments and organizational skills' (2005: 338). This implies – because the prospective entrepreneur needs at least some financial and skill resource – that many successful independent entrepreneurs are not from 'humble beginnings' but are more likely to have been formally employed in a 'large professionally run firm' (2005: 339). Thus, it is not surprising to find entrepreneurs working in large corporations rather than SMEs because, as economist Mark Casson has noted, it can take several generations to build a substantial business, and many drawn to the attractions of entrepreneurship decide quite sensibly to take their talents into existing large organisations.

Casson's starting point is that there have always been entrepreneurial talent running corporations: 'many of the most highly entrepreneurial individuals are the CEOs of large firms' (2005: 339). He's right. However, changing and extremely challenging economic circumstances in the 1970s (there was a quadrupling of the price of oil) meant that the traditional ways of running corporations started failing. *Excessive* reliance on bureaucratic and technocratic cultures wasn't working. New forms of innovative organisation were desired. Back in the late 1970s and 1980s when gurus, business scholars and corporate executives alike were pondering how to revitalise corporations, a renewed emphasis on entrepreneurship was seen as one of the ways forward (downsizing, the flattening of hierarchies, flexibility, outsourcing and culture change were some of the other strategies used: see Sennett 1998 for an assessment of the impact of these changes).

Some were sceptical about how existing divisional structures and overly bureaucratic cultures could adapt to the new entrepreneurialism (Morse 1986). Morse rightly recognised that three things would need to change if corporations were to become more entrepreneurial: the ability of individuals to earn entrepreneurial wealth within the corporation; personal autonomy in order to drive through innovations and initiatives in new structurally independent ventures or subsidiaries; and cultural change so that entrepreneurship within corporations was seen as the norm. All these things have come to pass. CEOs earn vast sums, corporations have disaggregated into looser semi-autonomous networks, and the cultures within organisations and society have become more self-interested and less worried about fairness and disparities of wealth. Hendry suggests that, largely as a result of the expansion of the world of business into ever greater aspects of society, 'the pursuit of self-interest at the expense of others, traditionally condemned as morally reprehensible, has come to be seen as morally acceptable and socially legitimate' (2004: 2). These changes have helped revitalise the corporation.

Early studies looking at corporate entrepreneurship – when it was one of many fashionable ideas – showed how difficult it was to foster new entrepreneurial ventures from within a divisionalised corporate structure (which are 'large agglomerates of widely diverse yet related businesses' groups into divisions whose general managers report to corporate management', Burgleman 1983: 223). Whilst recognising that entrepreneurially-minded individuals were able to create new innovations from within operational levels of the organisation, particularly if they were championed by their corporate manager, substantial obstacles, such as getting sufficient resources, remained in place because the new innovations often ran counter to existing corporate strategic objectives. Burgelman concluded that looser less divisionalised approaches would likely be necessary.

As corporations themselves experimented with different approaches to entrepreneurship, often following the advice of consultants, and guru-scholars, competing perspectives about the best way to transform the organisation emerged. Today although 'a large and growing literature on corporate entrepreneurship exists, there is no consensus on what it means, or at what level of analysis it should be studied' (Birkinshaw 2003: 57; see also Zahra et al. 1999, who agrees). Corporate entrepreneurship can nevertheless be defined as 'the development of new business ideas and opportunities within large and established corporations' (Birkinshaw 2003: 47). These developments include 'innovations (of all types) and new business creation through venturing' (Zahra et al. 1999: 51). Given the scope and breadth of the activities these definitions imply it is not surprising that four schools of thought – which are both descriptive and prescriptive in intent – have emerged.

Birkinshaw (2003) examines the excesses of entrepreneurship at the root of Enron (a large energy company that failed spectacularly in 2001 partly because of criminal activity; the next section looks at this case in detail) and uses it to great effect to examine how corporations should, and should not, become more entrepreneurial.

Table 7.1 The four schools of thought on corporate entrepreneurship

Corporate Venturing (or 'focused corporate entrepreneurship', Birkinshaw 1997: 208). This body of thinking argues that new business ventures need to be managed separately from the mainstream business, or they will not survive long enough to deliver benefit to the sponsoring company. It examines the organisational arrangements that new ventures need and the processes of aligning them with the company's existing activities.

Intrapreneurship (or 'dispersed corporate entrepreneurship', Birkinshaw 1997: 209). This approach focuses on the individual employee and his or her propensity to act in an entrepreneurial way. It works on the basic assumption that all large firms put in place systems and structures that inhibit initiative, so individuals have to be prepared to actively challenge those systems. It examines the often subversive tactics these corporate entrepreneurs adopt, and the things executives can do to make their lives easier or harder. It also considers the personalities and styles of individuals who make good corporate entrepreneurs.

Entrepreneurial transformation. Premised on the assumption that large firms can and should adapt to an ever-changing environment, entrepreneurial transformation suggests that such adaptation can best be achieved by manipulating the firm's culture and organisation systems, thereby inducing individuals to act in a more entrepreneurial way.

Bringing the market inside. This school of thought also operates at the firm level, but it focuses more on the structural changes that can be made to encourage entrepreneurial behaviour. It uses the metaphor of the marketplace to suggest how large firms should manage their resource allocation and people management systems, and it argues for greater use of such market techniques as spin-offs and corporate venture capital operations.

Source: Adapted from Birkinshaw (2003: 57)

He argues from an entrepreneurial transformation point of view – one that emphasises the need for an entrepreneurial culture throughout the organisation – and suggests that 'the job of senior executives is to develop a set of corporate systems and processes that promote such entrepreneurship throughout the organization' (2003: 48). However, in order for this to work there is a need to get the balance right between setting systems and processes that constrain entrepreneurship and those that can lead to a chaotic lack of control. In short he argues that too much entrepreneurship is dangerous.

Birkinshaw identifies four factors which need to be addressed if the corporation is to be successfully entrepreneurial: the *direction* or strategy of the organisation; the *space* or extent of freedom and autonomy that managers are given; the legal, regulatory or moral boundaries, *rules* and limits within which the organisation operates; and the *support* that managers and staff are given to do their job (a range of services are included, from information and communication sharing mechanisms to training and development initiatives). The model in Figure 7.1 illustrates where corporations should attempt to situate themselves – in the *ideal zone* where the corporation is managed with neither too much space nor too little *direction*. The ideal zone is where the corporation is succeeding through entrepreneurship. The centre box represents an overly constrained and static company. And the danger zone represents a business that is getting out of control; getting high on entrepreneurship.

Of course there are many other analyses and prescriptions for corporate entrepreneurship that we will not consider here (see Kuratko 2007; Katz and Shepherd 2004; and Sathe 2003 for book length treatments). Many of the prescriptions for

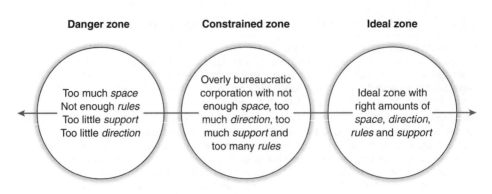

Danger zone	Constrained zone	Ideal zone

Too much *space*
Not enough *rules*
Too little *support*
Too little *direction*

Overly bureaucratic corporation with not enough *space*, too much *direction*, too much *support* and too many *rules*

Ideal zone with right amounts of *space, direction, rules* and *support*

Figure 7.1   Model of corporate entrepreneurship (adapted from Birkinshaw 2003: 51)

entrepreneuring-up the corporation help to make stronger businesses, and as the economy is dynamic, innovations of corporate form continue to develop. In recent decades the disaggregation of large corporations into loosely-coupled alliances and networks of subsidiaries – flotillas not oil tankers, remember – has been a noticeable innovation in corporate form. During the same period many nations have privatised previously state-owned enterprises in the telecoms, military industries, utilities, energy and airlines sectors, many of which have become global corporate players. As noted political scientist Sheldon Wolin argues, 'corporate power has increasingly assumed governmental functions and services, many of which had previously been deemed the special reserve of state power' (2008: 136). Arguably these previously state-owned enterprises are quite distinct and innovative corporate forms given that they often continue to operate at close proximity to state interests, receive subsidies and preferential state contracts, and so on.

Take the emergence of the privatised utility company. Some of their corporate behaviour seems akin to a form of private taxation, with little classical entrepreneurialism. Consider this description of the water utilities sector in the UK:

> **The privatisation of Britain's water companies in 1989 had nothing in common with the romantic notion of shareholder capitalism, where inventors and entrepreneurs have ideas, start businesses and sell shares to bold investors in order to raise money to help those businesses expand. [...] Far from being exciting new entrepreneurial ventures, the companies involved were settled operations that had been around in one form or another for almost two hundred years, and had benefited, for more than half that time, from steady infusions of ratepayers' and taxpayers' money. The most striking contradiction between water privatisation and Thatcherite free-market romanticism is the monopoly nature of the water companies. Millions of customers who have no choice of supplier, no choice but to take the water, and no choice but to pay for it. Millions of captive monthly payments in perpetuity: it is an investor's dream. (Meek 2008: 9–10)**

Schumpeter and other economists might point to the long-term good that arises, and to how over time the water companies will face the entrepreneurial forces of creative destruction; mergers, acquisitions and so forth. This may be the case, but from the customer's point of view what will change even then? As John Keynes, another great economist said, in the long run we will all be dead. The trouble with long-term arguments about the inevitable benevolence of capitalist dynamics is that they naturalise what is already happening. Almost any corporate behaviour becomes justifiable, because, the argument seems to imply, the forces of nature – creative destruction – will inevitably and eventually blow away the inefficient. We can assume that more investment monies are wrested from the customer than would be politically expedient from the taxpayer and that in a narrow sense the companies are now more efficient. Economists Netter and Megginson (2001: 381) explain that 'privatisation "works" in the sense that divested firms almost always become more efficient, more profitable, and financially healthier, and increase their capital investment spending. [...] However, there is little empirical evidence on how privatisation affects consumers'. The gains – including smaller more productive (better exploited) workforces – are however crucially framed around coercion; the customer has little choice and the provision of utilities is not directly and democratically accountable as it once was. The privatised form of corporate organisation may or may not be good for society as a whole (evidence regarding the mass privatisations of transition economies such as Russia's suggests that they contribute to 'sharp drops in life expectancy' (Stuckler et al. 2009)) – in the long run – but it is definitely a fair way from entrepreneurial behaviour as we classically understand it. As McCraw had written, 'only through innovation and entrepreneurship can any business except a government-sponsored monopoly survive over the long term' (2007: 496; see Schumpeter 1962/1942: 99, who also recognised that 'public utilities' were different). Are privatised utilities (and other such corporations) monopolies in this sense? To my mind some contemporary corporate activity is over-protected from the harsh gales of competition and not especially entrepreneurial.

There is a broader concern too at the interpenetration of the state and the corporation that utilities companies are only one aspect of. The nation state itself is changing and becoming weaker in the face of cross border activities by corporations and supranational institutions. Corporations are very powerful, and it matters how they address their problems. Their enthusiasm for entrepreneurship is undoubtedly having a significant impact on society more broadly. There is today a symbiotic cauldron of corporate sponsored lobbyists, consultants, and think tanks that undemocratically influence political outcomes. There is also a revolving door of political elites who take on corporate positions of one sort or another and of corporate leaders who come into regional, national and supranational government (and quasi-government) organisations in the form of board memberships, secondments and so on. There is corporate reliance on the state for 'contracts, subsidies, protection; for promoting opportunities at home and abroad' (Wolin 2008: 136). In many ways recent innovations in the interface between the corporation and the state have seen the competitive and profit-centred visions and missions of corporate culture replace the disinterested public service ethos (Hendry 2004). Some, in the US at least, have even argued that with it comes a lack of democratic accountability and an increase in corruption, venality and grey legal practices that seem an endemic aspect of the corporation (Wolin 2008). Corporate actions, and the manner in which they develop their businesses, are not then insignificant matters, and the disastrous aspects of excessive corporate entrepreneurialism can be seen in the next section, as we look at the demise of the Enron Corporation.

Enron: a case of too much entrepreneurship and innovation?

There are plenty of examples of how corporations claim that they are doing good *and* being entrepreneurial. There are not so many that admit to being drawn into illegality or grey, morally dubious practices. This suggests that there is a moral tension between entrepreneurial profit seeking and achieving other social and economic goods: a tension, not an incompatibility. Most companies strive to operate in morally neutral or even positive moral environments – think about Google's motto 'Don't be evil' – and the tension lies under the surface, not threatening the company or anyone else. But as we saw earlier, morally dubious and criminal activity is endemic to capitalism. Moral and legal boundaries shift with cycles of bust, regulation, boom, liberalisation, bust, and re-regulation. Morality is bound up in the structure of our world. Not all bad things in the world happen because of bad people: were Bush and Blair evil for starting a war in Iraq? Are bankers evil for ruining hundreds of thousands of peoples' lives? What about Enron?

The Enron Corporation was an energy conglomerate with a range of businesses in natural gas, electricity, communications, commodities trading and financial services. Prior to its collapse in December 2001 – from a position of being the seventh largest US corporation (Seeger and Ulmer 2003: 59) – it had been successively named by *Fortune* magazine as 'America's Most Innovative Company'. How did it collapse? Stein (2007: 1395) takes up the story:

> **Enron's recorded revenues reached a massive $100 billion (almost entirely based on its purported revenues in trading), making it the seventh largest company in the Fortune 500. However, this image disguised a chaotic reality characterized by an absence of regulation; the collusion of auditors Arthur Andersen; a range of illegal practices; intense internal rivalry; and highly dangerous risk-taking. During this time, a wide range of parties and stakeholders celebrated Enron as one of the most promising companies in the USA, praising it as an organization with an exemplary 'innovative' quality. Business academics such as Harvard's Gary Hamel, for example, wrote of Enron as having 'the almost magical mix of entrepreneurship with the ability ... to get things done' (quoted in Beard, 2003). This adulation lasted almost until Enron's collapse, and it was only in the latter part of 2001 that suspicions about Enron's activities became widespread. In August 2001, negative publicity was generated following an anonymous memo warning of an imminent accounting scandal, and in October 2001 the Securities and Exchange Commission (SEC) began an investigation. [...] this was the**

largest corporate bankruptcy in history. The consequences were widespread: thousands of Enron employees lost their jobs, their pensions ruined; Arthur Andersen (one of the 'big five' accounting firms) laid off thousands of workers and finally collapsed; the US Justice Department started a criminal investigation; senior Enron executives were in substantial legal and personal trouble, with one committing suicide; and the US business community was rocked to the core.

Many have offered explanations for the Enron bankruptcy with a variety of micro, individual-centred, and macro, environment-centred theories (Stein 2007: 1390–1392). Studies have tended to stress specific failures which relate, understandably, to the field of expertise or sub-discipline in which the authors operate (Boje and Rosile 2002: 315). So business ethics experts see it as a failure in ethics (Kuratko and Goldsby 2004). Experts in management communication see it as a failure in communications and responsible leadership (Seeger and Ulmer 2003). Experts in organisational psychology see it as a psychological failure to respect and react appropriately to external authority (Stein 2007). Organisational narrative experts see and emphasise the multiple stories seeking to explain the failure and the interests of those who tell the different accounts (Boje and Rosile 2002). And on it goes. Given that explaining Enron's failure is not the task at hand here, we, obviously, will focus on the role of corporate entrepreneurship (Birkinshaw 2003): Birkinshaw is an expert in, you guessed it, corporate entrepreneurship. This is not to argue that his is a better or truer explanation of how and why Enron collapsed, just more pertinent to our purpose. It *is* worth noting however, that Enron *was* an extremely innovative and entrepreneurial corporation and *was* also celebrated for it. Most explanations also frame their arguments with this in mind (see Seeger and Ulmer 2003: 70–82; also Kuratko and Goldsby 2004).

Birkinshaw framed his analysis of corporate entrepreneurship in terms of the model we discussed earlier (see Figure 7.1, page 122) and stressed the lack of direction, support and boundaries, and an excess of space as key contributing causes to the collapse. What this means is that Enron's enthusiasm for and application of entrepreneurship went too far. Let's look at the four factors in turn.

Firstly, Enron started with the specific goal of being the 'best gas distribution company'. As it grew and diversified it lost any 'overarching sense of where the company was going', and Enron's guiding *direction* became simply to be 'the world's best company'. The result was incoherence, vagueness, chaos and collapse (Birkinshaw 2003: 53).

Secondly, managers and staff at Enron were also given far too much *space*: so much so that CEOs often didn't know about substantial new Enron ventures when asked about these by journalists. The best staff were allowed to move around following the 'best' most exciting high potential projects and away from traditional revenue generating businesses. There was also an 'aggressive risk-reward mentality' which in turn disadvantaged the maintenance of those traditional businesses (2003: 54).

Thirdly, despite a 'relatively sophisticated control system' rules were regularly broken, and 'Enron's corporate governance practices and policing of its *boundaries*' were deficient. 'To avoid choking the entrepreneurial culture', serious rule-breaking was also treated with inappropriate laxity by senior managers (2003: 55). This reflects

Stein's (2007) view that external authority was seen as unnecessary nannying and interfering. I have suggested earlier that if profit is pursued aggressively and entrepreneurially without safeguards there are inevitably going to be rules and laws that are tested, probed or broken. In Enron's case, the attachment to entrepreneurialism became fetishistic and many boundaries were broken. Corporate entrepreneurship in this context asks managers and employees to walk 'a fine line between clever resourcefulness and outright rule breaking' (Kuratko and Goldsby 2004: 13).

Finally, 'Enron's personal development program [...] was almost entirely the responsibility of the individual'. Enron offered little *support* to staff because they were expected to act autonomously and entrepreneurially; it was a case of the survival of the most aggressively self-interested. This meant that 'pushy individuals did well, often at the expense of equally smart but less assertive colleagues' (Birkinshaw 2003: 56). Again traditional and established Enron businesses suffered, whilst the talent crowded into the new high-risk and unproven ventures.

All these factors contributed to Enron's failure. Corporate entrepreneurship initiatives were not applied in a balanced manner: 'Enron's demise was ultimately a failure of control and governance, but the seeds of that failure lay in a system that ratcheted up the risk–reward payoffs for individuals to such an extent that people were prepared to lie, steal, and cheat rather than miss their performance targets' (Birkinshaw 2003: 56). There are other reasons too. The moral bankruptcy of Enron and all the other dubious and criminal corporate practices (see Slapper and Tombs 1999; Clinard and Yeager 2005 for book length discussions of corporate crime) that have typified the recent entrepreneurial excesses suggest that there is a disjunction between the morality and ethics of business and society more generally. Hendry has argued that this disjunction represents the emergence of a dangerous form of 'bimoral' society which balances contradictory tensions between traditional ideas of moral behaviour with the self-interested and instrumental (greed is good) moral world of work and business. Hendry suggests that 'Events at Enron [...] and other large corporations have thrown into question both the judgement and moral integrity of business leaders and the ability of legal and regulatory systems of corporate governance to protect shareholders, employees, and other stakeholders from the excesses of entrepreneurial zeal' (2004: 1). Enron might be an extreme and emblematic example, but like Hendry and others cited in this chapter I would suggest that it does, at the very least, reflect some advisable limits to corporate entrepreneurship.

Conclusion

What would Schumpeter, who understood the vital role corporations play in processes of creative destruction, make of the contemporary business environment? Here's what his biographer Thomas McCraw thinks:

> Schumpeter often defended capitalism, and big business as well [...]. But he would never have condoned the behaviour brought into the public consciousness by the scandals of the 1990s and early twenty-first century: accounting frauds, outrageous executive pay schemes, back-dating of stock options, and

other looting of corporate treasuries by the very executives who were supposed to be their stewards. He would have considered these kinds of practices a betrayal of capitalism. (2007: 497–498)

Clearly something very important has been forgotten: 'the need for eternal vigilance and timely action by government regulators' (McCraw 2007: 498). Part of the explanation for this forgetting lies in the belief that unalloyed good comes from *aggressively* entrepreneurial economic expansion. With these ideological beliefs held by economic and political elites, and a consequently lax regulatory environment, the logic of capitalism slaps us hard in the face with inevitable, depressing, cyclical, results. Corporations and the economy rely on both internal and external bureaucratic mechanisms and routines that do much of the monitoring work once things are entrepreneurially pushed along in specific directions. What has gone wrong is that the engine of entrepreneurship has been pushed down way too steep a hill, and has crashed, with dramatic consequences for all of us. Here is a case for having too much of a good thing.

Summary

Rather than a narrow focus on theories of how corporations engage in entrepreneurship the historical development of the corporate form of organisation was explained. The vital importance of corporations was emphasised, and common misconceptions that place bureaucratic control as the antithesis of entrepreneurship were dispelled: bureaucracy is a vital control mechanism for all organisations, including entrepreneurial corporations. Different schools of thought explaining what corporate entrepreneuring is were discussed in the broader context of the socio-political importance of corporate behaviour. Many of the themes of the chapter were illustrated with an examination of the criminal failure of the Enron corporation; a company that suffered from too much entrepreneurship.

Further reading

Birkinshaw, J. (2003) 'The paradox of corporate entrepreneurship: Post-Enron principles for encouraging creativity without crossing the line', *Strategy and Business* 30(1): 46–57 (http://www.strategy-business.com/press/16635507/8276).

Burgelman, R.A. (1983) 'Process model of internal corporate venturing in the diversified major firm', *Administrative Science Quarterly* 28: 223–244.

Casson, M. (2005) 'Entrepreneurship and the theory of the firm', *Journal of Economic Behaviour and Organization* 58: 327–348

Hendry, J. (2004) *Between Enterprise and Ethics: Business and Management in a Bimoral Society*, Oxford: Oxford University Press.

Zahra, S.A., Jennings, D.F. and Kuratko, D.F. (1999) 'The antecedents and consequences of firm-level entrepreneurship: The state of the field', *Entrepreneurship, Theory and Practice* 24(4): 45–65.

8

Reflecting on Practice: Finance, Marketing and Networking, Strategy and Growth

Overview

This chapter has the following objectives:

- To develop a nuanced understanding of practice which stresses the link to theories of action through tacit knowledge.
- To argue that small firm practices in marketing, finance, networking and strategy are strategically oriented at achieving certain goals, and are practically achieved through improvisation, rather than through rigid adherence to rules and routines.
- To illustrate the key issues derived from research – and the author's own experience – that explain what small business owners actually do in relation to finance, marketing, networking and growth and strategy.

Introduction

As I explained in Chapter 1 this is not a 'how to' book. It's not a step-by-step guide or manual of best practice explaining how to start and run a successful venture. This is not to say that you won't have picked up a good deal of insight into how real businesses work. We are interested in how things are, to the best of our knowledge, not in how they ought to be. 'How to' books logically tend towards a fair amount of should and ought, and the best of these reflect the best of current practice. But they can never reflect the diversity or complexity of everyday enterprise and there is a tendency to ignore the less than ideal. They can also imply that the best practices of larger and entrepreneurial firms are also suitable to the smaller and less ambitious. We concentrate on what the research says about what smaller and entrepreneurial firms actually do. Or rather it draws on research about what entrepreneurs, owner-managers and their employees *say* they do. This is often different from what they actually do, or indeed from what they think they should be doing (Watson 1996). Thus, because of the emphasis on reflecting rather than telling, this chapter will emphasise the situated nature of practice; description rather than prescription. We begin by thinking about what 'practice' means, before looking at the practices of finance, marketing, networking and strategy/growth. Alongside these four sections we meet Paul and John again in our Fenderco case study, and I also reflect a little on my own entrepreneurial practice running a small independent record label business.

What is practice?

'All social life is essentially practical' (cited in Jenkins 1992: 68). So wrote Karl Marx in the nineteenth century. He was right. Too much is made of the distinction between theory and practice. In many ways this separation of the practical world of doing and a supposedly artificial world of ideas, thinking and reflecting represents a failure to understand the tacit 'theoretical' knowledge that is embodied in the ability to do things. Doing stuff requires an implicit theory about what is happening, even if explicit – theoretical – knowledge isn't always necessary. You could for instance read a book about how to ride a bike, but I wouldn't put much faith in your ability to actually ride one, if you hadn't ridden one before. But a lot of implied theory, ideas and concepts – mechanical properties of the body and machines, centre of gravity, road skills, danger and risk, geography, speed, acceleration, balance and so on – would lie behind the doing. Our understanding of how things work in the world underpins the doing. We rely on tacit knowledge a great deal: it's a short cut, an accumulation of what we know of the world. When viewing the first moving picture films people were fearful that the steaming train hurtling towards them would burst out into the auditorium: they didn't have a 'theory' about film or cinema screens.

Different groups develop their own specific practices. Cyclists do things differently from film-goers. Unicyclists have different practices from BMX cyclists; art house film buffs see their pursuit differently from your average cinema-goer. We can thus define practice as 'a set of socially defined ways of doing things in a specific domain: a set of common approaches and shared standards that create a basis for action, communication, problem solving, performance and accountability' (Wenger et al. 2002: 38). Thus unicyclists have a community forum (http://www.unicyclist.com/) which facilitates communication between members, and helps with technical tips and sets and monitors certain standards about how to behave (in relation to the road traffic laws, for instance). The above definition is derived from a book that emphasises the socially shared and agreed nature of specific practices; it stresses a community of practice. This raises an interesting question. What is the entrepreneur's community? Is it a community of fellow entrepreneurs? This seems unlikely. The practices and networks of different entrepreneurs vary a great deal, and the 'common approaches and shared standards' that constitute practice are likely to be determined more by business sectors than by some adherence to being an entrepreneur. Paul and John of Fenderco knew lots of port infrastructure professionals; they didn't know many other entrepreneurs.

Nevertheless, practices they have. And, despite the heterogeneity there are some commonalities that we can observe in the approach to marketing, finance, networking and strategy practices. The key point here is that how an entrepreneur in the computer software business does marketing will be different from an entrepreneur in an engineering firm, but they are both marketing. Indeed entrepreneurs and small business managers are not so different from the professional managers of any sized firm in this regards (Watson 1995). Moreover, to the extent that both entrepreneurs and managers identify with what they imagine the practices of their 'type' should be, they will have 'theories about the world and their place in it' (Jenkins 1992: 69).

This notion of practical activity and its underpinning ideas can be interpreted and explained in two ways. On the one hand you have those that emphasise the rule-bound and law-like essential nature of how people behave. This view, beloved by economists, argues that people do things for instrumental and rational reasons in pursuit of individual goals following rules and laws laid down by their peers, their community, or society. The other view, which I favour, argues that practically-oriented, discretionary, individual human behaviour is connected to cultural and historical contingencies and is 'improvisatory and strategic' in nature (Jenkins 1992: 68). This means that people actually shape the world they practice in too, and renew their practices to suit new circumstances. Rules do provide a context for how stuff is done, and people do often make rational choices in their decision making, but entrepreneurial practices are not determined simply by rationally following rules. The practices of those running businesses are strategically oriented at achieving certain goals, and are practically achieved through improvisation. In short, this means that what entrepreneurs and small business managers do, their practices, which we will describe and reflect upon in the following sections, take place in, and are affected by, specific circumstances. When considering the generalisations I make below you need therefore to bear this in mind.

_____ **Finance** _____

The author's story

Running a record label: finance

I learnt about the centrality of finance earlier in my life as a bright eyed and bushy-tailed 20 year old wannabe music entrepreneur. For four years I ran an independent record label as a limited company with a friend, Paul, and my brother, 'Funky' Ed (Down 2006: 1–2). We all put £500 pounds in to start the tapes rolling. We released 19 records over three years. It was mostly great fun, but a profitable business it wasn't. Neither did it pay a salary.

Towards the end, whilst trying to bridge a gap in operating cash, requiring us to put new bands into the recording studios and produce more records, we borrowed money in the form of a bank overdraft secured against the mortgage on the house I lived in with my brother. Unfortunately these records didn't sell that well and I couldn't clear the overdraft. I didn't want to risk our house further so we explained to the bands that we didn't have any more money and couldn't put any more of their records out. They went elsewhere. A year or so later a VAT bill triggered voluntary bankruptcy, a change of career and an extension of the mortgage by £12,000 (Paul, if you are reading this I'd still like your share of the debt back please!). If we had been serious about building a business we would have recognised earlier that we had expanded too quickly, had spent too much of our returns on new bands, and had not planned realistically. But we weren't really building a business. What we wanted, like many independent small music businesses, was to create enough of a buzz about the label or a band to secure a licensing deal – and a salary – with a larger record label. We had discussions – I now think of them as interviews – with various major record labels but unfortunately didn't manage to get 'the deal'.

Figure 8.1   The Pink Label logo

Activity

First rank and then discuss the following reasons for the record label's business failure:

a) poor financial planning
b) picking the wrong bands
c) not selling enough records
d) not persuading the major record companies to license the label

Read a brief history of the label at http://www.twee.net/labels/pink.html[.]

My own memory of 'doing' finance (perhaps it should be doing 'finance') when I ran my label is similar to the feeling I still get when going to the dentist. You know it has got to be done and that it's good for you, but it doesn't make it any more pleasant. Trips to the bank or the accountant were reality checks, and often the reality of where the business was at, compared to the hope-skewed picture I had in my mind, was, well, frightening. When it wasn't frightening (i.e. when the business was generating adequate revenues and not spending too much) seeing the accountant was still daunting. Most of the time I just looked at the bank balance – both the business and my own personal account, where one quite often helped the other out, with the personal one helping most – and acted accordingly. I was not a sophisticated practitioner of finance, and my business suffered as a result. Running a business is dependent on having and generating sufficient cash, and understanding – both knowing and practising – how to use limited resources efficiently is crucial to business survival.

Like my own modest beginnings most start-up finance is supplied by the personal savings and investments of their owners, their household or immediate networks. As a general rule we can say that 'the larger the start-up, the greater the proportion of debt, long-term debt, and outside and bank financing' that will be found in the firm (Cassar 2004: 262). Big bucks venture capitalist start-ups may be what we see most often in television programmes and in much entrepreneurship research, but it is actually a relatively rare form of small business funding. Jarvis has estimated that 'only around 10% of firms want to grow' and 'of these only approximately 10% will actually do so' (2006: 342–343). It's only growth firms that need venture capitalist funds. Much research attention has focused on this tiny fraction of firms because of their 'significant actual or perceived contribution to the economy' (ibid.: 343). Another reason for this attention is that publicly available data sets amenable to number-crunching are not as available for smaller more informal businesses. Thus compared to larger firms, because small firms are not required to disclose as much financial information and people will tend towards keeping it secret, our knowledge about how smaller firms use what kind of finance is not extensive (Jarvis 2006: 339).

Nevertheless, research has shown that once a firm has started they tend to rely on bank overdrafts or loans for their finance needs (Jarvis 2006: 344). Smaller firms also vary a great deal in relation both to how they source finance and how they use financial information and techniques. Generally speaking the larger the firm and the more formal its status, the more likely it is to have sophisticated financial practices. As firms grow 'what had been appropriate informal and tacit control by the owner-manager gives way to more formal, delegated processes of control' (Collis and Jarvis 2002: 101). Thus we can expect micro-firms, sole proprietorships and partnerships to be less sophisticated than limited companies. In terms of the latter 'there is a strong emphasis on controlling cash and monitoring performance in the context of maintaining relationships with the bank' (Collis and Jarvis 2002: 100). Collis and Jarvis's study of small but substantial limited companies found that 'periodic management accounts, cash flow information and bank statements' were considered the most useful sources of financial information, far more important than annual statutory accounts prepared for auditing and compliance reasons (2002: 105).

Though evidence now shows that most substantial smaller firms have 'relatively sophisticated' financial management practices 'that include formal methods of planning and control' (Collis and Jarvis 2002: 108), the majority of firms nevertheless will choose independence, control, survival and stability over growth (ibid. 2002: 101; Jarvis 2006: 341). There is also evidence that equity – 'the finance contributed by the owner(s) of the enterprise' (Jarvis 2006: 348) – and profits are often withdrawn by the owners of small firms, presumably in the form of income. As a consequence the majority of firms don't seek to get more money through selling a part of their firm. In other words, proportionally there are not many firms seeking external equity finance from venture capitalist (specialised investment companies) or business angels (informal individual investors). When more resources are needed small firms in the main will rely on banks and debt finance (which is money borrowed for an agreed period of time at a certain interest rate and repayment structure – i.e. a loan or overdraft). There is then a significant difference between entrepreneurial growth and other small firms in relation to finance.

Growth brings its own problems too. As Peel et al. note 'The fact that rapid growth often consumes cash, rather than generating it, has often caused financial difficulties for financially unsophisticated small firm owners' (2000: 19). This lack of sophistication also expresses itself most commonly in the lack of internal administrative resources – both knowledge and time – which are a key limit for many small firms, whether they are growth-oriented or not.

Small businesses therefore often look to make-do and stretch their finances without recourse to external finance. This has been called financial bootstrapping; pulling yourself out of trouble without the help of others. This might include getting family members to work for low salaries, going without a salary or taking an extra job, or even spending private money on the business, as I did from time to time. Other ways of bootstrapping include chasing people to pay you as quickly as possible by speeding up invoices, and on the other side, delaying payment as long as possible (Peel et al. 2000). Businesses also lease and hire purchase equipment, where costly items are rented rather than purchased outright, giving the advantage that 'it avoids a large capital outlay; it is cheaper; it helps cash flow; and it is easier to arrange' (Jarvis 2006: 348). Businesses also save resources by sharing costly items and important knowledge. Pollard (2007) for instance, in a study of jewellery micro-businesses found that subsidising the business via other household income (a spouse's salary for instance) was not uncommon, as was sharing financial knowledge with other businesses. Pollard's study showed that even where micro-business owners were co-located and running similar businesses their financial practices differed: she stresses the 'situated, idiosyncratic, and often very personal nature of the financial knowledges, practices, and networks' that typify micro-businesses (2007: 378).

Hence, many businesses, including my record label, operate within an 'economy of regard [...] where passion, exploration, and the sense of achievement gained from producing high-quality [goods and services], and not profit maximization per se, appear to be the key economic "test"' (Pollard 2007: 392). Many businesses, in the creative industries for instance, but also many 'normal' businesses, even in terms of their financial practices, seek merely to support a specific form of living. And whilst on the surface at least, this orientation will not necessarily enthuse growth-crazed policy-makers, clearly the passion for something beyond profit maximisation is also an important factor even for many more financially ambitious and entrepreneurial businesses. I don't suppose that Bill Gates would have been happy just selling dog food.

Another feature of smaller business financial practice is the use of trade credit, which refers to the supply of goods and services on a deferred payment basis. According to Peel et al. (2000: 17) 'the vast bulk of inter-firm sales are made on credit terms'. I didn't, for instance, pay cash up front to manufacture the records at the pressing plant. I would have these production costs advanced to me by Rough Trade, our distribution company, who would not pay me for records sold until the debt was cleared. Downstream, the bands would only get any royalty cheques if and when the recording and promotional costs were recouped. Upstream, no doubt similar arrangements were made between distributer and manufacturer, manufacturer and raw materials suppliers, and on and on.

Taken as a whole, we can see that financial practice varies a great deal between firms, with greater size tending towards a greater emphasis on formality and financial sophistication. Similarly, the life cycle of firms influences the types of financial practices favoured: 'When firms start up and as they grow they tend to rely on debt, but when the firm matures this reliance on debt declines' (Jarvis 2006: 355). Pollard's observation about micro-firms that practices are 'situated, idiosyncratic, and often very personal [in]nature' is perhaps applicable more widely.

Marketing

Let's start this section with another story about the record label I used to run.

The author's story

Running a record label: marketing and networking

In the world of small UK independent record labels in the mid-1980s short-term success meant selling enough records (vinyl 7 and 12 inch) to put the artists back in the studios to record the next product. Apart from the bands playing regular gigs (tours of universities were very good business; students were keen on the sort of fashionably obscure music on offer and had the cash to buy the records) virtually the only way to raise the profile of the acts was through the music press and radio plays. I spent much of my time doing two things. First and foremost persuading radio DJs like John Peel to play the records or to record and broadcast an in-studio session. Second, persuading music journalists – who were often as new to their careers as I was to mine – to review my new record releases or the band's gigs, and to write about the bands in magazines such as the *New Musical Express* (*NME*). The holy grail was a 'single-of-the-week' or a front cover page spread hailing the band as the next-big-thing. The front page of the *NME* featuring one of my bands (see Figure 8.2,

Case Study

page 136) guaranteed that thousands of young music-obsessed 'punters' would buy the record. To do the persuading I sent free copies of the records to DJs and journalists and tried to get them to come to the gigs. In my early twenties I would regularly go to three to four gigs a week, mostly on the guest list, which itself was a good indicator of how 'in' your activities were; how successful the 'marketing' was. In essence it was a social scene – or network – where more or less everyone involved was trying desperately to build their profiles and their careers as music promoters, record label managers, band managers, music journalists, photographers and musicians. Your success at getting bands watched, listened to, talked and written about reflected not just higher record sales, but also, ultimately, the likelihood of a career with a major record label. In essence – though I likely didn't understand this at the time – I was marketing myself as much as the bands.

Activity

What different marketing techniques and channels would an aspiring record label entrepreneur practice today?
How has technology affected the nature of marketing in the music industry?
How do creative industry entrepreneurs create 'buzz'?

One of the things that the above case study tells us about small and entrepreneurial businesses is that marketing techniques are often subsumed by activities inherent to the business itself. Having not completed any business education I was blissfully unaware that what I was doing when I was promoting my bands was called marketing. Many people who start businesses have a passion about the product or service and a deep belief about what they are doing. Thus it would have been somewhat pointless to tell me to sign country and western bands – or tell Bill Gates to start selling dog food – rather than indie pop ones, because they tend to sell more records. The point is that many entrepreneurial businesses are in the business of creating new markets, or as Stokes terms it they are 'innovation-oriented', starting 'with an idea, and then try[ing] to find a market for it' (2006: 324/330). Marketing is about getting others to buy stuff they didn't know they needed; teaching the consumers 'to want new things' (cited in McCraw 2007: 72, from Schumpeter 1934/1911: 65).

Nevertheless, in my business, I could have been more skilful at marketing my products. If I had understood marketing best practice I would perhaps have adopted a more professional approach which would have enhanced my understanding of the environment that my business was operating in. Being good at marketing is a 'key internal management skill that differentiates between surviving and failing firms' (Stokes 2006: 325). But often the textbook stipulations or 'theoretically based marketing practice[s]' (McCartan-Quinn and Carson 2003: 201) are not especially helpful. Small firms tend to have 'certain characteristics that cause marketing problems' (Stokes 2006: 324). These variously include a 'restricted customer base, limited marketing experience and impact, variable, unplanned effort and over-reliance on the

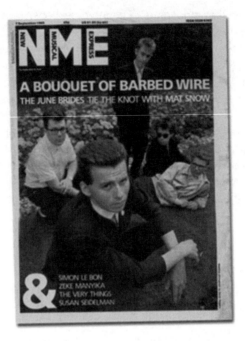

Figure 8.2　Front page of *New Musical Express* (NME) 1985 featuring a Pink Label band

© Derek Ridgers/IPC Media

owner-manager's marketing competency' (ibid.). These characteristics typified my own efforts too. However, professional big business marketing practices are not always appropriate. Would more market research – going and talking to competitors and customers (field research) or secondary information (desk research) – into the nature of my competitors and customers have made for a more successful business? Perhaps it would, but again, I still wouldn't have put out country and western music. Small businesses anyway have to be careful to maintain a balance between the need for good market intelligence and the cost of getting the information. Many successful entrepreneurs start out with a deep belief in what they are doing and it is deeply irrational. Competitor record labels from this time were not more successful because they did better market research. It was because they worked harder, 'shouted' louder, chose better bands, managed their finance better, persuaded major record labels to invest in their talent spotting, and they managed the promotional and reputation building process better.

Professional marketing practice might have helped, but as with many small businesses they often have limited control of the classic 'marketing mix'. This is often summarised in the five Ps: *product, price, promotion, place* and *people*. In my case the *product* – a vinyl record – was a creative collaboration between the artist, record label, record designers and studio producers. Like many small businesses which rely on wholesalers and specialised distributors, I had little control over the *price* or *place* (product distribution point of sale). Changes from the norm (such as discounts) would be negotiated with the label distribution company, with whom we had a contract, who would organise everything from the production of the records to distribution to the point of sale. *Promotion* and *people* were the main spheres of activity central to the business itself. As described above both of these activities were only indirectly oriented toward the customer. To influence the customer and create a market for our records we needed to convince the gatekeepers of reputational capital (radio, TV and the music press).

Stokes has suggested that given the limits of the five 'Ps' and traditional large firm marketing expertise, it is better to think of marketing and smaller entrepreneurial firms as four + four Is. Table 8.1 describes this marketing mix.

Table 8.1   Entrepreneurial marketing

Innovation	Incremental improvements and adjustments to practices rather than major inventions
Identification of target markets	'Niche' markets and customers, managing customer relationships
Interactive marketing methods: Influence	Using word of mouth marketing and personal referral and recommendation
Image building	Especially relevant in service businesses or those reliant on reputation
Incentives	Discounts, promotional offers, bartering, hospitality, etc.
Involvement	Participation encourages customer loyalty and enhances the effectiveness of word of mouth communication
Informal information gathering	External focus enhances the 'feel' for threats and opportunities

Source: Adapted from Stokes (2006: 332–335)

Small firms tend to focus on different tactics to attract new business, rather than viewing marketing as an enterprise orienting philosophy or strategy. Smaller firms therefore tend to have short-term, reactive approaches to their marketing activity, predominantly aimed at selling and promoting: an *operational* rather than *strategic* approach. Stokes suggests however that many small firms actually do far more sophisticated marketing practices than is commonly realised (2006: 330). Just because many entrepreneurs can't put the correct marketing term to the practice, it doesn't mean that they aren't engaging in market monitoring, targeting and relationship management. Thus 'it is all to easy to accept the owner-manager's comment that they "do not have the time or resources for marketing", when those same owners do indeed devote much of their time to building relationships with satisfied customers who then recommend the business to others. In other words, they spend considerable time and resources on marketing, but they call it by another name' (Stokes 2006: 330). The key difference between small/entrepreneurial and large, is the tacit nature of marketing practice. Thus even extremely professional growth-oriented entrepreneurial businesses often eschew traditional formal marketing planning, largely because longer-term plans tend to be made redundant by the changing environment (Collinson and Shaw 2001: 763).

Similarly small and entrepreneurial businesses make much of limited resources, and it is the management of network relationships, and the development of networking skills and competencies (Gilmore et al. 2001), which achieve what time, money and formal marketing expertise can't. 'Relationships with buyers, suppliers and others along the supply chain and in the immediate micro environment are used to identify which information [...] is relevant to their success and must be regularly collected and understood' (Collinson and Shaw 2001: 764). It is to an understanding of networking practices that we now turn.

Networking

Marketing is as obvious a key skill as it is crucial to the success of the business. Being good at networking and having effective networks is a newer and more fashionable practical skill. This section reflects on what we know about how entrepreneurs and small business owner-managers do networking.

One thing that is clear is how opaque the term networking is. Researchers often seem to be writing about very different things. One axis that separates business researchers is the empirical emphases. Some are interested in the qualitative content of the relationships. Others stress the frequency of the linkages. More theoretically, the concept of networks for some is a useful one with which to understand enterprise more generally. This is because, unlike some economic analysis which focuses on individual and abstract 'firms', networks force a view of entrepreneurship as inherently embedded in collective social activity. It is the inter-relationships between managers and entrepreneurs with others in society that is the focus of attention. As a result an extensive analytical apparatus has grown around the concept (summarised in Conway and Jones 2006). However, though the research reported on in this section draws on this theoretical nuance, the practice of networking is a little different and we will focus on how entrepreneurs and small business owner-managers go about using networks; how they are 'built, nurtured and mobilised' (Conway and Jones 2006: 307).

We all have relationships. We take them for granted. Yet all of us know, especially in work contexts, that when we meet and get to know someone that what they know or can do might be meaningful or useful to us. But relationships are complex and not reducible to evaluations of utility. The meaning of a relationship often depends on the quality of the interaction exchange (do the people like and trust each other?). Entrepreneurs and small business managers have relationships with a wide range of people and institutions. Of course, without external contacts the business could not operate (Chell and Baines 2000: 196). What excites policymakers and researchers about networking skills is not these everyday, obvious 'involuntary' relationships. It's how the successful business manager approaches *discretionary* networking that is of interest. Do successful entrepreneurs network more than the unsuccessful? If so when, and over what business function (marketing, HR, finance, information gathering, and so on), is the networking important?

There is, however, despite the seemingly positive case for extensive networking, a paradox at the heart of entrepreneurial networking behaviours. We know that many entrepreneurs and small business owners are fiercely independent and autonomous and are very short of the time and patience for chit-chat at business breakfast clubs and the like. On the other hand, we also know that extensive and wide ranging relationships can be very useful for business success. Can both be right? Just how important is networking to business success?

Early research into the content and context of network relations showed a lack of enthusiasm by small business managers to engage actively with others. Small business 'owner-managers tend to have relatively small and non-extensive networks with little resort to expected external contacts such as accountants and bank managers' (Curran et al. 1993: 23). The researchers stressed that this was not especially surprising as 'there is abundant research suggesting that owner-manager self-definitions stress independence very strongly […]. This produces a "fortress enterprise" mentality in dealing with the wider environment, and a low likelihood of participation in networks of all kinds' (Curran et al. 1993: 23–4). Others have shown that whilst this may be the case with owner-managers, growth-oriented entrepreneurial businesses seem to correlate with a positive relationship between active and enthusiastic networking and business success (Chell and Baines 2000). The empirical research has resolved our paradox: crudely put, entrepreneurs and owner-managers differ.

Two other factors can have a bearing on how entrepreneurs and owner-managers network. Firstly, the type of sector will influence the perceived need for network relationships and the expected norms of behaviour in the networks. Knowledge-intensive businesses and those where the product/service is based on reputation will tend to have more need to network than, say, a traditional manufacturing firm producing specialised widgets in their millions for a limited customer base. The nature and frequency of networking practice clearly depend on the type of business. Secondly, the temporal and spatial contexts of the relationships need to be borne in mind. A locally-oriented, traditional mature business will likely be set and formalised in the nature of its relationships. A new entrant competitor with international ambitions should be in a veritable whirl of informal networking activity, trying to persuade others to invest in their business or buy their products or services (Greve and Salaff 2003).

However, not all knowledge-intensive, early stage, high-networking businesses succeed, grow and prosper. If the extent of networking activity were the key determinant of a successful business then every economy would be thriving and we'd all be talking our heads off at networking events. Clearly, like many other attributes of successful businesses, it is the quality and not the extent that counts. The nature of the relationships that exist in networks is therefore important. Some relationships are strong and well established, others are weak. It is this balance between strong and weak ties that is crucial in understanding how networking functions in practice.

Strong ties are close and closed. Weak ties are loose and open. Counter-intuitive as it seems, it turns out that weak ties are very useful in spanning boundaries and creating the potential for also creating new opportunities and ideas. Equally however strong ties can be useful in providing emotional, information and financial support. In a famous study, sociologist Mark Granovetter wrote of 'the cohesive power of weak ties' (1973: 1360) in providing opportunities for gaining 'knowledge of the world' beyond immediate close strong family and friendship ties. Granovetter explains what this means: 'those to whom we are weakly tied are more likely to move in circles different from our own and will thus have access to information different from that which we receive' (1973: 1371). In short, our weak ties connect us to a wide range of different people, institutions and social structures. Stories about chance meetings on long haul flights leading to the start of new entrepreneurial ventures are legion (see Ziegler et al. 1992). It is the blend of strong ties, whether they are institutional or personal, carry high trust, and weaker ties, that bring new ideas and information, that is crucial to having the right connections for developing a business. It is this complex blend of ties that allows the entrepreneur to be both fiercely independent and autonomous and reliant on a wide range of relationships. Again, our paradox is resolved.

And, if you want to know what makes a successful entrepreneur, the skill at which you do the blending is a likely candidate. As Conway and Jones note, 'perhaps what distinguishes entrepreneurs is their ability to maintain and make use of their strong ties, as well as their effectiveness in initiating, nurturing and mobilising, weaker ties' (2006: 316). But as a budding entrepreneur, if all you do is work on your networks and forget to manage the business then clearly you will fail. Business is about selling stuff and making money, and whilst an extensive network and an active approach to maintaining relationships are invaluable, stuff still has to be sold.

Fenderco case study

Paul's – company director and entrepreneur – story about networking

The fendering and port infrastructure equipment industry is a little village really. Everyone knows each other. We come across the same people all over the world. It's mostly people like us, about the same age; same stage in their careers. There are not many people building ports: our database probably covers 60 per cent of the people in the industry. You bump into them. John and I go to quite a few seminars. It is a chance to meet up with old acquaintances. Much of what I do when I am not designing stuff is about managing relationships. We are forever sending and receiving rude email jokes to our closest associates. If I'm bored in the office, I quite often drive off to one of our project sites; arrange a meeting or something just to keep in touch, meet face-to-face with people and check on progress. You have to manage this stuff, especially because ours is such an international business. We have to fit in with their ways of doing business; you know 'gifts' and 'entertainment' and so on. Nothing scary, but you know how it is. Business in northern Europe is probably the exception in that sense.

Case Study

We have projects in virtually all the world's major ports, yet we are stuck here in the middle of England miles from any water! We are often a small player in a very big game, just a small piece in some very large projects, and one of my jobs is to ensure that we get recommended for the next project rather than our competitors. Key to this is making sure that the job goes well. Sometimes of course they don't, there are always problems, as you can imagine. The trick is to make sure that the important clients and project partners know your side of the story; this takes some skill. Sometimes it even pays to take a bollocking [being told off] from a managing project partner to make them feel better about the delay or the balls-up. It's better than pretending the problem doesn't exist. You can't afford to bullshit the paymasters. Taking the blame can be good business. I call it pleasing the customer. People remember your attitude, the way you helped out, took the blame or whatever. Its all about building and maintaining a relationship: being known for being trustworthy.

Activity

What role does trust play in network relationships?
Of the relationships Paul mentions or implies which are his stronger and weaker ties?
What skills and attributes does Paul show or claim?
Does Paul's story about taking a bollocking being good for business ring true, or is he just rationalising failure?

Growth and strategy

I have put growth and strategy together in this section because whilst smaller less ambitious businesses do behave strategically, it is generally in the context of a growing firm, with the changing organisational structures, roles and responsibilities it implies, that the *quality* of strategic practice becomes crucial to the firm's success. All firms behave strategically, and need to in order to survive (Storey 1994: 310); hence Burns's definition: strategy 'is a series of related tasks that, taken together, have a coherence and give direction to the firm' (2007: 129). All firms have a direction. Nevertheless more sophisticated strategic planning practice is normally associated with reasonably substantial or at least more aspirational businesses. Having a strategy implies doing disparate things, and connecting them together towards some sort of direction, a plan of action: a sense of wanting to go to a better, bigger, more prosperous place.

Back in Chapter 5 we looked at the difference between reactive and strategic smaller and entrepreneurial firms in the context of managing the employment relationship. We concluded that regardless of how skilled the entrepreneur was, how well organised the firm and how good the strategic decisions made, strategy could not be a perfectible science, but was rather something that could never entirely stop the leaky bucket of everyday business practice losing its water: human fallibility, environmental turbulence and dumb luck play too large a part in the fortunes of business. This is not to say that firms with clever and active strategies can't grow even in adverse market conditions (Smallbone et al. 1995: 59). The point is simply that strategic behaviour is not perfectible. If it was then most firms would grow and succeed.

As we noted in the finance section growing itself can be a dangerous business. Growth creates stresses which can trample the proverbial green shoots of a promising new venture. Growing businesses are also rare. But they are important. They can create new jobs. Back in Chapter 1 we first discussed the potential flaws in seeing all small firms as engines of job creation. I suggested that some growth firms might simply be the beneficiaries of organisational restructuring and the downsizing activities of larger businesses, rather than the providers of net job growth. Nevertheless, whatever the underlying balance of net and gross effects, expanding firms undoubtedly do create jobs. But growth is not inevitable once some threshold is reached: it is a discontinuous process, not something that is achieved through successive stages (Smallbone et al. 1995: 59). Growing firms often falter, contract and then grow again: experimentation and improvisation are the key, always. However, thresholds do arise, and one of the most important is bound up in the role of the entrepreneur or owner-manager. Put simply, can he or she make the shift from 'factory manager' to business-person? In other words, can the entrepreneur transform his or her management style and the firm's organisational structure to facilitate the delegation of operational level practices, and the shift to 'planning and higher level strategic functions' (ibid.: 60; Birley 1982: 85)? If the entrepreneur can manage this transition – and many actively avoid doing this by simply avoiding growth, or moving on to new ventures – then the business can grow.

Another key aspect of growing firms is that strategic planning is vital; firms that plan are more likely to grow (Woods and Joyce 2003: 182). Smallbone et al. put it this way, 'the clearest differences between fast growth SMEs and firms with lower levels of performance are with respect to their approach to product and market development' (1995: 59). This includes 'developing new products and services for existing customers, developing new markets, broadening their customer base, taking steps to make their products more competitive and in managing their product portfolio' (ibid.). It should be noted here that small firms can however find it very difficult to be as flexible as these stipulations suggest: often the firm is simply trying to create a market for a product or service, rather than manage a diverse range (Birley 1982: 85). One of the reasons for this relates again to the centrality of the entrepreneur. Not only does the management style and organisation structure often change with growth, the original goals of the business, which have been synonymous with the personal aspirations of the entrepreneur, also tend to change, broaden or dissipate as the business grows (Birley 1982). This is partly to do with the broadening of ownership and stakeholder interests that tend to accompany growth.

Clearly the heterogeneity of small business and the relatively limited number of high growth firms suggest that strategic practices in the majority of smaller enterprises are not all that developed. However, with more university educated managers and entrepreneurs, and the wide diffusion of knowledge embodied in practical strategic tools (these are just a few: competitor analysis, scenario planning, SWOT analysis, gap analysis and PEST analysis), some are now arguing that the notion of smaller firms being generally unsophisticated in their application of strategic practices is old hat (Woods and Joyce 2003). This argument stresses the inherent need for professionalism in successful ventures regardless of their entrepreneurialism (Watson 1995). Woods and Joyce also emphasise the increasing professionalism of management (2003: 191) and criticise the implicit suggestion that inspired entrepreneurialism can somehow do away with the need for competent strategically-oriented management. Their research shows that the more that a business uses strategic planning tools the better the businesses perform, and that 'those firms that were growing rapidly used more tools than those who were not, with declining firms using the fewest' (Woods and Joyce 2003: 191).

Woods and Joyce's research is a quantitative study capturing managerial self-reports about strategic tools heard about and used, which was then correlated to self-reports about firm performance. Undoubtedly their work clearly shows a link between knowing about and claiming to use strategic tools and successful growth, but what might be happening within firms and how extensively those tools are actually embedded would need to be the subject of qualitative investigation. Close-up ethnographic work tends to show a gap between managerial aspirations and the reality on the ground. For instance, the firms that Ruth Holliday studied all felt that 'growth was something which happened to a company'. Managers and employees all stressed their 'short planning horizons' and the fragility of firms in the face of environmental turbulence: 'Strategic decision-making tended to be a rather informal, *ad hoc* process' (1995: 136, emphasis in the original). Regardless, Wood and Joyce's findings are quite important and rather suggest that the heroic 'anti-planning' model of spontaneous and intuitive entrepreneurship is largely a myth. Their research shows managers as sophisticated users of the 'language of strategy': both in their use of tools and in the way they make sense of the world through 'practice and experimentation'; sticking to what works, ditching what doesn't (ibid. 192).

Conclusion

This takes us back to the beginning of the chapter. Practices, I argued in the first section, were not about a rigid adherence to rules and laws, rather they were 'improvisatory and strategic' in nature (Jenkins 1992: 68). So it proves. Each section of this chapter has shown how ostensibly rigid and rule-bound stipulations about how entrepreneurial ventures should practise finance, marketing, networking and strategy are, when placed in specific situated contexts, pulled and twisted by the maw of everyday practice, experimentation and improvisation. Tacit and explicit knowledge – action and theory – combine in practices. Thus, we have – as I promised – not learnt 'how to' do finance, marketing, networking and strategy, but have reflected on these practices. We can feel confident that how things happen in smaller enterprises is clearer than it was.

This chapter ends Part II, looking *Inside Enterprise*. We now look at the environment in which enterprise takes place more directly in Part III, *Outside Enterprise*.

Summary

The connection between practice and tacit knowledge, or theory, was stressed. It was argued that small business and entrepreneurial practices in marketing, finance, networking and strategy are strategically oriented at achieving certain goals, and are practically achieved through improvisation, rather than through a rigid adherence to rules and routines. These and other themes were illustrated by examples from research, the author's own experience at running a micro firm, and Fenderco. It was demonstrated that what small business owners actually do in relation to finance, marketing, networking and growth and strategy is often quite different from what they 'should' do.

■ ■ Further reading ■

Cassar, G. (2004) 'The financing of business start-ups', *Journal of Business Venturing* 19(2): 261–283.

Collis, J. and Jarvis, R. (2002) 'Financial information and the management of small private companies', *Journal of Small Business and Enterprise Development* 9(2): 100–110.

Conway, S. and Jones, O. (2006) 'Networking and the small business', in S. Carter and D. Jones-Evans (eds), *Enterprise and Small Business: Principles, Practice and Policy* (2nd edn), Harlow: Prentice Hall.

Greve, A. and Salaff, J.W. (2003) 'Social networks and entrepreneurship', *Entrepreneurship, Theory and Practice* 28(1): 1–22.

McCartan-Quinn, D. and Carson, D. (2003) 'Issues which impact upon marketing in the small firm', *Small Firm Economics* 21: 201–213.

Woods, A. and Joyce, P. (2003) 'Owner-managers and the practice of strategic management', *International Small Business Journal* 21(2): 181–195.

Part III

Outside Enterprise

Part II (Chapters 3–8) clearly did more than look 'inside' the smaller and entrepreneurial enterprise. Economic, psychological and sociological theories and
concepts were prodded and unpicked, what small business managers and entrepreneurs and their employees do was examined, and the entrepreneurial activities
of corporations were critiqued. Throughout I have argued that placing enterprising behaviour (be it individual or organisational) in broader patterns of political,
social and economic activity is not optional. There is though, more to be said.
What about globalisation? What about social changes, such as ageing populations?
What about government support for enterprise? The next three chapters (9–11)
address these and other topics and themes. We look outside the enterprise and turn
more directly to those broader patterns: what does enterprise look like set against
broader trends in the economy, society and politics?

9

Economic Contexts of Enterprise

Overview

This chapter has the following objectives:

- To understand how broad changes in economic context have influenced small scale and entrepreneurial economic behaviour.
- To analyse the competing explanations of globalisation and localisation, innovation and technology in the context of small and entrepreneurial business.
- To unpick the myth and hyperbole surrounding the economic importance of small firms in processes of globalisation and innovative clustering.
- To explain the economic context of innovation and technology in smaller and entrepreneurial firms, and stress the benefits and limitations that smallness can bring.
- To argue that economic contexts are more complex and diverse than often fashionable ideas highlighting the questionable importance of small scale economic activity. Suggest.

Introduction

A truly global economy is being created by the worldwide spread of new technologies, not by the spread of free markets. Every economy is being transformed as technologies are imitated, absorbed and adapted. No country can insulate itself from this wave of creative destruction. And the result is not a universal free market but an anarchy of sovereign states, rival capitalisms and stateless zones. (J. Gray 1998: 194)

These contextual forces for change, both economic and technological, are crucial to any clear understanding. In explaining growth in international economic interconnectedness – what is often called the new economy – Gray favours the creative powers of information technology over those of international market deregulation. Later we will find out why he thinks this. But that the last 30 years or so has seen a profound transformation in how economies function is not in doubt. This chapter locates enterprise within these changing patterns of market relationships.

A key point of discussion in these debates has been the relative power and importance of large and small enterprises. We first encountered this dichotomy in Chapter 1 in the debate between those like Birch (1979) who saw small firms as the engine of economic rejuvenation and job creation, and those like Harrison (1994) who were more sceptical and emphasised the interconnectedness of small and large enterprises and the continuing control that corporations exercised over economic structures. Below we unpack these competing explanations further and look at the role of smaller and entrepreneurial enterprise in the global economy: the extent to which enterprises operate at global and local/regional levels; the shifting nature of market and organisational relationships; the shift to flexible organisational strategies; and the role of smaller and entrepreneurial enterprises in the generation and exploitation of innovation and technology. But, before addressing globalisation head on, we consider some broader issues.

Back in 1990 James Curran wrote a paper warning that some of the models explaining the emerging 'new economy' and the growing importance of smaller scale economic activity were deeply flawed. To be sure, old notions dominant in the 1950s to the 1970s about the inevitable decline of small enterprise in the face of triumphant large scale activity were no longer tenable. However, lumping all small firms, entrepreneurship and self-employment into an homogeneous category, or ignoring the contribution of the duller, less dynamic forms of enterprise in order to make 'small firms' seem more dynamic and innovative, is plainly wrong. Not all small scale enterprise was equally dynamic or even a pertinent factor in the economic restructuring taking place. Ultimately, size is always relative to context and the confidence in which pundits speak of a 'small enterprise sector' is often misplaced given its inherent heterogeneity (Curran 1990: 130). Thus, there was, and remains, a good deal of wishful thinking, panacea-ism and over-simplification when it comes to talking about small scale economic activity and the new economy.

There is much continuity with the past too, and new theories and ideas seeking to explain the new economy often overstate the extent of change. The complexity and variation within sectors, geographies and so on are ignored and often the small, dynamic and entrepreneurial are forced to speak for the whole. Reality is more mundane, and despite the changes in the structure and increased importance of smaller enterprise 'the importance of the large enterprise remains undiminished' both in 1990 and today: 'The relative significance of small and large scale economic activities should not be seen as mutually exclusive. The complexities of economic structures can easily allow for increases in the significance of both to occur' (Curran 1990: 139–140). Explaining the relative importance of economic actors is not like some playground Top Trump argument about whether it's a Ferrari or Lamborghini that has the fastest top speed. It's just a tad more complex than that.

The rest of this chapter seeks to depolarise these debates about the relative importance of small scale economic activity in the new economy, and in so doing favours neither the boosters nor the knockers of the small. Small and large actors operate together in a complex concert of global, local, innovation and technological contexts. To ascribe any single reality to these processes is wrong.

Globalisation and the 'new economy': the nature of inter-organisational relationships

_____ The global... _____

There is a great deal of hullabaloo around globalisation. It is true that '[t]here has been a vast and unprecedented expansion in the volume of trade' (J. Gray 1998: 61). Audretsch (2007: 73) suggests that exports have grown as a percentage of world gross product from 10 per cent in 1960 to over one-quarter by 2005. '"Globalization" ... is a catchall word' (Sennett 2003: 181) which describes the decline of an old order of government that controlled capital flows and where large corporations repressed market competition. This is what entrepreneurship and innovation booster David Audretsch calls the old 'managed economy' (2007: 7). Events of the 1970s and institutional and political changes led to the release of pent up demand for product and services and an increased supply of capital:

> **Both supply and demand combined to spur corporations to adapt quickly to changes in market demand and money supply. Technological innovations via the computer made possible 'global real time,' the synchronisation of communications and financial transactions around the world. Last, and perhaps most important, a change in power: stockholders began to reassert demands for short-tern returns on investment, challenging management bureaucrats who had been content if things simply chugged along as they had before. (Sennett 2003: 180–181)**

One result of these changes, according to some, is the emergence of an 'entrepreneurial society' (Audretsch 2007).

For Audretsch it's also the triumph of the small over the large. However, Gray writing about the same processes and era disagrees: 'The growth and power of multinational corporations is enormous and also unprecedented. Multinationals now account for about a third of world output and two-thirds of world trade. Most significantly, around a quarter of world trade occurs *within* multinational corporations' (J. Gray 1998: 62). As I suggested in the introduction, too much energy is expended trying to resolve this apparent paradox. Corporations and other firms are symbiotically connected in complex relationships where the relative market power and influence are determined by sector, technology, geography, labour and capital supply and a whole host of other factors. It is a crucial mistake to see the rise of the internationalised high-tech small firm as a victor in some titanic battle between corporate dinosaurs and agile entrepreneurial ventures. If all you look at is firms, they are all you will see. Just because a large firm downsizes, outsources and spreads its activities around the globe (often called off-shoring or regime-shopping) it doesn't necessarily mean that it loses control. Some argue that in many cases downsizing and subcontracting strategies are being adopted to increase control as well as saving direct costs and improving productivity (Hancké 1998; Harrison 1994; Sennett 1998).

But isn't globalisation supposed to be predicated on the spread of free markets? What does Gray mean that free markets are not at the heart of a globalised economy?

His point is that in order for there to be less barriers to trade there needs to be new structure and regulation to achieve it. Freer markets aren't simply the absence of regulation. Gray goes further when he says that regulated and 'encumbered markets are the norm in every society, whereas free markets are a product of artifice, design and political coercion. **Laissez-faire** must be centrally planned; regulated markets just happen' (J. Gray 1998: 17). The differences that exist between national economies, their regulations on labour, wage differentials and so forth are what global competitive markets thrive on. It is these differences that entrepreneurs exploit. Totally free markets are an impossible reality; Gray calls it a utopia.

> **Laissez-faire** refers to the ideology of non-interference in the affairs of others, particularly with reference to government interference on economic matters. Markets should, in this doctrine, be left to operate 'naturally' according to economic laws.

Nevertheless business does now take place in a global economic context: 'Reduced barriers to international trade and investment coupled with advances in information technology have accorded opportunities for smaller firms – employing fewer than 500 persons – to emerge as multinational' (Prasad 1999: 1). Internationalised small firms 'tend to be larger, more capital rich, more productive and profitable and to have a higher export ratio than SMEs in general' (Buckley 1997). Obviously many such firms eventually cease to be small. They also often act in concert with other firms to provide integrated products and services. The car industry is a good example of how this integration works in practice. As Hancké suggests, for most car companies 'the actual value created by the company that owns the brand name, is below 30%; the rest is supplied by (often) small firms who supply specialised parts' (1998: 237). And, whilst the car industry is not seen as sexy, innovative and entrepreneurial in the same was as say Google, it is still a vital component of the modern economy: it makes up 8 per cent of GDP in the UK and employs one in ten of France's workforce (O'Hagan 2009).

However, there is no inevitable triumph of the small over the large in the car industry: 'By forging closer links with suppliers, the large firms did not give up control over the relationship' (Hancké 1998: 148). Through a combination of financial, quality and other control systems, such as just-in-time inventory controls, suppliers were forced to take more risk and responsibility for their role in the integrated and global production system. Instead of the fully integrated in-house production system of old, Hancké describes a form of large firm paternalism and concludes that 'even in the era of globalisation, economic and industrial adjustment can and often does follow a variety of trajectories. It can be co-operative, expressing trust between quasi-equals; market-organised, based on contracts and arms length relationships; or hierarchical, resulting from the power of one of the parties in the exchange' (Hancké 1998: 250). The study shows that globalised inter-firm relations do not necessarily place the smaller firm in the driving seat, however agile and flexible they may be.

Finally, Hancké's study also undermines another aspect of the hubbub associated with globalisation. It is often imagined that global firms, small or large, exist as free floating, almost virtual agents, without 'homes'. The structure of the French car industry suggests that whilst supply is more 'global' than it once was, such businesses are not totally spatially unattached. Hancké's study shows that national characteristics are still relevant. As with the unalloyed benefits of free markets, the extent to which entrepreneurial firms and corporations are free floating is often over done: 'the economy is not as indifferent to location as has been assumed' (Sennett 1998: 136). Moreover, the fact that businesses shop around for the best regulatory and investment friendly regime shows that the particular attributes of locations are indeed important. Most businesses retain strong cultural and economic links to particular nations, regions and localities. It is to a consideration of the local economic contexts and enterprise that we now turn.

... and the local

There is even more hullabaloo around the notion of innovative regional economic clusters. Alongside an increase in international business, the new economy has seen the growth of places like Silicon Valley in the US and Motor Sport Valley in the UK. These clusters are concentrated regional pockets of highly innovative, entrepreneurial and profitable businesses which interpenetrate in locally proximate and global networks. Every city and region wants to be prosperous, and many have looked to the analysis of successful regions to get a blueprint of how to develop their own regions. It is within these highly dynamic regions that the small high-tech entrepreneurial firm has come to exemplify a general model of economic development. The problem, as with the supposed triumph of the small business in the new economy, is not that this doesn't describe *a* reality only that it isn't a general one (Scott 2006). The supporters of clusters as a form of economic development and policy argue that myriad small firms combine in mutually supporting partnerships of 'trust, loyalty and reciprocity' to become globally relevant economic players (Taylor 2005). As we have seen with the relationship between large and small firms in the previous section, empirical research often shows that the realities of competitive pressures on making a profit mean that relationships are not always so cosy. Supporters of the cluster concept are often 'blind to the role of inter-firm power inequalities in shaping business relationships, choosing to privilege collaboration over competition' (Taylor 2005).

The promise of economic magic created by a mutually benefiting proximity of firms, which will produce something exciting that goes beyond (in wealth creation and job terms) the sum of their parts, has nevertheless stimulated economists, geographers and policy-makers for some decades now. Ever since the ground breaking work of Piore and Sabel (1984), which questioned assumptions about the advantages of large scale mass production for realising prospering economies, there have been billions piled into science parks, science cities and other policy initiatives seeking to enhance the linkages, connectivity and networks between small firms. The objective has been to seek to emulate the success of Italy's Emilia-Romagna region or Silicon Valley in the US where, 'small enterprises [...] worked together in closely integrated, economically powerful networks, which achieved high overall collective efficiency, enabling the firms to compete effectively in world markets' (Curran 2000b: 216). The idea is based on seeking to benefit from the flexibility and dynamism of smallness whilst maintaining access to external knowledge and expertise. Underlying these aspirations has been an assumption that mass production had had its day and that increasingly economic prosperity would rely on flexible and relatively small scale modes of production able to customise and specialise production methods through the application of new technologies. In 1984 Piore and Sabel rightly castigated the tendency of analysts to ascribe to large scale production the totality of competitive advantage throughout industrial history. Similarly today, their powerful insights aimed at establishing a more plural and heterogeneous view of economic production, have been bowdlerised into a similarly crass and totalising view that small is always best.

The reality of the local economic context is of course more complex. Small firms, and especially the more entrepreneurial, do not have inherent propensities to operate in localised networks (Scott 2006). In a detailed study Curran and Blackburn unsurprisingly conclude that different firms have different types of local connections. Some firms like local retail businesses are indeed connected to 'spatially proximate' markets. Others, the 'newer and the most rapidly expanding kinds of small businesses, are much less likely to be tied to "locality". [...] Using modern communications they deliver their "product", often intangibles involving knowledge manipulation rather than tangible objects, and maintain contacts with other businesses quickly and effectively, *increasingly regardless of spatial consideration*' (Curran and Blackburn 1994: 183, emphasis added). With globalisation and the internet this process of delocalisation has if anything accelerated and deepened. Curran and Blackburn's analysis of the local economy shows that many small and entrepreneurial firms, far from being locally concentrated and engaged, are becoming more internationally embedded, though clearly certain aspects of the business (for instance, employees of the firm will tend to live locally), will always tend to connect it to the local economy.

 ## Fenderco case study

Paul on why he set up in the middle of England miles from any ports

It's a bit silly really. Moving the business and living here was mostly to do with my wife, who thought Maltonbury was cute. It is. With the abbey and the pubs and all that. But I grew up here too. This is my home town. It's always felt like a safe haven to me, though I was initially a bit reticent about living in the same town as my parents. Coming back here and setting up this marine business in the middle of the Cotswolds seems a little obscure, always raises a smile when you talk to somebody. When I meet people at ports, up in Grimsby or Scotland they always ask 'Why Maltonbury?' 'It's a nice place to live and work', I tell them. There are a lot of high technology and engineering companies around. So finding staff is quite easy. We get quality people applying. But we're not really in this M4 Corridor cluster thing. It's sort of different here. We're not in the commuter belt – Silicon Valley – we're outside of that fortunately as the salary expectations are higher there, nearer London. So you know, it's an enjoyable town to live in and to work in, we've got good connections, an hour – a couple of hours to Manchester – hour and a half to London. You know, it's very central. Transport is quite important. It's nice to just get in a car and set off and know that whatever direction you take, you're not going to be sitting in a traffic jam. And, you know, it doesn't really make any difference to our business, wherever we are. The fendering industry is a little global village really. We're always meeting the same people all over the world. You bump into them at conferences and seminars. We're forever sharing jokey emails to mates all over. People are a bit surprised though when they find out where Maltonbury is.

Activity

What is the dominant rationale for Paul setting the business up in Maltonbury?

a) Proximity to main site of business
b) Personal and lifestyle reasons
c) Access to specialist knowledge
d) Ease of transportation
e) Access to funding support
f) Good pool of local labour

In what ways do the reasons given support a strong cluster thesis? Which reasons do and which don't?

However, this is not to suggest that internationally oriented, proximate and highly networked entrepreneurial ventures do not congregate and cluster around certain exciting locations (which may or may not be supported by government subsidies, low rents and tax breaks). And that is the point. Silicon Valley and other economic clusters are the exception, not a new universal economic model (Taylor 2005). They have however been very influential and for this reason it is worth looking at how they work. Take the Formula 1(F1) industry, or 'Motor Sport Valley' which surrounds London (Figure 9.1).

The counties surrounding London are a combination of pristine, leafy villages and dull but worthy commuter towns. It also happens to be where a large proportion of the world's Formula 1 race car constructors and suppliers are based. 'Motor Sport Valley' has emerged over many decades as a region where engineers, designers and managers develop their careers through successive roles with different companies. The industry is extremely fluid. Companies emerge, prosper and decline in tune with the success of technological developments, sponsorship, capital investment, and ultimately by fortunes on the track. Henry and Pinch showed that 'Motor Sport Valley is a close-knit knowledge community characterised by a complex mixture of cooperation as well as fierce competition' (2000: 206). By knowledge community they mean that employees in the industry have ways of thinking, doing and building their careers which transcend individual firms. This is just as well as many of the firms don't last very long. For those of you who are familiar with the sport another look at Figure 9.1 will show that of seven F1 constructors only two are now still fielding racing cars under the same name (Williams and McClaren). Henry and Pinch explain that Motor Sport Valley is similar to the software engineers of Silicon Valley who joke that they can quite often change firms without changing car parks. Geographical proximity is the key to how this industry works: 'in the high-firm death industry of British motor sport, engineers know that a location within the

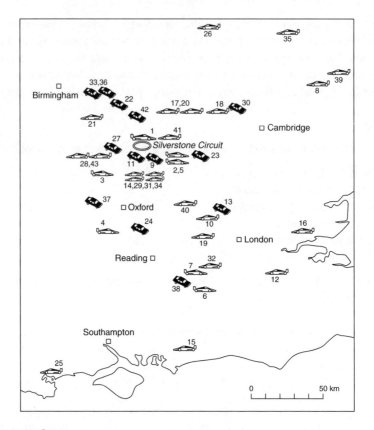

FORMULA ONE

1	Benson and Hedges Total Jordan Peugeot	5	Stewart Ford
2	Danka Arrows Yamaha	6	Tyrrell Racing Organization
3	Mild Seven Benetton Renault	7	West McClaren Mercedes
4	Rothmans Williams Renault		

OTHER FORMULAE and TOURING/RALLY CARS

8	Argo Cars	20	Magnum	32	Ronta
9	Audi Sport	21	Marrow-Jon Morris Designs	33	Rouse Sport
10	Bowman Cars	22	Mitsubishi Ralliart	34	Spice Racing Cars
11	BMW Team Schnitzer	23	Motor Sport Developments	35	Spider
12	Elden Racing Cars	24	Nissan Motorsport Europe	36	Total Team Peugeot
13	Ford Motorsport	25	Penske Cars Ltd.	37	TWR Racing
14	Galmer Engineering	26	Pilbeam Racing Design Ltd.	38	Valvoline Team Mondeo
15	G Force Precision Engineering	27	Prodrive	39	Van Diemen International
16	Hawke Racing Cars	28	Pro Sport Engineering Ltd.	40	Vector Racing Car Constructors
17	Jedi	29	Ralt Engineering	41	Vision
18	Lola Cars Ltd.	30	Ray Mallock	42	Volkswagen • SBG Sport
19	Lyncar	31	Reynard Racing Cars Ltd.	43	Zeus Motorsport Engineering

Figure 9.1   Motor Sport Valley: constructors (taken from Henry and Pinch 2000: 192)

Valley is likely to ensure continued employment without the need for a house move even if the name of the employer is likely to change relatively frequently' (2000: 206). It is this knowledge of employees and the region as a whole that is important, not the individual firms.

Ultimately however 'spatial or territorial proximity' is not 'a *necessary* condition for collaboration' (Freel 2000: 248, emphasis added). Motor Sport Valley is an exception and not a standard model for the new economy. Regional clusters should not be seen in isolation, but in context. It is often forgotten by those who wished to apply this model elsewhere that the success of these regions is often due to 'long-established local communities with strong social, political and religious infrastructures in sustaining the networks' (Freel 2000: 248). The success of Motor Sport Valley is predicated on a long history and culture of motor sport and aircraft engineering expertise which emerged after the Second World War (Henry and Pinch 2001: 1175). As with the introduction of unsustainable technologies in a development context, where tractors stand useless for want of simple repair skills in remote rural communities, policies promoting enterprising clusters and networks often fail: 'The difficulties of changing cultures and institutions, in short, have typically been grossly underestimated in attempting to introduce forms of entrepreneurship and the small enterprise from Western market-based economies' (Curran 2000b: 216).

Another aspect of the 'mesmerizing mantra' (Taylor 2005) of high-performing innovative regional clusters, is the role ascribed to universities. Universities are thought to be the sites of 'unexploited knowledge' which 'represents a key source of entrepreneurial opportunity' (Roper 2007: 337). This is a key basis of Audretsch's (2006) spillovers theory of entrepreneurship which Roper feels overplays the role of universities: 'Start-up rates have more to do with networks, culture or policy than the local availability of knowledge' (Roper 2007: 337). The likes of Audretsch (2007) and Acs (2006: 83) have sought to show that universities are key sites of innovation and entrepreneurship, and that is because the knowledge is picked up by regionally networked entrepreneurs.

This takes us back to the concept of opportunities we discussed in Chapter 3: are they created or discovered? I concluded that the objective/discovered notion was unrealistic and that human agency creates opportunities. They don't exist independently outside the human imagination and social interactions. With the spillover view, it is as if knowledge (and opportunities) is like some vast pot that boils over continuously, seeping through cracks, spreading out in unknowable and unruly ways. Some businesses will I am sure benefit from stumbling over these 'spills', but others, equally, will transcend proximity and get their knowledge needs from wherever (Scott 2006: 7). Research shows that the most innovative firms do indeed tend to have strong links with universities, but that these links can reach beyond the locally proximate (Freel 2000: 249).

The picture that emerges, yet again, is one of heterogeneity and diversity rather than rigid and homogeneous models of geographical patterns of enterprise development. There are, it seems, many ways for enterprise to be both global and local.

Innovation and technology

Innovation

Innovation! Innovation! Innovation! More than 'globalisation' and 'clusters' it is a word that really sets policy-makers' juices flowing. Almost every developed and developing nation is seeking to increase its rate of innovation and aims to foster technologically driven economic growth. Despite indicators to the contrary – our ostrich-like economic and political response to a warming planet – hopes for prosperous futures are sought in tackling and transcending our problems through technological innovation. Even where there is a sense that it is previous technological advances (e.g. fossil fuel exploitation) that are the underlying causes of environmental degradation and unsustainable practices, and that it is the exploitative nature of capitalist innovation that is the problem philosophically speaking (nature is a free lunch), practically it is to technology that governments and corporations naturally turn.

As we have seen in the previous section the weight of the world's problems, rhetorically at least, is often placed at the feet of the smaller enterprise. Not only is it received wisdom that small firms are more agile and dynamic in the new economy, especially when they 'cluster', but that they are also more innovative. This section examines these assumptions and finds them wanting.

What does it mean when we say a small firm is innovative? What is an innovation? Are the most innovative firms those that produce lots of new and successful ideas? To read the literature lionising the innovativeness of small firms, it would seem that it's simply about how many innovations a firm thinks it has to hand. Of course, not all ideas are equal. Some ideas are truly transformative and disruptive, others less so. As Mark Freel puts it: 'Innovation is not categorical but a matter of degree' (2000: 253). This points us yet again to the distinction between smaller enterprise and entrepreneurship. Innovation lies at the heart of entrepreneurship. One can run a successful small firm without innovating very much, but being an entrepreneur implies doing something exciting, creative and new. The figure of the entrepreneur is often seen as a 'prime economic mover', an economic revolutionary if you like (Curran 1990: 134). This is because, in the Schumpetarian sense 'he/she sees *new ways* of ordering and managing resources to use them more effectively, that is, more profitably, in relation to existing or emerging market opportunities' (Curran 1990: 134, emphasis added). What are these 'new ways' of doing things?

According to Schumpter there are five types of innovation:

- **The introduction of a *new good* – namely one with which consumers are not yet familiar – or of a new quality of a good.**
- **The introduction of a *new method* of production, which needs by no means to be founded upon a discovery that is scientifically new, and can also exist in a new way of handling a commodity commercially.**
- **The opening of a *new market*, namely a market into which the particular branch of manufacture of the country in question has not previously entered, whether or not this market has existed before.**
- **The conquest of a *new source of supply* of raw materials or half-manufactured goods, again irrespective of whether this source already exists or whether it has first to be created.**
- **The carrying out of the *new organisation* of any industry, like the creation of a monopoly position (for example through trustification) or the breaking up of a monopoly position (Schumpeter 1934/1911: 66).**

Note that Schumpeter does not mention or imply anything about small firms. According to Thomas McCraw, Schumpeter could be somewhat inconsistent regarding the issue of firm size and innovation. But taken overall his approach was that 'size in and of itself does not preclude innovation, and [large firms] can promote it in ways that would not occur in small business' (McCraw 2007: 639). McCraw is insistent however that this did not mean that Schumpeter supported small over large, or large over small. The structure of the economy has changed since Schumpeter's days when large industrial agglomeration was where much innovation took place. Big firms had all the money to invest in R&D (research and development). In many respects given what we discussed earlier in this chapter, they still have. Big firms are innovators because they can 'afford to gamble on new techniques. They were willing to absorb losses in some of their new ventures because they could be confident of profits in others (McCraw 2007: 164). The economy as a whole is structured and dominated by increasing economic concentration and by the very large corporation. Dynamic enterprises do start small and become corporations, some maintain smallness and power in important niches, but to ascribe smallness as the defining attribute of economic renewal is a mistake. And, whilst successful entrepreneurial ventures must almost by definition have a degree of innovativeness, small firms are by no means inherently innovative: 'Most inherit an existing enterprise or purchase an established business or simply replicate an existing, proven, form of business. The small corner shop, for instance, is a much more common form of small scale economic activity than any mould-breaking activities which might be labelled "entrepreneurship"' (Curran 1990: 134). Most small businesses are 'hugely *uninnovative and conservative*' (ibid.).

Nevertheless, because of the shifts in the organisational structures of industries – flotillas of coordinated activity rather than slow and unwieldy oil tankers (see Chapter 7) – that I have described throughout this book, the stock of more innovative business has likely increased. One of the purposes of restructuring has been to create more communicative business units that can realise entrepreneurial and employee creativity. But this reflects the structure of the economy and the nature of discourses about what constitutes innovation, as much as it does anything inherently new about business activity.

Given the faith placed in innovation as a way of solving problems, defining and measuring the innovativeness of an economy has become a growth industry in both academic, corporate and policy spheres. Acs (2006) suggests that one of the reasons why smaller firms have been the focus of attention is because of the way 'the innovation process' has been measured differently over time. In the past R&D investments were counted as a proxy for innovativeness. Then came the numbers of patents, as it was realised that R&D was an input rather than an output figure. Counting patents has its limitations too as different industrial sectors have different propensities to produce them and patents don't always reflect real innovations, but can reflect market capture/blocking behaviour, stopping competitors from using technologies. More recently direct measures of innovative outputs have been used, although this has limits too: not all 'innovations are of equal importance' (Acs 2006: 79). This shift in measurement preference, and of course, greater understanding of the relative importance of the smaller enterprise in a changing economy, has meant progressively more small scale enterprise activity being included in discourse about innovation. However, all measures provide consistent and comparable *proxies* for what is actually a complex and context specific process, as we saw in Motor Sport Valley. But amongst this ambiguity it *is* safe to say that small entrepreneurial firms (especially those internationally oriented high-tech businesses) are amongst the most innovative and account for an increasing proportion of innovativeness in many industries.

However, it is important to recognise the extent of sectoral specificity. Building aircrafts, automobiles, oil and gas plants is a job for big corporations. There wouldn't likely be many Jumbo jets around if we had to rely on small firms. And, whilst companies like Airbus and Boeing, and Ford and Renault, rely on a vast flotilla of small and large suppliers and service companies, no doubt more now than in the oil tanker past, it still requires the bigness of the corporation to marshal the capital resources and the vision. Smaller firms tend to be prevalent in newer industries such as biotechnology and information technologies: Acs concludes that 'the relative innovative advantage of large firms tends to be promoted in industries that are capital-intensive, advertising intensive, concentrated and highly unionised. By contrast, in industries that are highly innovative and composed predominantly of large firms, the relative innovative advantage is held by small enterprises' (2006: 88). Given the context specific nature of innovation there will always be limits to understanding the rate and frequency of innovation in the economy as a whole.

Not only do small and large organisations tend towards different sectors in terms of innovativeness, they also have different attributes relating to the control and exploitation of innovations. Acs has suggested that '[s]mall firms are superior in commercialising new knowledge; large firms are superior in their ability to appropriate returns from these innovations, either by buying property rights or acquiring small firms' (ibid.). What this means in practice is that a large firm will often buy a smaller one which looks as though they have a truly innovative product. Some high-tech small firms actively embrace being taken over as a way of realising personal wealth for the entrepreneur/s and/or as a way to access international markets that would otherwise take years to build through organic growth (Keeble et al. 1998: 328). In other cases, as with the dot com bubble of the late 1990s, the potential of a new market producing a paradigm shifting idea can sometimes get ahead of the real economy's ability to realise a profit from it. Not all innovative ideas come to market.

Some entrepreneurial and innovative firms resist the temptation to sell out and build and grow independently. What do these innovative small firms look like? Research shows that the most innovative firms will tend to collaborate with their suppliers and involve their customers in product development. Small innovative firms need to forge linkages such as these in order to gain the knowledge and expertise they lack. These linkages are not without dangers for the firm however, as the more open a firm is to collaboration the more the possibility that the innovative idea might get stolen arises (Freel 2000: 248). And, whilst some industries like Motor Sport Valley will tend to cluster around certain regions and localities, many businesses will innovate regardless of local proximity. Innovative small businesses tend to be export-oriented and will occasionally have links with universities. But being near a university is no guarantee of innovativeness. This goes against the hype typical of enthusiasts for industry–university interaction: 'there is little evidence available to substantiate the role of near-to-university science parks in encouraging small firm innovation or more generally, improved performance' (Freel 2000: 248). In this regard the key attribute of innovative small firms lies in the quality of their collaborations: it is long-term, frequent and enduring linkages, and 'the role of interpersonal dynamics and trust', that are crucial (Freel 2000: 259).

Fenderco case study

Paul talks about his innovation and design philosophy

I get a real kick out of making Fenderco's products look good. Design should be authoritative. It should embody function and style. So often the best designs look very elegant. I like to use contrasting colours to highlight the innovative aspects of our designs. One job we got in Scotland was embarrassingly profitable, which gave us the space to make sure it worked *and* looked really good. You don't always get the chance to do this. This one job led to others as the word spread about how it looked. People at port authorities care about this sort of stuff. It's where they work. No reason for it to look rubbish. We put together three colours for a moving jetty and the moving part was red over a gray fixed mass. It looked brilliant. I didn't get the opportunities to sell this sort of thing to customers when I worked for Europort; they were just too big to be bothered by that sort of detail. You know, an any colour as long as it's grey sort of thing. Not that I am professionally trained as a designer or anything. I just did basic engineering till I was 20 or so and then learnt what I know now from my first job. I'm always learning stuff. My philosophy is if it looks right it probably works well. I've always enjoyed innovative and elegant designs, especially if it conceals the workings. To an extent, this keeps the competition from nicking your ideas too. Innovation is about learning stuff from different contexts. When I walk round the factories that actually knock our stuff together I will stop and chat with the welder or fitter. These guys know what they're about and a fair few of the ideas I get from redesigning stuff to be simpler, more elegant and the like, come from them. They do the work after all, and they can tell me if it's a pig of a job, if it can be done differently; quicker, stronger, smarter, cheaper. It's all very much a learning process. You've just got to talk with people: suppliers, sub-contractors, everyone. Even the company bookkeeper can innovate: what do I know about managing an office!?

Activity

In groups discuss the innovation process Paul is describing. Answer the following questions.

Is creativity and innovation a social or individual process?
Are there business limits to good design?
Is Paul innovating or creating good design? Are they the same?

New things are not inherently better because they are new. New things and processes are often introduced in order to solve certain problems, but inevitably they will create others. Unintended consequences and unforeseen problems result from technological innovation. The automobile certainly allowed for faster distribution and transportation, but increased speed also caused death and injury from accidents and increased fossil fuel pollution. The rise of the internet and a consequent decline in print journalism may not appear to have a downside, but internet news delivery has been destroying the US journalism and newspaper industry. Internet news services in the main are not as yet monetising their product or attracting sufficient advertising revenue to employ as many journalists and reporters as once were employed in newspapers. As a consequence internet providers rely on recycling and re-circulating news originating in the print media: 'the parasite is slowly consuming the host' (Simon 2009). The result has been a decline in serious news reporting and journalism, which many hold up as a foundation stone of democratic society.

Once a technology has been adopted, others are often discarded. Cars and trucks replaced a different form of technology, the horse. There are therefore path dependencies associated with the adoption of technology; we can't un-invent or un-use the computer. It is this aspect of technology – the incremental, step-by-step, process of development – that provides a great deal of opportunity for enterprises to produce products and services. Cycles of technological innovation, redundancy and obsolescence have in recent decades accelerated enormously (Keeble et al. 1998: 328), in part no doubt fuelled by the booms in ready credit and consumption. Technology begets more technology. Technology creates new opportunities; new problems to solve.

New technology does not become part of our world without effort. Companies, small and large, are formed. Technologies are developed and then placed on the market. Competing technologies vie for access to our cash and it isn't always the best technology that wins. One would think that consumers would choose the cheapest and highest functioning products, and in most cases they probably do. But the success of new technologies is not just about functional and economic advantage. Munir and Phillips (2005) argue that firms – they focus on the story of Kodak, the photography and camera firm – do more than simply present a palette of new technologies to consumers. They show how consumers were 'taught to want new things' (cited in McCraw 2007: 72, from Schumpeter 1934/1911: 65) through advertising and marketing. Indeed Kodak was responsible for turning photography from an elite, highly skilled and artistic pastime into something everyone could do. The simple portable Kodak cameras of the time produced an inferior picture quality and were initially a business failure. Advertising and the reinvention of what photography meant – the creation of the photo album, popular photo magazines, the 'snapshot' as a way of chronicling family history, separating taking the photo from developing it – was as much a social project as it was a technological one (Figure 9.2 and 9.3). New technologies create new things, but things such as portable cameras only really become meaningful once new concepts and social activities develop to use the thing. This is why not all new technologies are successful: people have to enjoy finding uses for them. What Kodak did in the past Sony is doing today: 'they have been portraying hard prints as a relic that belongs to the past and stressing the necessity of saving images in cyberspace' (Munir and Phillips 2005: 1683). Thus it is the degree to which a business (what Munir and Phillips describe as the 'institutional entrepreneur') 'can manage meaning of the technology and embed it in the everyday lives of potential consumers that determines how disruptive the technology will be' (ibid.), and not necessarily the nature of the technology itself.

This indicates a potential limit to the extent to which small entrepreneurial firms, on their own, can be transformative. Managing the meaning of technology and embedding it in everyday lives requires more than just the capacity to bring technological innovations to market, it demands the sort of power and influence that corporations exert. For Google to disrupt and transform our lives it had to be entrepreneurial and innovative, but it also had to grow into a large corporation.

A focus on the social and economic power (managing meaning) required to embed technological innovations is also reflected in Schumpeter's different forms of innovation, presented above. Note that he does not specifically refer to new technology. Innovations can be technological, as in a new type of machine or electrical circuit, but they don't have to be. Innovations can also refer to processes and new ways of organising (Pittaway et al. 2004). Equally, new technologies needn't be machines. A horse can be a technology. Thus the distinction between technology and innovation can be a difficult one to isolate. This perhaps explains one of the reasons why there has been so much intellectual excitement about high-technology small firms. The technology may be difficult to understand – be it in bioprocessing, nanotechnology or information technology – but imagine it in a small firm under the control of a technically-oriented entrepreneur, then it becomes something tangible in a way that technologies like horses and process innovations aren't.

To be sure, small and dynamic high-tech businesses have received a great deal of academic and policy attention in recent years. Earlier I stressed the need to avoid characterising the whole economic context by reference to high-tech geographically-clustered global entrepreneurial firms. This is not to say that these firms are not important. Firms like these can destroy old industries, form the basis of whole new industries and realise economic growth and create jobs. The hype often gets out of hand however and as Peter Buckley notes small firms have their limits: 'All the evidence suggests that SMEs will not, in aggregate, be the major suppliers and transferors of technology in the world economy, but they can fill crucial niche roles' (Buckley 1997: 77). It is this niche filling role that is crucial and it also shapes how these types of businesses behave. Research has shown for instance that because of the niche markets that these firms operate within they have to internationalise their activities very early on (Keeble et al. 1998: 338). A small Swedish firm can be a world leader in the supply of specialised instrumentation and diagnostics equipment in the bioprocessing sector, but given the limited scope of

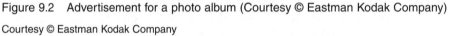

Figure 9.2   Advertisement for a photo album (Courtesy © Eastman Kodak Company)

Courtesy © Eastman Kodak Company

Figure 9.3   A Kodak Moment, 1916 (Courtesy © Eastman Kodak Company)

Courtesy © Eastman Kodak Company

the industry in Sweden it would be foolish not to see the whole world as a market. Keeble and his colleagues conclude that 'technology intensive firms' often exhibit strong international networks and also tend to 'exhibit above-average levels of local networking with respects to research collaboration and intra-industry links' (1998: 338).

When the small firm is operating within a new niche, taking risks with untried technological applications, competition may be less severe. The dot com boom was a story of venture capital being seduced by the technological promise which failed to deliver. When new technological ideas bloom like this, there may initially be just a few key players who will fight it out to make the technology succeed. The documentary film *Startup.Com* shows this process for real. The film describes the birth and eventual death of a dot com business called govWorks.Com. It shows how the firm's entrepreneurs convinced venture capitalist to invest millions. GovWorks.com's idea was to develop an online application that enabled people to do business with local government: to pay things like parking tickets on the internet. What a great idea! Unfortunately despite growing quickly to employ around 200 staff and spend much of the investment cash, the software was never reliable enough, and they struggled to generate sustainable revenues. The business eventually failed and was taken over by a more successful competitor.

This pattern of new ideas, unproven risky technologies, and small firms willing to try everything to get to market and to get it to work is familiar, but doesn't necessarily describe how all new technologies emerge. Where it does, it's because the barriers to entry are often relatively low, allowing smaller firms the 'time' to create a niche market. As novel technology becomes more reliable, less of a risk and more obviously profitable, larger businesses will tend to look for ways, through joint venture, licensing arrangements or acquisition (Acs and Preston 1997: 4), to exploit the opportunities. And, 'as sectors become more mature larger firms tend to dominate and the remaining small firms are likely to occupy narrow niches, unattractive to larger firms' (Cooper 2006: 248). These 'cycles' of risk, technological application, entrepreneurial dynamism, and maturation are complex and vary from sector to sector. Cooper (ibid.) for example points out that when compared to the length of time and amount of capital required for applying new ideas in the biotechnology sector, the translation of ideas into products in the electronics industry is very fast. We see again that small entrepreneurial firms are part of a broader economic context of technological innovation and not isolated agents.

Conclusion

The overall story here has been one emphasising the complexity and diversity of economic contexts and the ease by which fashionable ideas get blown out of proportion to try to do conceptual work way beyond their true application. Small entrepreneurial innovative firms are important, but let's not get carried away. Size isn't everything. Economies are very complex with a vast range of differently sized and organised private firms, government funded and/or run organisations, charitable organisations and so on. It is the interconnectedness of these organisations that is really important to understand.

Summary

The chapter has discussed how broad contextual changes have restructured the economy such that small scale and entrepreneurial economic activity is more important than it once was. This can be seen clearly in the competing explanations of globalisation and localisation, innovation and technology in the context of small and entrepreneurial business. It was argued that a great deal of hyperbole is written about the importance of small firms in processes of globalisation and innovative clustering. Similarly though smaller firms can be innovative there is nothing inherently innovative about smallness. Overall the chapter has argued that economic contexts and the structural changes that emerge are more complex and diverse than often fashionable ideas about the small firm and innovative clusters suggest.

■ ■ Further reading ■

Audretsch, D. (2007) *The Entrepreneurial Society*, Oxford: Oxford University Press.

Curran, J. (1990) 'Rethinking economic structure: Exploring the role of the small firm and self-employment in the British economy', *Work, Employment and Society* Special Issue (May): 125–146.

Freel, M. (2000) 'External linkages and product innovation in small manufacturing firms', *Entrepreneurship and Regional Development* 12(3): 245–266.

Hancké, B. (1998) 'Trust or hierarchy? Changing relationships between large and small firms in France', *Small Business Economics* 11: 237–252.

Henry, N. and Pinch, S. (2000) 'Spatialising knowledge: placing the knowledge community of Motor Sport Valley', *Geoforum* 31: 191–208.

Keeble, D., Lawson, C., Lawton Smith, H., Moore, B. and Wilkinson, F. (1998) 'Internationalisation processes, networking and local embeddedness in technology intensive small firms', *Small Business Economics* 11: 327–342.

Munir, K.A. and Phillips, N. (2005) 'The birth of the "Kodak moment": Institutional entrepreneurship and the adoption of new technologies', *Organization Studies* 26(11): 1665–1687.

Scott, A.J. (2006) 'Entrepreneurship, innovation and industrial development: Geography and the creative field revisited', *Small Business Economics* 26(1): 24.

10

Social Contexts of Enterprise: Cultural Centrality, Diversity and Marginality

Overview

This chapter has the following objectives:

- To demonstrate the importance of a social and cultural understanding of enterprise, entrepreneurship and small business.
- To illustrate how social change creates new entrepreneurial opportunities.
- To explain the social dimensions of family, immigrant/ethnic and criminal enterprises.
- To introduce the concept of *entre-tainment* to discuss the emergence of entrepreneurially-oriented contemporary culture.

Introduction: what is the 'social context'?

This chapter looks at ways in which our society and culture interrelate with enterprise. This should not be seen as an addition to the supposedly more important economic significance of enterprise. Societies, cultures or economies are equally significant for everyday life, depending of course on the sorts of relationships and activity you are engaged with at particular times. They are different ways of describing the same relationships and activities.

What do we mean by society? Often equating to the nation state in common sense use, more precisely it refers to the relationships and structures that people create and organise. Thus social contexts can refer to a dizzying range of activity: in fact almost everything we do. As we discussed in Chapter 4, even creating a sense of self is social in nature. Similarly most, perhaps all human activity will have its economic and political dimensions. Nevertheless, some aspects of human behaviour are generally perceived as more socially relevant than others. The main ones relate to class, family and gender relations, crime and deviance, race and ethnicity, and demography. As we progress through the chapter we will see that many of these issues are relevant to a discussion of enterprise.

In addressing society in this way, we uncover many of the facets of enterprise that don't quite fit the stereotypical picture of a white, male, economically rational entrepreneur. Ethnic minorities, family, criminal and Indigenous entrepreneurs are often discussed in splendid isolation. The approach here will be to place these discussions in broader contexts of social and cultural trends, and to avoid categorising them as marginal in the sense of being less important than normal enterprise. However, these facets of enterprise *are* marginal in the sense that society more broadly identifies them as an other, different from the norm. This marginality can however be interpreted and used for both negative and positive purposes. Thus Indigenous groups can use their distinct and marginal identity to effect positive change in society. Criminal entrepreneurship is marginal not in the sense of being unimportant – though it is not often discussed by enterprise scholars – but in the negative sense of being outside the mainstream and morally proscribed. For these reasons it makes sense to discuss these social aspects of enterprise via the concept of marginality.

Okay, I get society, but what has culture to do with enterprise? Before answering this the notion of culture should be understood. There are many different definitions and competing understandings, but at its core scholars normally refer to aspects of life bound up with the symbolic, learned, and linguistic, our beliefs and ideas, customs and ways of life (dress, mannerisms and so forth), and our popular (and 'high') culture (art, music, film, newspapers, TV, etc.). This is a big topic. To make it more manageable we concentrate on how enterprise is depicted and mobilised in cultural media.

This is not a typical topic in enterprise textbooks or research, but it is interesting, and I think increasingly important in understanding what enterprise represents. Many of you will have noticed the cultural impact of television programmes such as *The Apprentice* and *Dragons' Den*. But equally it is also noticeable how the growing number of voluble media-savvy famous entrepreneurs such as Richard Branson appear in the media to comment on this or that topic. The entrepreneur is a powerful cultural character who has an influence on us all. This is also a central aspect of the discourse of enterprise. The discourse of the entrepreneur as hero figure (and the many other aspects of the entrepreneur: the man of the people; the crusader for the customer and so on) is an important cultural archetype, with many implications that we briefly explore at the end of the chapter.

The chapter is organised in the following manner. The first section looks at underlying social changes and incorporates a discussion of social class, demographic change including age and geographical mobility, the nature of the individual, gender and family and social and cultural attitudes. The second section looks at marginal aspects of enterprise (including discussions of family, immigrant/ethnic, Indigenous, and criminal enterprise). The third section briefly explores the cultural importance of enterprise and entrepreneurship, which is noticeable in, but not limited to, the rise of TV *entre-tainment* (i.e. *The Apprentice*). The final section summarises the chapter.

Enterprise and social change

Over the last few decades societies around the world have been changing quickly. Though one can argue about the extent, nature and geographical variability, it is difficult to avoid concluding that our grandparents' world was very different from ours. That's history for you. We can summarise this under the following headings.

Class

It is often assumed today that we live in classless societies. Whilst it may not be so easy to fit yourself into the middle- or working-class categories as it once was, there are still many differences between groups of people. We have become so used to thinking of ourselves as unique individuals that terms such as these have fallen out of fashion. This doesn't stop companies categorising people into socio-economic groups for the purpose of establishing relative spending power, nor does it stop governments categorising people for this and that purpose. Despite our changes in attitudes there are still structured hierarchies and inequalities between groups of people: societies are still stratified.

In terms of thinking about enterprise, certain classes of people – those with access to financial capital, knowledge and education, relevant labour market expertise and experience – are more likely to be able to start and succeed in business than others. Overall though class is very unfashionable among enterprise scholars, and there is scant research in this area, which is a shame because seen in class terms, the types of people engaged in enterprising activity varies amazingly. To be sure, the upper-class or high-status rich are over-represented in the ranks of the famously and grandly enterprising, but you will also find unemployed and illegally enterprising window cleaners. There have also been interesting changes in the composition and nature of social classes.

The 'old money' rich have been joined by increasing numbers of corporate and self-made millionaires: celebrities, internet and telecommunications entrepreneurs. Many more women and ethic minorities form part of these new moneyed elites than in the past. In part, in Britain at least, this is due to changes in attitudes and opportunities brought about by enterprise culture policies. The middle classes have grown and become ever more diverse as more and more people now work in service and professional roles. Other changes in the structure of employment opportunity mean that more and more people are turning towards self-employment and enterprise as a means of supporting themselves and achieving social advancement.

Demographic change

Two demographic changes are having a profound effect. Firstly the shifting age composition of Western nations, particularly in Europe, and secondly, changes in populations caused by geographical mobility, caused by either immigration or urbanisation. None of these trends have deterministic influences on what people are actually doing with their lives, and in particular how they go about being enterprising, but certain specific impacts can be identified which have an influence on the nature and characteristics of entrepreneurship and small business.

The ageing population is increasingly seen as a problem (in terms of declining government taxation revenues and more people being reliant on welfare and healthcare provisions). One of the proposed solutions is to encourage older people to be more economically active; work longer; start businesses; or at least to engage in more social enterprise or volunteering. Shifting age compositions will also lead to growth in the numbers of older entrepreneurs, but more importantly growth in the entrepreneurial opportunities in markets that appeal to older people. The 'grey' dollar will be spent on assistive technologies, differentiated healthcare and a whole range of other new products and services.

Looking at geographical mobility, many European nations are now providing homes to large new immigrant populations. Many people will choose enterprise (or be forced into 'necessity' entrepreneurship) over the alternative of insecure, low-paid employment because of their qualifications not being recognised, or because it provides a better opportunity. Urbanisation (the shift towards people living in cities) is a feature in both developed and developing societies, producing both threats and opportunities to enterprise activity. We will consider aspects of immigrant enterprise in a later section.

The individual, gender and family

In Chapter 4 we saw the impact that changing notions of the individual and self-identity were having on how entrepreneurs are understood. We found that the individual – the person – had historical attributes such that someone even a few hundred years ago would have had a very different sense of themselves as a person than they would do today. Here we briefly consider the ways in which our social relationships to each other and the institutions that structure them (e.g. family, gender norms) are changing the social environment in which enterprise takes place.

Western societies are becoming more individually oriented. Society comprises of more and more single occupancy homes. Single? Lonely? You are not alone. People are marrying less and later in life. They are also divorcing more. Many couples choose not to have children. Birth rates have been in decline; societies are getting older. The traditional family is in decline. Single parent families are common. There is less social interaction between parents and children. Social bonds in many areas of our lives are weakening, and becoming temporary and transient.

At the same time our notions of gender have also changed. Gender – the psychological, social and cultural differences between men and women – has become a political issue in many nations, and equality between men and women an expected social norm. Despite these changes in social attitudes and the law, women still face discrimination and an inferior status in all societies. In Western societies many more women work now than in the past. The man is no longer assumed to be the bread-winner. What it is to be a man or a woman is different to what it used to be, and social expectations about gender are far broader than they once were.

Aldrich and Cliff (2003: 574) have argued that these changes are likely to have profound influences on entrepreneurship and the formation of small firms. They suggest that the changes in the 'family system' will likely create new opportunities for entrepreneurs: the sale of supermarket prepared all-in-one-meals for example is booming. Opportunities are emerging in individualised products, household services and related products in cleaning, cooking, childcare and shopping which are all innovations that respond to our increasingly atomised and busy work-oriented lives. 'Dual-earner' families – those with two parents working full-time – in particular provide many opportunities for the canny entrepreneur: someone or something has to look after the children. Products that do this are being lapped-up by time-poor parents. Services such as dating agencies and relationship-brokering (group holiday services, club events, and so forth) are all doing very nicely, thank you very much.

Changes in family composition will also influence patterns in the formation of businesses. Will the preponderance of single parent families produce more or less family business entrepreneurs? Aldrich and Cliff argue that whilst smaller families may mean that nascent entrepreneurs will perceive less risk in their start-ups, the small family size may also hinder these because of the lack of family-based resources. Turning to gender, we can see that the existence of discrimination against women and a 'glass ceiling' which halts promotion and pay equality might act as an incentive to start their own firm. But equally for some, having to manage work, home and children may make starting their own business look like a job too far.

Trends in individual social behaviour, family composition and gender dynamics are clearly having a significant impact on the enterprise environment. Given the complexity of the changes the implications are unsurprisingly not straightforward or uni-directional.

Social and cultural attitudes

One of the areas of social change that has created particular and obvious entrepreneurial opportunity has been what might be termed 'lifestyle'. Perhaps because of the growth of disposable income and consumerism more generally people find themselves with more choices about how to be: what to wear, what to read and listen to, what to think, what to eat, who to believe. People even have choices about how to care for and decorate their 'birthday suit': body care products, make-up, tattooing, and piercing are just some of the products and services to choose from (Figure 10.1). Underlying these changes have been fundamental shifts in the conduct and attitudes of many, which have been exploited and further stimulated by entrepreneurs who are creating new opportunities for consumption, choice and individual expression.

There are many facets to these changes. One fundamental factor in the rise of personal freedom has been the decline in authority of the traditional organised religions. Though new forms of spirituality, quasi-spirituality and new evangelical religions have taken their place, the terrain for personal freedom has changed irrevocably. These new forms of spirituality have in some cases spawned large associated industries such as those corporate mega-churches run by 'pastorpreneurs', and the products and paraphernalia associated with 'New Age' thinking. Shifting

Figure 10.1   Freedom to choose

© iStockPhoto

attitudes to sexuality have become one expression of these changes, as the availability and acceptability of contraception created new lifestyle choices, and for many the time to consume and explore these opportunities. Popular culture emerged with the development of mass media technologies (e.g. television), and in important ways celebrated and encouraged the growth of individual expression and experimentation, with successive waves of fashion, music and lifestyle choices. Entrepreneurs readily exploit these shifting attitudes and continually offer new variations to choose from – both responding to and stimulating different cultural tastes and leisure pursuits.

Political developments and fashions have played a part too. A contemporary example is the concern people are now showing about the environment. Many in the West are increasingly keen to adopt green lifestyles, whilst at the same time striving to maintain their standard of living. Entrepreneurial opportunities here are perhaps in their early stages, as the political necessities of saving water and energy and sustainable production (e.g. organic foods) become more urgent and the green political discourse gathers pace and substance. Already though, corporations and SMEs round the world are understanding the importance of appearing green: opportunities abound.

Other technological changes have shrunk the world and created the phenomenon of mass international travel. On one dimension the world is becoming more homogeneous as globalised products and services (Starbucks, McDonald's, and so on) spread their net wider and deeper, and people expect to have their products and services available everywhere. But other opportunities exploit our desire for the authentic, individual experience. Mobile phones and texting have created new ways of communicating: new languages create new forms of social behaviour and entrepreneurial opportunity. Virtually too the world has got a lot smaller. But the internet has done a lot more than enable faster communication. It has created whole new worlds of social interaction and possibilities for personal freedom, including the creation of new identity narratives. In Second Life – a virtual world with its own currency and possibilities of individual personal reality – a new virtual economy has been created. Email, Google, MySpace and YouTube are all having profound impacts on what we do with our lives and on our social and cultural attitudes: here too are whole new frontiers for enterprise and commercial exploitation.

I could go on. Though many arguments are made about the way in which we may have gained personal freedom, only to be imprisoned by consumption and an irrational desire for individual uniqueness, our focus here remains limited to the ways in which enterprise responds to and helps create the social context. It is clear that changing social and cultural attitudes have a strong relationship to the nature of entrepreneurial opportunity.

We turn now to look at how these patterns manifest themselves in terms of the diversity of enterprise.

Diversity and marginality

Family business

Not so long ago academics, policy-makers and business gurus thought that the small family firm was likely to disappear, to be replaced by ever larger and more efficient divisionalised and vertically integrated corporations. **Nepotism**, hereditary management and emotionalism were not compatible with business rationalism, professionalism, bureaucracy and entrepreneurial efficiency. How wrong they were! Family involvement with the economy and all it entails has proved extremely persistent, and any number of articles (e.g. Chua et al. 2003; Steier et al. 2004) have shown that in terms of the numbers of firms, gross national product and in numbers of employees the family firm is still very significant.

Nepotism is favouring your own family or friends in an unjustified manner.

But what do we mean by a family business? As with most things relating to enterprise, though at first sight it seems obvious, definitions often become overly abstract, vague and lacking in meaning in their attempt to capture and cram in the variety of activities encompassed. Simply put, a family firm means a business which is owned and controlled by a family. But it can also mean a husband and wife managing a non-owned franchise (are they still a family if they are not married and without children?), or a family not managing a business but retaining control through ownership. There are many variations, which encompass very different types of economic activity and family ties.

Part of the point of this definition debate is to try to determine whether family firms are special in terms of economic performance. Thus 'while there is no universally accepted definition of a family firm there seems to be a theoretical consensus that a family's ability and intentions to influence business decisions and behaviour are what distinguish family and non-family firms' (Steier et al. 2004: 295). Fair enough. But establishing a positive relationship between family ownership and business performance is a 'very difficult link to make' (Storey 2002: xi). Regardless of whether searching for the holy grail of economic growth is your thing or not, the recent interest in family business is a long overdue recognition of its continuing social and economic importance.

If we think more carefully and broadly about family and its diverse place in particular cultures across the world, we can add greatly to our understanding of enterprise. The family firm *is* different, but not because of any particular special performance quality, but because of the 'closeness' of the social and emotional relations within the firm (Storey 2002: xii). The family firm very particularly and obviously does not just have economic goals, even if we make the rather dubious assumption that all normal small and entrepreneurial firms do. This more-than-just-economics-perspective reflects a now classic view of the firm that sees it as unavoidably embedded in its social contexts (Granovetter 1985). Given these attributes we maybe need to see family in a different way. As we have witnessed elsewhere in the book, enterprise scholars will have different interests in studying enterprise. Some emphasise efficiency, performance and fit with the economy and others, issues of control, gender and power. Despite these fundamental divergences, conversations between the different emphases do take place and academics like Denise Fletcher (2002) have sought to integrate thinking about family business research. She supports thinking about the family firm as a cultural and discursive construction. This approach recognises that different sets of people (academics, policy-makers, and so on) use notions or discourses of the 'family' and 'family firm' for different purposes. Fletcher's three discourses are:

- **Rationality discourse**: The view that in order to pursue an efficient and flourishing business, 'irrational' family influences (emotions, obligations and so forth) need to be managed and constrained.
- **Resource discourse**: The view that the family can provide nurturing, support and emotional labour resources (such as the support of the owner-manager by the spouse) helping the business and individual members to develop.
- **Critical discourse**: The view that emphasises the manner in which commitments to family and/or business can undermine individual freedom and be an arena of control (such as the exploitation of the emotional obligations of children or spouse, to further the owner-manager's personal aspirations for business success).

Each of these discourses can contribute to understanding the family firm. Within the *rationality* discourse for instance is an interest in the process of succession: how a family firm manages the transfer of ownership and control. Research often restricts its view to problems of maintaining firm performance in what is often a far more significant, messy and emotional *family* crisis. Owner-managers might have favourite siblings. Siblings might have other ideas. There is always death, sickness and divorce. These family scenarios are obvious and often crippling for a business, especially in a succession crisis. Can the rationality discourse really capture this messy emotional reality?

In a *resource* discourse view however the 'problem' of succession will be seen through the variety of social relations that might occur as a result of the need for change. Succession becomes the context for a broader discussion about how family interacts with business: about how the interaction between family desires and aspirations acts as a guide and support for the trans-generational development of the business.

The association of entrepreneurs and dynasties is a common one. It was Joseph Schumpeter who suggested that part of the motivation for an entrepreneur was 'the dream and the will to found a private kingdom, usually, though not necessarily, also a dynasty' (1934/1911: 93). The message that a trans-generational trans-feral of money and status – a dynasty – was an entrepreneurial objective shows how the family can act as a resource.

When thinking about how families use business as a vehicle for trans-generational social mobility, particularly those with 'no other chance of achieving social distinction' (Schumpeter 1934/1911: 93), I always think of *The Godfather* films based on the books written by Mario Puzo about the rise and tribulations of a mafia family in the US. This epic saga shows how that family solved the problems of succession and business success, risking the security and harmony of family relations in exchange for social, economic and political upward mobility. For the Corleones as with many other family businesses normal living was often deferred and suspended. For some families starting at the bottom of the business ladder (perhaps with a corner shop or a takeaway restaurant), they will make many sacrifices to get on.

Home-based or class activity

Watch the trilogy of films, *The Godfather I, II, III* (1972, 1974, 1990), directed by Francis Ford Coppola (note that these contain strong violence). The films show the story of an Italian-American family and their gradual rise to prosperity, power and notoriety through their involvement in criminal enterprises. Think about the following questions whilst watching the film and discuss the film and the questions in class as the basis of a discussion.

How did the family's business activities change over the years? What opportunities did the business respond to?

In what ways did the family organisation help and hinder the business?

How would each of the different family business discourses – rationality, resource, critical – explain the role of the family in the business activities depicted in *The Godfather* films?

In what ways do the films help us understand family and immigrant enterprise?

The power of the family head can often override the desires and aspirations of others in the family. Michael Corleone initially wanted nothing to do with the family business. Indeed his father had also hoped that he would not have to be involved. But the needs of both family and the business (it is difficult to distinguish between home and work in a family enterprise – the business *is* the family) meant that he was drawn in with ultimately disastrous effects on his emotional and family relationships. This is fiction, but real family businesses will often exhibit these stresses and strains (Hamilton 2006; Holliday 1995). The *critical* discourse highlights these more negative aspects of family business, and new opportunities for understanding then emerge.

Succession from a critical discourse perspective becomes an intergenerational arena for potential exploitation and oppression. Sons and daughters can be emotionally blackmailed into carrying on the family firm. The contribution of non-managing spouses can go unrewarded in succession related changes. No doubt family firms can be dreadful places with over-controlling and bossy patriarchs, but it is easy to overdo the negative aspects of family firms. Recent research has shown that simplistic notions of male owner-managers and female 'support' on the one hand, or patriarchal exploitation on the other, belie complex and fluid social and interpersonal dynamics (Hamilton 2006: 263). This perspective has the power therefore to make apparent the emotional and relational subtleties of family business, as well as pointing out the more negative aspects.

In this section I have shown that once the enterprise stereotype is dispensed with, we can see a greater diversity and relevance for the term family. However, this ambiguity does not mean that the term is not valuable. The various academic discussions I have referred too have shown the relevance of family in discussions of small and entrepreneurial firms. Ultimately, it is perhaps more important to think about what a family dimension can add to non-family aspects of enterprise, than to think of it as a category in and of itself.

Immigrant/ethnic enterprise, religion, and Indigenous entrepreneurship

We know already from our earlier discussion in this chapter that enterprise at the margins of society has certain differences from normal entrepreneurship and it is the light that is thrown on the processes of enterprise more generally that is particularly important when studying these margins. In the next three sections we look at these aspects of enterprise and the role of religion.

Immigrant/ethnic enterprise

It has long been thought that cultural, racial or ethnic groupings have particular entrepreneurial attributes: some cultures or races of people are just better at enterprise than others. In this section we look at the development of research in this area, which on the whole shows that whilst the group people belong to has a bearing on their propensity to be successfully enterprising (research has shown that ethnic immigrant Chinese tend to demonstrate more of an enterprise orientation in most settings than Afro-Caribbean people, for instance), the main reasons for this have been shown to reside in complex and situated factors relating to particular historical, social, economic and cultural contexts, and *not* because of innate racial characteristics. This conclusion is not simply born of political correctness and a desire to be fair-minded, but of careful empirical research, some of which is discussed below. Whilst individuals may well be biologically predisposed to certain types of behaviour which might be more likely to lead to enterprising activity, the forms that enterprising behaviour can take in the real world are so diverse (from corporate entrepreneur to criminal mastermind to community activist), and the contexts in which the individual finds itself so powerful in shaping specific individual outcomes, that it is wrong to speak of racially-determined entrepreneurialism. There is no enterprise gene!

As with our understanding of family business, arguments about migrant enterprise reflect broader shifts in understanding. Initially immigrant enterprise was understood as a process of 'acculturation lag', whereby immigrant families will use family businesses to irrationally hold on to otherwise declining traditional aspects of society and a strong commitment to family **solidarity**. Latterly, this holding on to outmoded values and attributes has been interpreted as a strength rather than a weakness, because of the way in which strong traditional bonds of trust and social solidarity benefit the ethnic community in its business endeavours. These usually include an ethos of hard work and self-help, family solidarity and strong social networks. Traditional views of ethnic or migrant business 'tend to underplay socio-economic considerations, and concentrate on more "ethnic" resources of minority groups' (Ram et al. 2001: 355), with social relations such as class and gender being particularly ignored. More recent research has criticised this 'culturalist' view for over-particularising the ethnic minority business family (making it appear too positively distinct and special), as well as assuming an overly harmonious family-based environment, whereas the reality often shows conflict and exploitation within firms in ways that are similar or indeed worse to normal businesses (Ram and Jones 2002).

> **Solidarity** refers to the union of interests shared in order to achieve more than they would individually.

An example of how this approach reflects the complex reality of immigrant enterprise can be seen in a description of the differing impacts of solidaristic obligation – the bonds of obligation between members of specific cultural and ethnic groups – in two different ethnic groups in Indonesia in the 1960s. Both native Balinese and overseas Chinese businesses in Java were constrained by these obligations. However, the Chinese businesses generally performed better than native businesses because their position in society as an ethnic minority and the existence of clearer leadership structures meant that the social obligations did not lead to inefficiencies in the running of the business. For the Balinese businesses solidaristic obligation created social welfare: 'if you go into a Balinese business "there are a half-dozen directors, a book-keeper or two, several clerks, some truck drivers and a hoard (*sic*) of semi-idle workers; if you go into a Chinese concern of the same size there is just the proprietor, his wife, and his ten-year-old boy, but they are getting even more work done"' (Granovetter 1995: 144). For Granovetter, 'cultural understanding and practices do not emerge out of thin air; they are shaped by and in turn shape structures of social interaction' (1995: 143).

If one adds to this the dizzying diversity of contemporary immigrant minorities in most developed nations, simple arguments about inherent cultural superiority in enterprise become even less convincing. Take for instance the Chinese **diaspora** in Australia. This includes a vast range of people, from the 'undocumented Chinese dishwasher from the PRC to a millionaire ethnic Chinese businessman from Hong Kong, Malaysia or Indonesia' (Collins 2002: 118). In other words the contemporary immigrant is extremely diverse in their origin, class and ethnicity, means of immigration, religious background and so forth, and 'rates of entrepreneurship for ethnic Chinese immigrants vary considerably, casting doubt on culturalist explanations (the Chinese are good at business) of ethnic entrepreneurship' (Collins 2002: 120). Rath (2002) suggests that underlying much research into immigrant enterprise is a prior intellectual commitment to the hard work and enterprising spirit of immigrants which assumes that 'native' people lack those capabilities. The reality is that the establishment of immigrant niches needs to be seen in the context of the historical, social, economic and political contexts in which they emerge. The traditional values of immigrant communities are not in themselves going to make ethnic entrepreneurs successful. This depends on the specific settings in which the values and the way they are deployed as resources exist as well as the way they are received by others in the specific social context.

> **Diaspora** is similar to dispersal or dispersion but specific to particular groups of people who originate from a particular homeland and are often described as a community: thus, the Chinese diaspora.

Religion

Similarly, the religious affiliations of ethnic and immigrant communities are often said to be a positive social resource for enterprise. The connection between enterprise and religion has a long history. As the power and relevance of organised religion seem to be persistent features of human society, it is not surprising that enterprise scholars are finding religion increasingly interesting. This new interest also reflects broader currents of contemporary history, where despite an overall increase in **secularism** in the world, important pockets of fundamentalism (in the newer forms of Christianity and Islam) in particular nations are arguably having increasing influence on secular matters.

> **Secularism** refers to the belief that the organisation of modern life should be free of religion and a matter for the individual.

Indeed, many major economic and social theorists have argued that capitalism itself owes its dynamism to the Protestant Christian Reformation of the early-modern period. Max Weber (1995/1930) famously argued that in Protestantism the individual's duty to God subsumed everyday life; the individual accumulation of wealth, hard work, self-control, rationalism, and entrepreneurialism assured the individual's salvation. Getting into heaven became the individual's, not the church's, responsibility. As a means of explaining why capitalism emerged when and how it did, religion probably does have something to say, because Protestantism has had such a profound impact on history, but what of specific affiliations in contemporary contexts?

Just as Weber has been criticised for over-particularising the impact of Protestantism (in that Christianity more generally – including Catholicism – was also compatible and conducive to capitalist development) contemporary research is suggesting a mixed view of the impact of religion on entrepreneurship is appropriate. For instance, Ram and Jones (2002) are rather scathing in their description of the way in which particular religious affinities have been linked to success in family entrepreneurialism: if Christianity, Confucianism, Islam, Hinduism *and* Sikhism can all underpin entrepreneurial success, then how valuable are these as explanations? Other evidence (Drakopoulou Dodd and Seaman 1999), looking at a large sample of entrepreneurs in the UK, confirms that there is little evidence to suggest that being religious makes you more or less likely to be a successful entrepreneur. Others have argued that rather than religion or culture being the determining factors for the entrepreneurial success of particular groups, broader regional historical contexts need to be considered. The ethnic Chinese in Southeast Asia have, for hundreds of years, found themselves in favourable economic situations in comparison to native businesses (Jones and Wadhwani 2006a). There is no denying that a religious affinity *can* be a contributing factor to success, but it is doubtful that a general link can be sustained, or that one ethnically-linked religion is any more likely than another to produce successful entrepreneurial behaviour.

Yet this does not mean religion is not an important and interesting influence on entrepreneurship in specific environments. If we go back to Indonesia, ethnic-Chinese businesses are still being as successful as they were in the 1960s. Today, however, new religious movements are making an impact on the characteristics of ethnic enterprise. Koning (2009) has found that many Chinese businessmen have been turning towards charismatic or evangelical Christianity. She argues that for this ethnic minority it makes sense to adopt this Western-oriented and global religion because it provides solace in times of trouble. Specific religious networks and organisations can also provide practical social and business capital resources. Finally, their affinity with a global religion means that they identify their position in relation to the wider world, rather than the Indonesian national environment where they are a marginalised minority. We can see therefore that religion can be dynamically important to how entrepreneurs construct a sense of themselves, particularly when their religious affinity is strong.

Indigenous enterprise

In the context of understanding diversity Indigenous enterprise is of interest to us for two reasons. Firstly, many nations have substantial populations of Indigenous peoples and it is interesting to understand differences in enterprising behaviour, particularly in comparison to other minorities. Secondly, because of their often disadvantaged and minority status many governments are attempting to use enterprise support policy to help improve their situation. This is interesting because it is contentious, and illuminates many debates about the impact of enterprise in contemporary society. Government activity towards Indigenous people has historically been not much short of disastrous, even up to – and some would argue including – recent times. Who's to say that contemporary enterprise encouragement policies will, ultimately, not have similarly negative impacts?

Most Indigenous peoples round the world have been seriously disadvantaged by history. Their stories are invariably ones showing colonial subjugation, violent suppression and exploitation, death from diseases brought by conquerors, racial discrimination, stigmatisation and social marginalisation. It is not surprising that many colonial powers have felt the need to apologise for the behaviours of their forebears. This is not just a problem from the past. Many Indigenous populations still face staggering disadvantages and life expectancies for many are substantially lower than national averages. It is not surprising that Indigenous peoples are much less likely to be enterprising than the norm. Policies aimed at redressing their historical disadvantage, including those aimed at encouraging enterprise, are mostly quite new.

Australia is a good example of how enterprise is now seen as a way of improving the socio-economic standing of Indigenous peoples. Many academic, political and Aboriginal activist voices have called for policies to encourage more Aborigines and Torres Strait Islanders to set up their own businesses. The dominant view is that supporting Indigenous enterprise start-ups will help to alleviate socio-economic disadvantage, thereby improving their life-chances and decreasing their dependence on the state in terms of receiving passive welfare (Hindle and Rushworth 2002; Peredo et al. 2004). Others claim that in encouraging more engagement with Western capitalistic practices, which they perceive as being incompatible with Aboriginal and Torres Strait Islanders values (and indeed are also seen as the cause of their problems), their identity and socio-economic position will be further undermined. Both sides of the argument have valid points to make, particularly when you consider the poor track record of government management of Indigenous issues.

My own research in Australia has shown that an engagement with enterprise can be empowering for Indigenous people, in the sense of providing an identity (the community-orientated entrepreneur) which can override the damage caused by stigmatisation and racial discrimination (Reveley and Down 2009). Similarly Scott Simon discusses the empowering effects against the stigma of racism in Taiwan (2003: 174). His research describes the case of a female Aboriginal craft dealer, Yuma, who is a member of the Tayal tribe, an Austronesian Aboriginal minority which has acquired a stereotypical reputation for violence, crime, laziness and drunkenness from the dominant Chinese Han Taiwanese minority: Simon talks of Chinese 'mainlanders [who] now comprise approximately 13 percent of the country's population, but have long controlled the reins of power' (2003: 10). Enterprise 'has allowed [Yuma] to take control of her life, and affirm a positive Aboriginal identity in ways that would have been difficult in many workplaces' (2003: 187).

In response to those who would argue that such engagement with enterprise will further erode traditional culture, Simon argues that 'much of that has been lost through decades of [...] colonialism and industrial development' (2003: 187–188): the choice for Aboriginal people in Taiwan as it is in Australia is not tradition vs. enterprise, tradition has already been lost and cannot be retrieved. Both Simon's and my own research shows that Indigenous people are often motivated not just by profit and the good life, but also by bringing self-respect and material resources into their communities, as Indigenous entrepreneurs are often community activists too.

In comparison to other immigrant ethnic groups Indigenous peoples often face even more severe problems relating to racial discrimination and a lack of access and opportunities in the mainstream economic environment. Whereas immigrant groups often use their 'internal group resource endowments', including those value-based resources related to religion, to create enterprises in order to ameliorate their disadvantage in the 'opportunity structure' (Ram et al. 2001), Indigenous people have until recently not been able to call upon enough 'resource endowments' to follow this route. In other words, in order to be successful entrepreneurs there needs to be at least some resources – capital, experience, expertise, education, cheap labour, compatible religious-moral values, and so on – to draw upon. Indigenous people in the main have been so disadvantaged that this has not been possible.

Criminal entrepreneurship

Criminal enterprise is largely ignored by enterprise scholars. In being ignored the impression is given that there is a gaping chasm between normal enterprise and 'abnormal' – illegal, criminal or deviant – enterprise. The reality is that enterprising illegal behaviour is extremely common. Internationally, in addition to differences in laws between nations (which many exploit as entrepreneurial opportunities), different cultures also have different tolerances for 'gifts', bribery, corruption and so forth. What might be illegal in Britain might also be illegal in Greece, but in terms of actual custom and practice, this might be perceived as perfectly normal and morally neutral behaviour. Any discussion of criminal or illegal enterprise needs to recognise that the 'normal' is socially constructed and not necessarily confined within the boundaries of legal statute. Whilst laws governing behaviour are a reasonable guide to what is perceived as normal and morally good, they are certainly not one and the same thing.

The reason why criminal enterprise exists is because there are those who are able to access the opportunities to generate profit by supplying products and services that break laws. Criminal enterprise relies on those who demand products and services such as drugs and prostitution, and it is also characterised by a need to respond to the same environmental changes that face normal businesses. The normal business entrepreneur will also look to exploit opportunities in nominally legal but grey areas of the law: entrepreneurs are known for being creative, bending the rules, and pushing the boundaries of what is acceptable (Fadahunsi and Rosa 2002: 399). Even predatory criminality (such as sex trafficking, robbery, intellectual property crime, internet identity theft, money laundering, and so on) is based on the realisation of opportunities.

This is not a marginal matter: there are all manner of opportunities to make a profit by breaking laws. It is probably not putting it too forcibly to claim that corruption and illegality in business behaviour are common around the world. This is because for many people around the globe the rule of law is not as rooted in civil society as it is in Western societies. Even in the West crime and the formal economy are certainly no strangers to each other, even if behavioural expectations and norms in conducting business are predominantly based on trust, obligation and legal adherence.

Why is it ignored? The answer, one that is applicable across all business studies disciplines, is that by and large the study of small business and entrepreneurship has a prior ideological commitment to entrepreneurship as a positive moral good: an unambiguously Good Thing. Rehn and Taalas (2004b) suggest that if one looks at the enterprising criminal analytically they appear similar to normal entrepreneurs (ibid.): they look for opportunities, they take risks, they create organisations, they are profit seeking, they destroy, create and innovate. Enterprising behaviour is not inherently good or evil, rather the moral worth of the activity very much depends on the historical and situational context, how it is perceived, and by whom.

And just as normal business is not all entrepreneurial, illicit enterprise also varies a great deal. Before we even get to the properly criminal we can talk of the *grey* economy which describes those economically hidden activities associated with domestic and voluntary work, the *mauve* economy which describes micro-business activity at the margins of the *white* or formal economy, and the *black* economy which Goss has described as 'illicit or undeclared activities of individuals and small businesses' (1991: 92). Even much of the black economy is not especially or dramatically criminal and might be termed 'evasive' enterprise, in that it is illegal because of the avoidance of taxation and regulatory obligations rather than because of its predatory or organised criminal nature (Goss 1991: 95).

Law breaking and enterprise have had a long, intimate and colourful past (see Hobsbawm 1985). Clearly this is most obvious in organised criminal gangs such as the mafia and the triads. But there have always been legends such as Robin Hood (who stole from the rich to give to the poor), and those created around historical figures such as Jesse James, Ned Kelly, Al Capone (who saw himself as a modern Robin Hood), Song Jiang in China and the Kray Twins are widespread and pervasive features of most societies, reflecting deep social ambivalence in relation to the rule of law and criminality. Often, like famous entrepreneurs, those that engage in illicit enterprise have been depicted as lovable rogues and though the bandit cultural hero is perhaps becoming an historical figure (though piracy and banditry are still very prevalent in many parts of the world), contemporary cultural renditions of criminal enterprise are far from universally negative. In the stories our cultures construct about crime, both cops and robbers are often ambiguous in their moral attachments, and the tales often revolve around the resolution of this ambiguity, for good or bad depending on the type of film or book. In culture at least we can realise that criminal enterprise is a broad zone of social engagement, not two distinct activities separated by a gaping chasm, as is normally implied in the entrepreneurship literature.

> ## Home-based and in-class activity
>
> Watch the Martin Scorsese-directed film *GoodFellas* (1990), which is another gangster film (also very violent). The film depicts the organised nature of the criminal enterprise and the moral ambiguity inherent in building an enterprising and entrepreneurial criminal career. After watching both *GoodFellas* and *The Godfather* trilogy, answer the following questions and discuss the films and the questions in class.
>
> > In what ways, if at all, were the gangsters behaving entrepreneurially?
> >
> > What are the differences between legitimate and criminal enterprises? What differentiates criminal and non-criminal entrepreneurship?
> >
> > In what ways do the films help us understand criminal enterprise?
> >
> > Why can it be profitable for entrepreneurs to exploit 'grey' areas where there is confusion about the letter of the law and the ability of law enforcement agencies to enforce the law?

Perhaps the most interesting place in the world that shows the importance of illicit enterprise is in contemporary Russia. After a period of 'personalised political redistribution' – that is the expropriation of previously state-owned business into the hands of a small number of powerful oligarchs – following the collapse of Soviet Russia (Anderson 2007; Kuznetsov et al. 2000: 105), normal business has developed into a very strange beast indeed.

Volkov (1999) has written about the violence that has emerged in post-Soviet Russia to fill the gap made by a vacuum in the state's ability to exercise effective control over the commercial environment. Today the state is in a much stronger position but this does not necessarily mean that there is less illegality: the economy is still rife with violence and illegality in which many aspects of the state itself are heavily and directly involved (Anderson 2007). To run a business in Russia one often needs to employ protection agencies. These vary in nature from those run by state police and security forces acting as private entrepreneurs, legal private protection companies, to illegal private organised crime outfits. Many of today's Russian entrepreneurs are former state police and intelligence officials, and the 'large protection companies are in fact privatised segments of the state security and intelligence organs' (Volkov 1999: 750). What these enterprises do is act with force or its threat to enforce compliance to contractual and business obligations. The business climate is a generally uncertain one where trust is low and entrepreneurial risks are extremely high (in some cases ultimately high: assassination is an occasional solution to a business problem). It is not unknown for whole businesses simply to be stolen by force. The reason this system has developed is because:

> criminal groups were simply more efficient than the state organs in solving day-to-day problems of the new Russian entrepreneurs. Because of a predatory tax system and inefficient state protection and arbitrage, the transaction costs incurred by using private rule-enforcers were lower than the costs of legal economic activity. (Volkov 1999: 744)

To repeat (as it is an important point), what all of this tells us about crime and enterprise is that there is nothing inherently morally good about enterprising activity. Given different political, legal, social and economic contexts those individuals and organisations able and willing to exploit opportunities will do so in a variety of ways, some of which might not be legal. There are many parts – perhaps the majority in geographical terms – of the world where 'safe and righteous' (Rehn and Taalas 2004a: 246) Western notions of enterprise are extremely inappropriate, where, as in Nigeria, 'illegal practices are so widespread that they are a norm' and where 'traders do not view illegal trading as immoral' (Fadahunsi and Rosa 2002: 397). Criminal enterprise forces us to re-evaluate many of the ideological certainties of the moral worth of enterprise.

This section overall shows that our assumptions about what is normal enterprise are culturally specific. Each of the topics discussed in this section has shown that common Western 'safe and self-righteous' views and assumptions about enterprise are fairly tenuous. This is not only relevant for the consideration of the *social* contexts of enterprise, but also challenges some central theoretical and analytical notions of what enterprise and entrepreneurship are. Discussion of these marginal topics undermines economistic notions of the entrepreneur as an individual rational profit-maximiser, and forces us to re-evaluate this view of normal Western enterprise too.

The cultural place of enterprise: entre-tainment

This final short section of the chapter is about the broader cultural place of enterprise within society. The most obvious way in which to tackle this in a simple and direct manner, given the vagueness and ubiquity of the term enterprise, is to limit our investigation to the character or figure of the entrepreneur. We look at two short examples below of how the entrepreneur is depicted, one in a UK newspaper and the other in a reality TV show.

We already know that like enterprise the clarity of the term entrepreneur is not exactly robust. As a figure depicted in newspapers, books, films and the like, 'the entrepreneur' used to be a more marginal and nationally specific figure than he is today (using 'he' in this way is not meant to be sexist: culturally the characterisation of the entrepreneur in the media is predominantly male). In 1960s Britain for instance, to be called an entrepreneur was to infer that the individual was a maverick and potentially disreputable and untrustworthy: the sort of character who might sell you a dodgy second-hand car, or swindle the government. This notion of the entrepreneur is just about still with us – as the lovable rogue that keeps the stodgy-trapped-in-their-routines establishment figures on their toes and fights on behalf of the consumer against the faceless corporation. By and large though a more globalised, heroic and less morally ambiguous character is today culturally dominant. Instead of an untrustworthy chancer, he is invariably seen as a heroic, daring, innovative creator and risk-taker (Gates, Branson, and the like).

Home-based activity

Using Wikipedia (www.wikipedia.org/) **and Google** (www.google.com) **as a starting point find out how each of the businessmen and entrepreneurs shown in Figure 10.2 got into trouble with the law. Answer the following questions:**

What are the dominant discourses and narratives describing these entrepreneurs? Are they described as good, unlucky, or just bad men?

To what extent do you think that the behaviours of these entrepreneurs are typical? Were they simply unlucky in getting caught?

What is your dominant mental picture of 'the entrepreneur'? Try to describe how you feel about the entrepreneur as a cultural figure.

Sources:

http://en.wikipedia.org/wiki/Jeffrey_Skilling

http://en.wikipedia.org/wiki/John_DeLorean

http://en.wikipedia.org/wiki/Alan_Bond_(businessman)

http://en.wikipedia.org/wiki/Madoff_investment_scandal

So how is the entrepreneur depicted in cultural media? There has not been very much research done in this area but Nicholson and Anderson have shown how a UK newspaper changed its orientation to the entrepreneur from a 'reverence to ridicule' over time (2005: 168). Nicholson and Anderson speculated that the newspaper's earlier glorification of the entrepreneur was a social response to the optimism of the rise of entrepreneurialism in the 1980s as an economic ideology: 'Similarly, the recognition, by 2000, that entrepreneurs were not the panacea, created the backwash of disapproval' (2005: 168). This research helps us understand the importance of culture in creating shared meaning regarding the character of the entrepreneur. In one UK newspaper then, the entrepreneur is not lionised today as much as they were. The dominant cultural view is still emphatically positive, but one assumes that the more negative rendition will have an effect on the readers of this particular newspaper. Culture reflects not only what's actually going on in society, but through it being consumed and digested, it also helps reconstitute how being an entrepreneur is done in reality.

Another example of how an enterprise culture is produced, one that is perhaps more representative of the prevalence of the entrepreneur as contemporary folk hero, can be seen in the rise of the entrepreneurial reality show or *entre-tainment*. Such is the attractiveness and popularity of the idea of becoming an entrepreneur it has become part of our entertainment culture. Reality shows such as *Dragons' Den* – which asks aspiring entrepreneurs to pitch their ideas to a panel of successful millionaire business people, who will then decide which idea to invest in – are essentially etiquette guides, about how to be and how to behave in particular social

Figure 10.2   A rogues' gallery: left to right, Alan Bond (Rod Tyler/AFP/Getty Images); Enron's Jeffrey Skilling (Dave Einsel/Getty Images News/Getty Images); Bernard Madoff (Courtesy US Dept of Justice); John DeLorean (© Roger Ressmeyer/CORBIS)

contexts. *Dragons' Den* shows people – both participants and viewers – what, and what not, to do in order to be a successful entrepreneur. The point of *entretainment* is to show us what the character of the entrepreneur is all about: it helps creates a cultural stereotype. It is entertaining because we see people succeeding and failing to meet the grade; to fit the stock character of the entrepreneur. In the process we also see and enjoy people being humiliated and rejected or validated and accepted. The participants undergo a systematic and ritualised examination, not simply of the business idea, but ultimately also of who they are as a person. Being enterprising equates to an aspect of our identity: 'are we fit to be an entrepreneur?' becomes as important a question as 'is our idea any good?' TV shows such as these certainly reflect the practice of entrepreneurship, but they also influence, however superficially, how that social practice is done: it will certainly influence how the participants develop their businesses. How many nascent entrepreneurs have been inspired to act or are maybe scared witless because of *Dragons' Den*?

Our cultural stereotype of the entrepreneur is not the reality, which we have seen in this chapter overall is extremely diverse and complex. What we see in our newspapers and particularly on television is a stripped-down, simplified version that promotes the positive social, moral and economic virtues of that behaviour, and in part encourages people to engage with enterprise. But why has the boring world of business plans, revenue forecasts and running a business become so culturally popular? Maybe it is because it reflects a social need in an era of increasing divisions of wealth to feel that material success, self-fulfilment and social mobility are possible through starting a business. Like becoming a soccer or baseball star, the rags-to-riches syrupy story of becoming an entrepreneur has emerged in recent decades as a strong cultural narrative.

Research into the intersection of enterprise and culture is not well developed, and is perhaps ignored by the mainstream enterprise scholars because of the critique of the exclusively positive rendition of entrepreneurialism that it implies. But asking questions of the social and cultural significance of enterprise is not a criticism of enterprise as such. Rather it forces us to consider carefully why our societies currently lionise the character of the entrepreneur, despite the seemingly myriad variety of what counts as entrepreneurial activity we have seen described in this chapter.

Summary

The chapter has shown that enterprise is extremely diverse, and likely to be found in all societies and cultures. Social and cultural influences on enterprising behaviour are fundamental and not marginal. Family, immigrant/ethnic and criminal enterprise were discussed as examples of the often ignored diversity of entrepreneurship behaviour, and the implications for thinking about enterprise more generally were highlighted. The cultural place of enterprise and the character of the entrepreneur in particular were discussed, specifically focusing on the depiction of entrepreneurship in newspapers and *entre-tainment*.

▣ ▣ Further reading ▣

Fadahunsi, A. and Rosa, P. (2002) 'Entrepreneurship and illegality: Insights from the Nigerian cross-border trade', *Journal of Business Venturing* 17(5): 397–429.

Fletcher, D.E. (ed.) (2002) *Understanding the Small Family Business*, London: Routledge.

Ram, M. and Jones, T. (2002) 'Exploring the connection: Ethnic minority businesses and family enterprise', in D.E. Fletcher (ed.), *Understanding the Small Family Business*, London: Routledge.

Rehn, A. and Taalas, S. (2004a) '"Znakomstva I Svyazi" (Acquaintances and connections) – *Blat*, the Soviet Union, and mundane entrepreneurship', *Entrepreneurship and Regional Development* 16(3): 235–250.

11

Political Contexts of Enterprise: Governments and Smaller Enterprise

Overview

This chapter has the following objectives:

- To explain the role of government in shaping the environment of small scale economic activity, in the sense of practical economic policy and more general ideological objectives.
- To examine different explanations of the purpose of government intervention in support of smaller firms and enterprise discourse, and the practical issues surrounding the evaluation of policy impact.
- To list and analyse different types of policy and policy instruments, including: financial and fiscal; information and counselling; administrative deregulation and simplification; education and training services; and sectoral and issue-specific policies.
- To examine specific UK and US national approaches.

Introduction

At various points in this book mention has been made of the role governments and other political actors have in shaping the environment for enterprising people and organisations. In this chapter we will look at how governments adopt a stance towards and use the idea of enterprise to achieve their aims.

The vast majority of governmental activity that affects small businesses, the self-employed and entrepreneurs is subsumed within broad economic and social activities: policies influencing taxation and interest rates that affect us all. Most people would agree that the state has a role to play in facilitating economic and social stability, and the laws and policies a government implements and maintains will normally reflect an aim to achieving this. Enterprising activity is just one aspect of a government's responsibility in managing a nation's affairs. The emphasis a government will give certain policies will change over time to reflect the importance of a particular problem or opportunity. When a government feels threatened by the aggressive actions of another country, they will respond with appropriate policies of a military or diplomatic nature. When the economy is seen to stagnate a government will attempt to introduce policies to encourage more – and more successful – economic activity. Attitudes toward the role of government in society differ, as does the extent to which the state pervades everyday life. Because there are legitimate differences in views about what causes problems, even about what problems exist and about how to best exploit opportunities, different policies are offered, discussed and implemented.

In recent decades in the developed economies, in the previously planned economies of Russia and China, and even in developing economies, governments have to varying degrees, and in different ways, supported policies targeted at enhancing enterprise. There have been three dimensions to this. Firstly, governments have aimed at enhancing and extending economic prosperity. Secondly, they have used self-employment and enterprise support policies as a form of social welfare: that is, encouraging the un- or under-employed to re-engage with economic activity. These aims are clearly interlinked and mutually reinforcing. There is also a third dimension which sees government actors mobilising the ideology of enterprise to attempt to change economic and social behaviour. An example of this can be seen in the UK in the way that current education policies are formulated with explicit enterprise objectives and agendas, and in the ways that government agencies themselves have been restructured to function more like private businesses.

In certain countries enterprise support 'industries' have emerged, variously addressing all three of the dimensions above. Enterprise policy provision can be described as an industry because in some countries it is populated by a complex array of organisations, some of which are run directly by government, and others that are contracted by government institutions to provide training, information and funding services to people and businesses. In short, government funding creates a market for stimulating enterprise.

As the enterprise industry has grown, so too have the academic disciplines researching enterprise. A good deal of the funded research into small business and entrepreneurship is undertaken at the behest of governments wishing to evaluate policies and understand the problems and opportunities surrounding policy initiatives. Even where the funding link is not direct, much research justifies its findings and research rationale by reference to its effect on policy debates. Academics are involved with and benefit from involvement with the enterprise industry (it is always worth bearing in mind the reasons why a piece of research was conducted, and who funded it, when you read research articles).

The idea of enterprise – as we have seen, some people call this the enterprise culture or discourse of enterprise – is now so ubiquitous and strong a feature of contemporary society that it has begun to inform and guide areas of government policy previously underpinned by different dominant ideas. Such is the transformation of both work and the structure of economic organisation, that an education policy in some nations is now explicitly recognised as needing to reflect the self-employed and enterprising realities of future work lives (Gavron et al. 1998).

Below we will look in more detail at how education policy has been changing, but it is important now to emphasise the emergence of enterprise as an underlying ideology which shapes government activity.

Ideas about the role of government in our lives change over time. Some have argued persuasively that the idea of enterprise and entrepreneurialism has been mobilised by governments as a response to a desire to open up public services to market pressures and customer choice. Yet as Steyaert and Katz (2004) point out the idea of entrepreneurship in this governmental setting loses some of what we would normally associate with it. The ideas of autonomy and self-employment get left out and instead enterprise becomes an idea which 'is used as a means of increasing control over the bureaucratic organization by coupling customer acceptance and performance outcomes to budgets' (2004: 187). The notion of enterprise in this context is not one of thrusting individualism and can do-ism but of using the enterprise ideologies of markets and customer sovereignty to justify and shape managerial control. State sponsorship of enterprise is not simply aimed at increasing economic prosperity or political stability and social cohesion (through the maintenance of adequate levels of employment). It is also used as an idea (or ideology) to achieve a range of political and managerial goals.

Historically support for small business has been aimed at protection from the monopolistic efficiencies of large corporations, which can push important economic and social activity (i.e. local shops) out of business. In post-Second World War America small business was supported for social and political reasons (Gilbert et al. 2004: 315): ensuring full employment via a central tenet of American life and the ability to start a business. Similar protectionist policies aimed at protecting farmers continue to this day on both sides of the Atlantic, despite the free market rhetoric. However, with the profound restructuring of the global economy, which has favoured a greater diversity of organisational forms, and in particular a growth of small scale economic activity, enterprise policy has become a keystone of economic management for growth and new employment.

Another aspect of the contemporary political context of enterprise is the extent to which the autonomy of nations to make decisions in the economic sphere is subject to supra-national governance, and internationalised market forces more generally. Governments are not all powerful; to a certain extent they have given up certain powers to corporations in order to promote deregulated, liberalised and harmonised free markets. However, in facilitating globalisation governments have also needed to ensure that their interests – and the interests of the people they represent – are protected. In place of particular and national regulations, increasingly governments are looking to adopt or indeed are effectively compelled to adopt supra-national and international forms of regulation and governance. Organisations and inter-governmental fora such as the *G20* (http://www.g20.org/), *International Monetary Fund* (http://www.imf.org/external/index.htm), *European Union* (http://europa.eu/index_en.htm), *World Trade Organization* (http://www.wto.org/), and important meetings such as the *World Economic Forum* at Davos in Switzerland (http://www.weforum.org/en/index.

htm), all have ideological and more substantive attachments to promoting enterprise, as well as other ideologies such as free trade and globalisation itself. National governmental policies also need to be seen in the light of these supra-national commitments and obligations.

This chapter is structured as follows. First, we delve deeper into what the economic and social purposes of enterprise policies might be, before looking at specific types of enterprise support policies and instruments. We look at financial and fiscal measures, information and counselling services, education and training initiatives, and the issues surrounding administrative deregulation and simplification. We then develop an understanding of the complexity of the different stakeholders involved in the enterprise industry. Though keen to avoid too much parochial detail, in a later section I present a short case study on how different national governments have addressed a growing interest in 'grey' or mature-aged entrepreneurship. The conclusion reflects more broadly on the role of government and enterprise, looking again at the third ideological dimension.

What are the purposes of policy?

Historically government enterprise policies have rested on certain assumptions. The first of these is that it is small firms and entrepreneurial growth that can create more employment. The second is that increasing the numbers and growth potential of small firms and entrepreneurs will lead to increased economic prosperity. The difficulty however is in understanding how greater employment and economic prosperity might be achieved. Unsurprisingly there is a large literature which has sought to prove one way or another how best to do this, and rather than presenting all the arguments and empirical data, this section opts instead to discuss the underlying factors which constrain government activity in achieving these purposes.

In a market economy free market economists will usually argue that governments can justifiably intervene when there is a market failure and it can be shown that there will be 'post-intervention welfare improvements' more generally which will outweigh the cost of implementing and administrating the policy intervention (Storey 1994). The problem is that it is difficult to know for sure whether subsidising the formation and support of small firms or the self-employed is actually necessary and beneficial. Storey has argued that 'subsidies to one group have to be raised by increased taxes or reduced relief to other groups, and it has never been shown that the *net* effect of subsidising small firms is to create more wealth in the community' (1994: 255). Academic debate on this point continues and it seems unlikely to be unequivocally resolved.

Even the link between entrepreneurial activity and economic growth is in doubt. Harding, in the UK **Global Entrepreneurship Monitor** (GEM) 2003 report, stated that 'policies toward entrepreneurship often take as their base an

Global Entrepreneurship Monitor (GEM) 'is a not-for-profit academic research consortium that has as its goal making high quality international research data on entrepreneurial activity readily available to as wide an audience as possible. GEM is the largest single study of entrepreneurial activity in the world' (http://www.gemconsortium.org/).

assumption that there is a causal link between entrepreneurship and economic growth and productivity. [...] GEM global [...] over the last five years has found little or no correlation between opportunity entrepreneurship and GDP growth'. Harding concluded that the real contribution of policies to encourage entrepreneurship (at least at the individual and direct support level) may be the jobs created and the 'greater well-being at a community level and the consequences for social cohesion and inclusion' (Harding 2003: 23). In simple terms this means that in helping people to become self-employed when jobs might be thin on the ground can help people feel like they are part of society, not outside it.

In practice, despite the difficulties of finding proof of a positive correlation between entrepreneurship and growth, organisations such as GEM and government actors operate on the assumption that there is. Even if empirical analyses of specific policies are often inconclusive, some historical interpretations (Landes 1998) suggest that a positive relationship exists, at least in terms of economic growth. The problem that remains is attributing causation to government promotion of enterprise in particular contexts.

Resolving diverging views and understandings of the underlying economic philosophy of supporting enterprise is not easy. As we discovered in Chapters 2 and 3 the basis on which knowledge claims are made is not definitive and absolute. Findings can always be criticised. Facts cannot speak for themselves. Making political and social decisions are therefore inherently difficult. Allied to this is the enormous complexity of government activity which means that issues of working out cause and effect and the balancing of conflicting policy objectives are not always easy to resolve: money spent on encouraging and educating people to become more enterprising might be better spent on making people healthier, or the environment less polluted. 'Better' is something that people have to agree on, it depends on who and what your interests with.

Then there are unintended consequences to consider. For example, teaching and encouraging people to be more enterprising may create more and better businesses. But it might feasibly also exacerbate a future superannuation/pensions crisis. How? As a result of success in such a policy there will likely be less people paying automatic direct employee contributions. This is because the self-employed generally will have more choice about whether to save for the future than employees. Success in one policy area might have profoundly unexpected negative implications in another.

Complicating the picture even further, are the number and diversity of different constituents or stakeholders that policy can be directed at. Enterprise policy-makers need to decide whom they wish to benefit: entrepreneurs, small business owners, the self-employed, social entrepreneurs, female entrepreneurs and so on. Once decided, governmental institutions need to decide the criteria by which people will fit the classification. Clearly individuals will attempt to maximise benefits by attempting to fit the criteria and reap the benefits. If the criteria are too loose and easily met, policy benefits (resources, grants, information, tax relief and so on) may help the wrong people. Too hard, and the right people may miss out. So having a policy to help, say high-tech entrepreneurs, might entail a complex and costly administrative infrastructure, all of which adds to the cost–benefit equation.

It should be repeated however that even for the most enterprise enthusiastic government, enterprise specific policies always constitute a relatively small aspect of total activity. The setting of taxes, interest rates, the general impact of public spending (defence, health, education, and so on), and the management of inflation are by far the most important issues connecting government to real people running real businesses. The ebbs and flows of economic performance affect entrepreneurs, just like the rest of us.

To show the inherent difficulties in setting policy the example of taxation and small businesses is instructive. Taxation on small firms generally falls proportionally heavier than it does on large firms, who can invest resources to maximise tax efficiency (namely avoid paying them). Many governments have attempted to reduce taxes to level the field in favour of small firms. Where such initiatives have occurred, policy-makers have also argued that this would act as an incentive for more small businesses to expand, reinvest and become more entrepreneurially growth-oriented. The reality is, as usual, more complex. Whilst some owner-managers certainly take the initiative, the majority of small business owners are only interested in achieving a certain level of income and will either take more money as income, or take more leisure as a result of a liberalised tax regime. However, all is not doom and gloom. The picture grows ever more complex if we consider the effects of this increased income or leisure. Whilst the original economic policy intentions of growth encouragement may not be met directly, in taking more income or leisure the small business owner might nevertheless benefit the economy overall by consuming more and benefiting other businesses. Setting policy is a tricky business. Unintended consequences abound.

Once enterprise policies have been set, complex administrative infrastructures tend to emerge to manage and guide the implementation process: the aforementioned 'enterprise industry' comes into being. As with all organisational activity, the competencies, capacities and structures of the industry will have an influence on the quality of the outcomes. In the UK context there has been sustained criticism of the fragmented and messy nature of enterprise support provision. Historically, government bodies engaged in enterprise support have been short-lived and geographically inconsistent. Problems relating to duplication of provision from different government or non-government agents, and the lack of uptake of the services provided because they are deemed irrelevant to the needs of real small businesses, are but a few of the problems that can beset the provision of effective enterprise support policies.

Further generic problems remain. First is the problem known as *displacement*: how can we be sure that if we subsidise one small business, that we are not forcing the exit or displacement of another unsubsidised one? Second, we have the problem of *deadweight*. This refers to the problem of being unable to know what would have happened if we had not have made a decision and implemented a given policy. How are we to know this? Third, there is the issue of *additionality*:

what exactly are the net positive outcomes that can be attributed to the policy initiative (Curran and Storey 2002: 169)?

Finding answers to these problems would (and does) cost a great deal of money in conducting careful evaluation research, which in itself adds to the overall costs of introducing and implementing the policy. The difficulties of proper evaluation are so great that actual evaluations are often criticised for being superficial and illustrative. Part of the problem of effective evaluation is the nature of the vested interests of those who conduct or commission the research. Policy-makers will tend to favour commercially-oriented evaluation researchers – and types of research methods (normally with a strong emphasis on quantitative methodologies) – who depend on future contracts, rather than independent academics (Curran and Storey 2002: 169). Indeed Curran and Storey have anyway suggested that 'the sheer **hegemonic power** of notions such as "the entrepreneur", "entrepreneur", and the "entrepreneurial society" since the late 1970s has discouraged serious assessment of policies promoting the small enterprise' (2002: 164). The effects of displacement, deadweight and additionality are still largely unknown.

It seems that there are a lot of reasons not to be cheerful about the formulation and provision of enterprise policies. There are nevertheless good reasons why governments will continue to pursue them. So while Curran and Storey may well be correct in their conclusion that in the UK the health of small enterprises is such that support is no longer required (2002: 175), the real reasons for continuing enterprise policies are perhaps more ideological and political than economic. The economic rationalism of government rhetoric – we will all be better off if we do these things – is less important than the way in which a certain way of life – individualism, opportunity, autonomy, self-reliance and so on – is promoted and deepened. Winning hearts and minds is the real issue, not boosting our wallets. This is not so strange when we look at the US, where as we saw above, small business support policy historically has been often explicitly justified in terms of supporting the American way of life (Gilbert et al. 2004) rather than promoting economic growth.

Hegemonic power refers to the predominant influence or power of a particular group over others.

Types of policy and policy instruments

This section describes the different types of policy instruments (specific support measures). Policy specifics will vary greatly from country to country, but generally they fall into two inter-related target categories: at the level of the enterprise or individual and at the level of infrastructures, creating a good environment for enterprising activity.

Financial and fiscal

An example of the latter can be seen in how governments encourage the birth of new enterprises and existing enterprises to grow via a manipulation of the financial and fiscal environment. Firstly, there are changes in fiscal measures. The taxes businesses pay can be reduced, expenditure or consumption tax exemption thresholds can be raised, and other taxation incentives to stimulate investment can be introduced. But as we have seen, some business owners will take more income and leisure rather than working harder or investing more, if taxation is relaxed. Secondly, governments and their agencies can offer direct and indirect financial incentives in the form of competitive awards for the development of innovative products; subsidies on costs, including business premises, often aimed at creating clusters of related high-tech firms; loan guarantee schemes, where the government agrees to pay or guarantee a certain percentage of the loan from a bank should the business fail; providing gap venture capital and other funding, reducing the risks to direct private investment; measures to ensure the prompt payment of debts, a problem which tends to hit smaller firms hard; and direct grants and low interest loans, particularly to encourage certain business behaviours such as developing quality systems or stimulating more training.

Information and counselling

A major motivation behind many policy instruments is the perceived difficulty that many small firms have in getting information to help achieve a given business goal. Business knowledge about accounts, financing (where to get it, how to manage it, and so on) and how to market effectively are all areas where governments have sought to extend a helping hand through advice agencies. Much of my own time in the first year of running my record label was spent learning about all sorts of things which I had no idea were so important, and which had very little to do with making music. Many of the most important I chose to ignore or didn't realise I needed to know. Today in the UK there is no shortage of people prepared to help businesses, most of them funded through government agencies. Some of the available help exists at the end of a phone or at the click of a mouse, but more intensive and specific advice and counselling is also often provided, to help new firms improve their operations or overcome crises. Similarly, government funded agencies will often facilitate the sharing of information via networking initiatives. This might be to encourage the sharing of technical information or international export experiences, or simply to provide a context where businesses can meet each other. The overall purpose of all of this activity is to improve the internal efficiency of the enterprise.

Administrative deregulation and simplification

We have already seen that small firms lack economies of scale. This also applies to the taxation regime, in that they often don't have the resources to find ways of minimising their obligations, which include the administrative costs of taxation and other legal obligations such as health and safety, environment and discrimination legislation. In recent years many nations have sought to liberalise some of the 'burdens' on smaller firms. The impact of administrative liberalisation may have a positive effect on the health of a small business, but as Storey has suggested, the *net* effect of such policies may not necessarily be beneficial to society more broadly (1994: 256). Tiresome and expensive red tape for the small business owner is an important guarantee of a safe workplace for their employees, a guarantee of safe, quality products for consumers, and an insurance against environmental abuse. Whilst there has been little objection to measures streamlining administrative processes originally designed for large organisations, the liberalisation of labour and other standards has met with opposition. In the context of a restructured economy where fewer people are working for large organisations in permanent full-time jobs, there is a danger that administrative liberalisation might simply be a euphemism for the erosion of labour standards. The reality for most small firms is likely to be less sinister. Despite the rhetoric of being the small business's friend, governments often struggle to actually reduce the administrative burden. Visions of small firms behaving like Victorian sweatshops as a result of removing administrative requirements are often hyperbole. Changes are often innocuous, and overall compliance burdens fluctuate as they do in many spheres of life.

Education and training services

Governments, though powerful, are relatively constrained when it comes to shaping the economy. Good fiscal management, sensible spending and careful investment in the infrastructure will not necessarily insulate the economy from a world economic recession or increases in the price of energy. Though its implications are often overblown, we live in a global environment, where nations benefit and suffer together from the results of economic change. Where government might be expected to have a more profound effect on the nature and health of the economy is in shaping and transforming people's attitudes, expectations and likely behaviour in relation to work. In other words, in shaping how they learn about the world: education.

Both in the EU and the US there have been significant voices, amongst the general chorus of praise, doubting the overall economic effect of the enterprise policies in the last few decades (Holtz-Eakin 2000), particularly in relation to arguably unrealistic hopes in the form of job creation and the generation of legions of high-growth businesses. As we have discussed above, it is difficult to know if and how much all the activity has helped. Maybe partly as a result of these reservations, increasingly policy has been turning toward changing people's attitudes to enterprise via a variety of educational measures. The US is invariably used as a measure of entrepreneurial success, it being the place where the extent and depth of the entrepreneurial spirit is seen as strongest. Countries which perceive themselves as lacking or under-developed entrepreneurially, often seek to create an enterprise culture and often attempt to emulate US cultural attitudes to enterprise.

The UK in particular has over many years, and via a variety of shifting policy emphases, attempted to create such a culture. In particular government efforts have been directed at enterprise education. In addition to the broader cultural aims, specific and pressing labour demographic issues are also pushing government to incorporate more enterprise education. Gavron et al. (1998: 43) have argued that 'The rapid growth of the graduate population and the concurrent decrease of job opportunities in large firms point to the need for graduates to see SMEs as a positive alternative and to gain appropriate skills'.

There are many specific measures that the state uses to create these types of attitudinal and educational changes. At the simplest level government departments will campaign and engage in outreach activity. These are often instigated in conjunction with specific substantive programmes, and will involve the mobilisation of media resources channelling the particular governmental agency's message. Because government often funds schools and universities they can also direct or attach incentives for these institutions to introduce changes to the curriculum. All education is governed by certain rules and standards.

Subjects such as business studies with explicit enterprise components are becoming increasingly common. In the UK both school and university students will often have an opportunity to run their own business as part of their studies, and the momentum more generally in the EU is gathering to increase the extent to which business, entrepreneurship and enterprise skills are taught throughout the education system.

There is some debate however, about whether more entrepreneurs will be created as a result, or, simply people with better business skills. Deciding how to educate people to become more enterprising is inherently difficult. UK based critics such as Allan Gibb (2002) doubt very much that the current learning philosophies in most schools and universities are capable of generating more and more successful entrepreneurs. However it is taught, enterprise education as a whole is certainly not a bad thing. The knowledge and self-confidence that people gain can lead to the identification of new opportunities; for business and in life. Against this, some have argued that education might act as a socialising and controlling influence undermining creative energies. How many hero entrepreneur stories start with dropping out of university? Does the business plan constrain entrepreneurial energy and imagination? Political initiatives in this area, as with any other 'social engineering' aims, would seem to be a long-term and tenuous process. However, as I have argued throughout the book there have definitely been profound shifts towards the creation of entrepreneurial societies in many Western nations, partly no doubt as a result of shifts in education.

Sectoral and issue-specific policies

Most governments will also have explicit social objectives in mind when formulating enterprise policy. There is of course a fundamental link between the aim of

Figure 11.1   The Enterprise Education Trust helps people to realise their potential through business and enterprise

Courtesy Enterprise Education Trust

economic prosperity and the amelioration of social deprivation and disadvantage. In a direct sense however, social policies can often have little connection to explicit economic ends. Economic development will often be used rhetorically to justify specific initiatives. The reasons given for the policy might emphasise the economic benefits of reducing tax-payers' burden, and getting people working and supporting themselves. However, the direct and immediate reasons for encouraging entrepreneurship in, for instance, deprived ethnic communities will more than likely be cultural and social (for instance, aimed at encouraging greater integration and social inclusion).

Socially directed enterprise policies are targeted in many directions and sectors, mostly aiming to redress forms of disadvantage and discrimination. These might include the encouragement of older entrepreneurship; help towards immigrant populations and ethnic minorities; the encouragement of female entrepreneurship; the protection and development of rural businesses; the protection of community services (local shops and the like); and the development of social enterprises.

The most important social measures are those directed at long-term unemployment. Economic restructuring in the West and the withdrawal of traditional manual and factory employment have had disproportionate regional effects in most countries. Formally prosperous regions of heavy primary and secondary industry are now often sites of extreme deprivation and long-term unemployment.

Enterprise policies aimed at ameliorating long-term unemployment are often viewed with suspicion by recipients (and by academic critics) who perhaps rightly feel that their plight is the result of government supported structural changes in the economy and that attempts to help the problem by creating an army of self-employed plumbers and aromatherapists are simply 'band-aid' policy. Enterprise policy directed at social ends operates within broader more profound contexts of the state pursuing measures aimed at improving competitiveness, free trade and other structural features of the international economy. These are the tensions and contradictions in government behaviour, where the need to deal with the outfall of systemic change is accepted and regional adjustments (high unemployment) are managed, without necessarily trying to address the underlying structural problems.

An example of the complexities of enterprise policy directed at the second social dimension can be seen in an interview I conducted with a former enterprise agency manager. He was recalling a story told to him by a recently graduated local government agency officer. The officer was conducting research into young people's attitudes to enterprise and entrepreneurialism in a deprived area of the North East of England. One particular youth responded that 'enterprise was for losers'. The young researcher was shocked and uncomprehending at this. In the context of that youth's life, where the majority of his community had only distantly been the holders of real jobs, enterprise meant state-led unemployment measures. He did not aspire to enterprise. What he wanted was mainstream success: a BMW company car and a secure corporate job. Enterprise, by becoming an instrument of social welfare policy for the unemployed, becomes something for 'losers'. Though seemingly perverse, the young man's response was perfectly rational. He desired to become more than another government subsidised plumber or aromatherapist. Clearly, this was not what the government wanted.

Setting policy is a tricky business.

Fenderco case study

Paul's opinion on government support

We don't really go in for all this government support business. When we started up we looked at it and there wasn't much really available to us, you know. The time and effort involved in getting any of it wasn't really worth it and we looked at it for other things like technology and innovation development grants and so on. It was so complicated. We didn't have the resources to get it in the first place and we would have had to apply for another grant to get the resources to make a grant to apply to! You end up having to be professional grant appliers, if you get my drift.

There seems to be a certain type of company that the government agencies go for. It's difficult to put your finger on it, but somehow, the companies that win the awards and get the grants all seem to spend all their time doing that. Some of them are really quite large companies that don't really need the money. I mean their technologies or innovations have all been sorted out already. They have departments set up to bring this sort of cash in. Then there are smaller companies where it seems that's all they do. They never seem to go anywhere: they are all 'executive director' of this and 'chairman' of that, when it's just one man and his dog. It makes me laugh. Here we are employing people, growing, and producing innovative stuff. We haven't got the time to get into that game. It's a lot of bullshit really. Looks like the government is helping the small firm, you know. We just keep our heads down and get on with it.

Businesses we work with who get this sort of stuff tell us that it can be a nightmare. The money always comes with strings attached and there are lots of people poking around your business, audits and all that, making sure you have spent the money in the way you said you would. It's all too much hassle.

Activity

Why might Paul be wrong to expect that government support should come without 'strings attached'?

Should government agencies give more support to succeeding or struggling businesses? List the reasons for each scenario.

What should the average citizen expect from government business support policies?

National approaches: a case study of US and UK approaches to encouraging mature-aged entrepreneurship

The extent of enterprise policies in most developed nations is such that a detailed examination of national programmes would be confusing, especially in a textbook such as ours, where we are trying to gain a generic understanding. This doesn't mean that we should avoid detail altogether. In this section we are going to briefly compare the United Kingdom and the United States, focusing on enterprise policies aimed at encouraging and supporting older entrepreneurship.

Changing population demographics are currently exercising the minds of most governments in the Western world. The UK and the US are getting older. There are less people being born, they are living longer, but not working longer (at least not yet). The problem therefore is that there may not be enough economically active taxpayers to support the older economically inactive population in providing their everyday welfare needs and health care. There are many other aspects to the problem, such as recent cultural changes to the saving and spending patterns of older people, who by and large don't feel as inclined to pass their money on to their children, and as a whole tend to underestimate the amount of money they will need to support themselves in old age. Added to this, employers have also been scaling down their retirement commitments claiming that they cannot afford such generous pensions and maintain profits, especially in labour markets which are increasingly flexible and transitory. They are also less likely to be employing people until retirement age, with redundancy for the over-50s a common occurrence, and re-employment sadly not as common. It isn't difficult to see why this problem gets politicians scratching their heads.

Governments are trying to address the general problem – which has been called the 'demographic time bomb' – via a variety of measures, particularly changes to the provision of retirement pensions. But governments have responded to these challenges in different ways, depending on the extent of the problem and the relevant behaviours of the population as regards saving, work and the like. In the US the problem of an ageing population is perceived as less acute than it is in Europe. It is nevertheless exacting the minds of policy-makers and Alan Greenspan (former Chairman of the US Federal Reserve Board) has spoken of the pressure that the ageing population will put upon tax receipts if the current levels of social welfare and medical taxation are maintained (Greenspan 2004). In the UK the government has been encouraging people to save more for the future, explaining that the state pension will be insufficient to meet most people's needs in the future. Prolonging the working life of the ageing population has been discussed as a possible solution and the retirement age for women has been changed from 60 to 65. The availability of 'real' work is however, often limited for older people, not least because employers perceive a lack of relevant skills in this section of the labour market. Ageism legislation in the UK has been introduced to counter prejudice, where a lack of relevant skills is not the case. The UK government has also been exploring the use of self-employment and business start-up as a potential solution to this problem (Curran and Blackburn 2001). The argument being that self-employment is a viable option to prolong the working life of an older person in a climate where ageism constrains opportunities in the labour market.

Differences between national approaches are instructive, so we now look at how the UK and the US are responding with particular references to their enterprise policies to older people.

UK enterprise policy

Government policy, currently implemented by the Department for Business Innovation and Skills (BIS) and its Enterprise Directorate (http://www.berr. gov.uk/whatwedo/enterprise/index.html), has long been criticised for failing to improve the quality and coherence of government support for small business (Curran and Storey 2002). Government agencies and a plethora of other state sponsored and private sector business support agencies have been tasked with enhancing the environment for entrepreneurship and small business and to build an enterprise culture. This has involved: encouraging a more dynamic start-up market; building small business growth capability and access to finance; encouraging enterprise in disadvantaged communities and under-represented groups; improving recipient experience of government services; and developing better regulation and policy (Harding 2003). Regionally enterprise support is currently coordinated through a net of Regional Development Agencies (RDAs) and more local Business Links (BL); one-stop-shops providing help to people interested in enterprise. Provision of central government and EU funding for initiatives generally flows through these institutions (RDAs and BL), however private and not-for-profit enterprise support and training companies on a competitive tendering basis deliver most of the actual initiatives. There has been much criticism of these public/private interfaces, and the general 'piecemeal and poorly specified' nature of the policies introduced and implemented (Curran 2000a). Furthermore these institutional arrangements and the competitive tendering for delivering contracts have been criticised for encouraging the proliferation of support organisations and initiatives and a consequent dilution of available funds to too many providers (Curran and Storey 2002).

Government initiatives directly relating to older people are currently focused at enhancing employability and reducing unemployment, often through differential welfare benefit incentives (people get more benefit money if they decide to try self-employment). Policy initiatives are not explicitly aimed at enhancing the enterprise potential for economic growth and development. This is not to say however that initiatives do not aim to promote self-employment and business ownership, and one initiative in particular – PRIME – has an explicit enterprise focus.

PRIME (the Prince's Initiative for Mature Enterprise; http://www.prime initiative.org.uk) is a wholly owned subsidiary of the charity Age Concern and is a not-for-profit company whose aim is to release the untapped potential of people in their 50s, 60s and 70s. PRIME is not a large organisation and like many in the 'enterprise industry' survives on a mix of short-term competitive funding, charitable funds and direct grants from central and regional partners. These partners include Help the Aged, RDAs, the EU and government departments. PRIME does not provide a consistent national coverage and the exact nature of its activities varies from region to region, depending on the nature of the funding available. In addition to providing loans for enterprise training, PRIME campaigns and encourages the over-50s to look into considering self-employment and business start-up. PRIME also acts as a focus for research into and knowledge about older people and enterprise.

PRIME engages in a number of activities, which include publicising the benefits of self-employment at events and exhibitions, workshops and outreach events; working in conjunction with unemployment agencies; and working together with organisations linked to the interests of the over-50s. Their approach might be described as a holistic one that seeks to develop and mentor the person interested in self-employment towards 'enterprise readiness'. Overall PRIME is a typical component of the UK 'enterprise industry', providing a privately run niche service at the behest of central or regional state agencies. PRIME's activities do not amount to a concerted and specific centrally driven policy aimed at encouraging enterprise in older people (Figure 11.2).

Taken as a whole, the UK government activity in this area is focused at getting older unemployed people back to work. Even where the focus is more enterprise explicit – as in its aspects of the PRIME initiative – it is nevertheless piecemeal and fragmented in its approach. Too critical an assessment is probably not appropriate. Policy in this area need not be an issue of entrepreneurial dynamism and job creation. Broader issues regarding older people, work and society need also to be taken into consideration when making assessments. The benefits of PRIME need not be measured solely by the numbers of new start-ups, but by regarding the problem of older un- and under-employment as a broader social and education issue. Viewed this way, relatively inexpensive inputs from organisations such as PRIME might be seen as providing intangible life skills benefits leading to lower levels of inactivity.

US enterprise policy

The Small Business Administration (SBA) dominates enterprise policy in the US. It is a federally organised government agency with regional and more local district offices across the country. The SBA's mission statement is to 'maintain and strengthen the nation's economy by aiding, counselling, assisting and protecting the interests of small businesses and by helping families and businesses recover from national disasters' (http://www.sba.gov). The SBA and its various resource partners (who implement the SBA's policies) provide a range of services to small business. These include: technical assistance (training and counselling); financial assistance in the form of a range of loan options, but primarily acting as a guarantor of loans made by private and other institutions; contracting assistance; and helping small business interests via advocacy, and the formulation of laws and regulations. In recent years the SBA has been centrally involved in disaster assistance recovery.

In terms of the intersection of enterprise policy and the ageing population, there are no explicit measures encouraging older entrepreneurship. This perhaps reflects aspects of the US enterprise environment which are instructive in understanding the embedded context of policy support for enterprise. Firstly, the infrastructure of enterprise support is generally less geared towards alleviating unemployment. Though the SBA implements socially-oriented policy in the form of assistance to minority businesses, historically its main objective has been to protect the interests of small business (Anglund 2000) and to foster and support small business and enterprise skills. More recently small business policies have taken on a more social and redistributive quality, ensuring that all sections of the population, particularly the economically disadvantaged, have 'equal access to capital'. Aoyama states that '[s]mall business policy in the US is primarily a corrective measure to sustain competitive markets and offset discriminatory behaviour', though the US now has policies to promote small firms in specific industrial sectors and by enhancing inter-firm networks (1999: 224). Assistance to older individuals is subsumed within general programmes (though there are specific programmes for ethnic minorities, women, veterans and young entrepreneurs).

However, and secondly, this may reflect the different cultural orientations to enterprise in the US. There is a far greater expectation of, and aspiration to, becoming self-employed or starting a business in the US. As in the UK, structural changes in the economy have meant that many older age people will retire or be made redundant

Figure 11.2 My Unique Gifts – a small business established with the help of PRIME workshops

Courtesy PRIME Initiative

earlier than the traditional 65, and often they will find 'bridge employment' in paid work or in self-employment (Singh and DeNoble 2003). The absence of specific programmes perhaps reflects the profound cultural embeddedness of enterprise throughout society and perhaps a more economically active older population. Though it might also be the case, as Singh and DeNoble imply (2003: 222), that the SBA and older age institutions (such as the National Council for Aging – http://www.ncoa.org/) need to do more to help and encourage older enterprise.

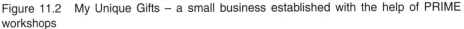

Home-based activity

Look at the various websites I have mentioned in this chapter or the website of the business, enterprise or innovation government agency, department or ministry in your country and find out what they say and do to support smaller and entrepreneurial business.

How do the different websites write about small and entrepreneurial firms and their role in society?

Broader considerations

We have looked at what the government *does* in relation to achieving economic and social aims; the first and second dimensions. In this final section we look in more depth at the third ideological dimension of politics and enterprise, and other broader aspects of the political context of enterprise.

Firstly, though this book often describes enterprise as if it were the same all over the world, we know that it isn't. Enterprise is culturally embedded: it means something specific to people depending on where they live. As we saw earlier the political underpinnings and functions of the US enterprise system are significantly different from the UK's. This suggests that national – even regional – policy shouldn't be divorced from the cultural context. According to some academics one of the underlying problems of applying enterprise policy is that it fails to accord enough attention to the embeddedness of enterprise in the 'wider cultural, social and political environment' (Curran 2000b: 212). Governments will often look to other countries to see what policies are being successful and will then attempt to replicate and apply a policy in their own country. For instance, the core values or cultural uniqueness underpinning US small business policy have been described as representing a 'guardian of free competition' approach. Japanese policy on the other hand reflects a more statist approach emphasising 'overall industrial development' (Aoyama 1999: 222). Just as each nation or region will stress different cultural and moral values more generally, the political structures and the policies they generate will tend to be related. This tendency for the international transference of policy ideas by governments without due regard for the cultural and historical uniqueness of national environments is a common criticism (Gibb 2000).

Nevertheless, whilst these culturally embedded relativities exist, deeper and more pervasive ideas such as economic rationalism tend to transcend these differences such that all governments will generally favour economistic methods of analysis and research in policy matters. Arguments about enterprise policy centre on and are often limited to the mobilisation of economic statistical evidence, and the quality of research designed to support a course of action is often determined by the rigour of the method employed and not necessarily on the quality of the insights generated. Researchers contracted by the government are not predisposed to present findings that don't fit with political objectives. Questions about the purpose of a given policy and whether it is the right course of action for the particular cultural milieu are not often asked. The result, as Storey has written, is that 'Too often there are "findings" from questionable research which have entered "received wisdom", and which are quoted by the "enterprise industry"' (1994: 294). In other words, the dominant ideology of economics and the prevailing political 'received wisdom' will tend to bracket out certain policy options, just as they will favour others.

A second broader consideration is the impact of the enterprise culture on government organisation and political activity itself. Such is the significance and power of the enterprise idea – or what some call the discourse of enterprise – that much of the machinery of government is being shaped by it. We saw earlier in this chapter how Steyaert and Katz (2004) suggested that the UK government is using certain aspects of the idea of enterprise to effect changes in the way government agencies operate: that they become more like businesses. Hendry makes a similar argument, and asks how appropriate it is to encourage government to organise itself around the entrepreneurial principles of self-interest and unaccountability. His answer is the same as that of Steyaert and Katz: whilst 'Government and the public sector [continue] to embrace the rhetoric of enterprise, [they] have resisted the reality' (2004: 56). In other words, governments talk about their activities as if businesses were being run, but are actually overly bureaucratic and hierarchical. Is this a good thing? Personally I would prefer that my public services are democratically accountable and run by people interested in the common interest and public service rather than themselves. As we saw in Chapter 7 too much entrepreneurship can be a bad thing.

A related consideration is the relationship between government and business. Undoubtedly it has changed. Some have taken a positive approach to the new enterprising role of government and have suggested that government has shifted from being an 'overseer' or supervisor of business, regulating and constraining business, to being 'that of a partner of business' (Gilbert et al. 2004). Certainly, earlier industrial policies have emphasised the role of government in protecting people from the excesses of capitalism. Gilbert et al. (2004) argued that because capitalism has changed toward the exploitation of knowledge (and not capital), governments are now required to be in partnership with business in fostering and encouraging the start-up and growth of new enterprises. Whether the underlying reasons why government protected its citizenry have in fact now disappeared is debatable. Governments certainly work closer with business, but whether this is a good thing, in democracies at least, is a matter for the ballot box. It depends on your view of the moral logic of capitalism.

Thirdly, there is the long view to consider. Explanations for things will often look different after some time has passed. Some, for instance, have argued that the 'promotion of the enterprise culture in the UK might be [interpreted as] more a coping mechanism – a way of seeing forces seemingly beyond the control of people and government which were having a devastating effect on jobs, communities and the welfare state, in a more positive way': in other words the economic restructuring of the 1980s and 1990s could be seen 'as a source of new opportunities' (Curran 2000b: 215). Governments that challenge the great forces of history – structural economic change – tend to have short terms of office. But this doesn't mean that they do nothing to ameliorate the impact of change on their populations. We have already seen that policies can act as 'band aids'. This notion of government acting as a coping mechanism via initiatives to ameliorate deep and unpleasant systemic changes was made apparent to me whilst talking to a local government officer about the plight of former ship, coal and steel workers. In the long run he said the problem will be solved, politically at least: the unemployed men will grow old and die.

Finally, there is of course politics. You know; the interminable staged-managed stuff you see on the news. Governments and their key players strive to get re-elected, to implement their policies and make a mark on the nation. To do this they need a degree of popular legitimacy. Policies therefore must be seen to be administratively and politically viable and to address specific politically relevant problems. Political parties, civil servants and to others who work in governing all have vested interests as well as political ideals to protect. Small business – like health care, law and order and education – is a political pawn, as well as an element of rational policy making. An example of this can be seen in the US, where Anglund, in an insightful historical analysis of US small business policy, argued that during the 1980s and 1990s the 'small business job [creation] causal story [was] extremely viable in the political sphere' (2000: 132). This story – originated by the political establishment's acceptance of Birch's (1979) research as gospel, which we discussed in Chapter 1 – was that the support of small business was good because it helped protect and generate jobs. People are still arguing about what was and is true on this score. Regardless, promoting small business proved to be politically popular.

To conclude this chapter, we should ask again: what is the purpose of policy? We have learnt why there are enterprise policies, what they are and what they can and can't achieve. Certainly SMEs, entrepreneurs, enterprise and small firms are key to many a government's thinking about the economy and society. The question, as Curran and Storey (2002: 175) have asked, is what do we do if enterprise has become an overly dominant aspect of public policy? Is it morally right that governments continue to support such policies if SMEs and the environment for entrepreneurship are now so strong? Others such as David Storey and his colleagues who have researched public policy in the UK for decades, have looked at the evidence for the long-run impact of the billions of taxpayers' pounds that have been spent on developing an enterprise culture and economy in the UK and have shown that the impact is difficult to discern in the aggregate (Storey and Van Stel 2004). Yet enterprise support managers working in the enterprise industry will argue that their efforts have turned around the lives of many individuals. What should be apparent from this chapter is that the purpose of enterprise policy is complex and it is not likely to disappear any time soon, regardless of the evidence.

Summary

The chapter explains the role that government has in shaping the environment of small scale economic activity, both in the sense of practical economic policy, such as setting taxation and more general ideological objectives. Different explanations of the overall purpose of government intervention in support of smaller firms are discussed, and the role of governments in fostering enterprise discourse is assessed. The problems of ascertaining whether policy interventions have positive social, political, or economic net benefits are examined. Different types of policy and policy instruments are examined, including: financial and fiscal; information and counselling; administrative deregulation and simplification; education and training services; and sectoral and issue-specific policies. UK and US national specific approaches are briefly discussed. Broader political issues about the role of governments and their influence of enterprise and vice versa are discussed.

Curran, J. (2000a) 'What is small business policy in the UK for? Evaluation and assessing small business support policies', *International Small Business Journal* 18(3): 36–50.

Curran, J. and Storey, D. (2002) 'Small business policy in the United Kingdom: The inheritance of the Small Business Service and implications for its future effectiveness', *Environment and Planning C: Government and Policy* 20(2): 163–177.

Gilbert, B.A., Audretsch, D.B. and McDougall, P.P. (2004) 'The emergence of entrepreneurial policy', *Small Business Economics* 22: 313–323.

Holtz-Eakin, D. (2000) 'Public policy towards entrepreneurship', *Small Business Economics* 15: 283–291.

Steyaert, C. and Katz, J. (2004) 'Reclaiming the space of entrepreneurship in society: geographical, discursive and social dimensions', *Entrepreneurship and Regional Development* 16(3): 179–196.

12
Conclusion

Overview

This chapter has the following objectives:

- To reflect on the moral content of enterprise activity.
- To understand entrepreneurship as a form of social action.
- To restate the situated and context-rich approach to enterprise adopted in this text.
- To comment on what you may have learnt and found useful, having read this book.

Introduction

Normally at this stage the textbook author either seeks simply to summarise what has been covered or starts to wax lyrical about the futurology of his or her topic. I want to avoid both. It would be a dull conclusion simply to repeat what has been said before. And, for the latter strategy, who knows what the future direction of research will be? It will rather depend on the problems that society and the economy throws at us. There are not many authors who are as lucky or prescient about the future as John Gray writing about the possible future of global capitalism in 1998: 'Global *laissez-faire* may break down in an unmanageable crisis of the world's stock markets and financial institutions. The enormous, practically unknowable virtual economy of financial derivative enhances the risks of a systemic crash' (1998: 198). Gray wasn't entirely convinced by this future, and now as I write this book it looks like the bust hasn't been quite so bad. Or, rather, it seems that governments' use of taxpayers' money has saved the day and re-created the trust that was squandered so recklessly by financial institutions. But we can be sure that 'unmanageable' or not, the financial crisis of 2007–9 will shape the environment for enterprise and entrepreneurship for some time to come. It is a routine-breaking event, and out of such turbulence people effect change and create entrepreneurial opportunity.

Rather than summarise or ponder the future, I want to do two things before we finish. First, in the next section, there is a final substantive issue that I want to address that has been skulking around various chapters, making unannounced appearances here and there. This muted interest has been in the morality of enterprising behaviour, and I think it's fitting and not uninteresting to spend a little time to use this topic to draw some broader conclusions. I then reflect more directly on what you have studied and why, and what the knowledge you have developed might be useful for.

First we meet the guys from Fenderco one last time.

Fenderco case study

Simon (the researcher), Paul, John, Mark and Will in the pub talking about cars and motorbikes one Friday night

Simon: I've never really liked Jaguars to be honest, they have always seemed a bit too … you know…. So what you gonna get then? Now the company seems to be doing so well. You must fancy getting something nice.

Paul: Yeah things are pretty good I suppose. We certainly need to get rid of the profit, tax wise, that's for sure. And it's not like we can gold plate the office kitchen taps: there is only so much investment we can make. We aren't an asset rich company; there is only so much the accountant can do. So we were thinking about replacing our cars as it happens. We have worked bloody hard the last few years. We're not quite in Aston Martin or Ferrari territory just yet, and anyway that's not my style. I was thinking of a Merc: nothing too fancy. What about you John?

John: Well that Volvo I've got is no slouch, you know. But I have been thinking about a TVR. The wife can get rid of that little Peugeot then. 'Bout time we got something out of all this work and stress.

Mark: What about us? We've been slaving away helping make the profits, you bastards get to spend it all. [said in a warm, jokey manner]

Will: Yeah! Us down-trodden workers get nothing. The bosses always win. [both exaggerate a sense of mock outrage for comic effect]

Paul: Oh dear! You've caught us out! Oh bugger, John, what are we going to do now that the workers have found us out? Oh deary deary me! You workers can take what your given; the way you two work, you're lucky to have jobs: you bastards! [also said with jokey warmth and mock exaggeration – shock, horror – at being found out intending to spend company money on personal luxury]

John: Don't worry, you'll get you're share. Joking aside, we've always seen you right haven't we?

Will: Yeah right, all we're likely to get is a Christmas turkey for a bonus!
[general laughter]

Simon: On that note, does anyone want another pint?

Activity

What are the moral, social and legal norms that underpin the distribution of rewards implied by the above dialogue? Discuss these norms without making prior judgements about the moral virtues or lack of them in current arrangements.

If there are different nationalities in your group, what differences in moral, social and legal norms might you see in different national contexts?

_____Enterprise and morality_____

The distribution of rewards implied in the above dialogue and discussion activity is unremarkably normal – to us. Entrepreneurial reward is legitimate and morally sanctioned in contemporary developed societies. Baumol (1990) has shown that the forms of, and rewards given to, entrepreneurship have differed over history. His historical review of entrepreneurship shows that those with entrepreneurial dispositions in past societies, when business and commerce were not so highly esteemed activities, sought power, riches and status via whatever 'rules of the game' prevailed at the time (ibid.: 894). In ancient Rome the rules (social norms and structures) meant that budding entrepreneurs were rewarded by gaining political office, land and collecting rents. Commerce could provide for wealth but it did not confer high status. In the earlier Middle Ages in Europe land and castles brought wealth and hence military prowess was the premier entrepreneurial route. Even in early twentieth-century Britain wealth through commerce and industrial production was treated with snobbish disdain from the aristocratic political and landed classes.

And there are also societies today that have alternative norms underlying reward distribution for entrepreneurial effort. Indeed, even in contemporary developed societies 'no modern capitalist is purely economic man' (Baumol 1990: 904); economic considerations are not the only factors in determining moral norms. My own research into Australian Indigenous entrepreneurs has shown that there are strong social and moral norms which mean they will tend to share their rewards in ways that benefit their community (Reveley and Down 2009). They ignore these norms at the risk of being seen as illegitimate, and not part of the community. These differences reflect the variance in moral norms: different entrepreneurial objectives depending on the 'rules of the game'. As Anderson and Smith also note, economic activities are 'embedded in non-economic social relations and shaped by moral values other than instrumental rationality' (2007: 479). When medieval warlords sought to capture lands through murder, war and terror it was not through coolly calculating relative returns on investment: might was right; 'this type of entrepreneurial undertaking obviously differs vastly from the introduction of a cost-saving industrial process or a valuable new consumer product' (Baumol 1990: 904).

We see here that entrepreneurship has no 'divine' moral compass (Rorty 1989: 59). Enterprising activity in itself is not inherently morally good. Morality is bound up intricately with everyday life, in the rules of the games we play. As philosopher Richard Rorty has written, morality is the 'voice of ourselves as members of a community, speakers of a common language' (ibid.). People and the communities they play a part in combine and build moral norms about what is good and bad behaviour. When we say that something is immoral, it is because we imagine a large group of people who share common ideas about how things are and how we should behave. If an immoral act is 'done by one of us, or if done repeatedly by one of us, that person ceases to be one of us' (ibid.). It is important therefore that entrepreneurial acts are seen as legitimate in this sense: that they remain one of 'us'.

Those individuals and organisations that engage in enterprise and entrepreneurship play an important role in societies as agents of change. Richard Sennett writes that, '[c]reative destruction, Schumpeter said, thinking about entrepreneurs, requires people at ease about not reckoning the consequences of change, or not knowing what comes next. Most people, though, are not at ease with change in this nonchalant, negligent way' (Sennett 1998: 30). As a result, those engaged in enterprise – in forcing change – hold a special and delicate moral place in our societies. Mark and Will may well accept the distribution of rewards in Fenderco, and so share the social and moral norms of our society, but they will also expect to share in those rewards. They expect Paul and John to do the right thing. Comedy and laughter in the above dialogue are a way of allowing real differences to surface and make them known; to communicate normative moral expectations.

Because of their role in creating change entrepreneurs often serve to push the boundaries of what 'us' means. In a very real sense entrepreneurship is a 'form of social action' (Goss 2005: 217) which helps reshape societies. But entrepreneurship also needs to be perceived as legitimate. In recent years entrepreneurship has been held in high regard, and yet, as we saw in Chapter 7, the likes of Hendry (2004) would argue that there is a moral disconnect, a bimoral social disjunction, whereby traditional ideas of moral behaviour have become disconnected from the self-interested and instrumental (greed-is-good) moral world of economic rationality, where just about anything goes so long as it's good business. The entrepreneurial excess – particularly where we see monopolistic, rent-seeking and criminal behaviours in large corporations – that we have noted at various times throughout this book places stresses on how much part of 'us' entrepreneurship really is. In this sense enterprise activity is in danger of losing its moral legitimacy.

This is also partly the case because, as David Goss suggests, entrepreneurship has itself become routinised. In the sense of becoming institutionalised through education (courses like the one you are studying) and through culture (television programmes), but also in the sense of government and corporate enterprise and innovation policies. The danger is that if the engine of change itself becomes routine, then how will society and economies react and adapt? Goss is optimistic and notes that 'the more routine entrepreneurship becomes, [...] the more its interactional and emotional effects will provoke some individuals to innovative reactions' (2005: 216–217). People will always strive to challenge and change routine structures: 'as long as human beings engage one another socially and experience the emotions thereby produced, there will be scope for entrepreneurial action' (Goss 2005: 216). So if

Hendry is correct and there is increasingly a moral disconnection separating 'us' from business entrepreneurship, then perhaps we will start to see 'new and emerging forms of entrepreneurship' (Goss 2005: 217) that will challenge the current rules of the game: perhaps we shall see more entrepreneurship in social and political fields.

Enterprise and entrepreneurship as forms of social action will always find routines to challenge. The role of academic research must then be to ensure that entrepreneurship as a discipline doesn't get overly fixated on the routine *economic* manifestations of entrepreneurship, where furthering economic progress, business growth and performance becomes the only point of interest: to ensure that we see enterprise as both an economic and social and political activity, and a form of social and moral action that connects entrepreneurs to 'us'. By using concepts and theories that highlight the connectedness of entrepreneurship activity to everyday aspects of life, we re-legitimise rather than fetishise it. The story underlying the ideas, concepts and theories I have favoured in this textbook is one that seeks to maintain the connection between economic activity and other aspects of life.

Finally, this discussion implies that enterprise research and knowledge should be willing to recognise that the *content* of enterprise activity is relevant. *What* entrepreneurship produces is as important as the *manner* in which it is produced. Though destructive and productive entrepreneurship may share similarities in terms of process, I think it matters what impact the activity has on 'us'. An entrepreneurial Indigenous business promoting cultural awareness among tourists and distributing profits to the local community is better enterprise than an innovative, but legally dubious, loan-sharking business, exploiting the desperate. Entrepreneurship based on manipulative and damaging services or products is less desirable than produce and services that serve the public good. Many enterprise scholars will argue that it is not the role of the scientist to make moral judgements: we should focus on general processes, they will say. But if moral neutrality applies to different *forms* of enterprising behaviour, it should also logically apply to enterprising behaviour in general. It doesn't, because the positive moral worth of enterprise is generally assumed, without reflection. The negative content of entrepreneurial activity – the destructive, 'grey' and the illegal – is generally ignored. It shouldn't be, and I have tried to redress the balance by showing enterprise processes in a range of *situated* and *content-rich* contexts. Yet, research into entrepreneurship still needs to do more if this failure is to be redressed. Without a good grasp of the different content of enterprise we can't readily characterise its moral worth. Recent experience has shown us that we can't simply assume that all enterprise is good for us.

What have you been studying, and why? And, what can you do with this knowledge?

Textbooks generally pretend to describe their discipline dispassionately. In reality these are attempts at creating them anew. There are right royal intellectual battles taking place over the ideas described and explained in this book: enterprise is not an homogeneous discipline. Throughout I have been open about how and why I am drawing up the boundaries of the enterprise map. But I have made no pretence to hide that a definite approach has been favoured. I have not, as some do, tried to pretend that there is only one worthwhile perspective. Each of the broad schools of entrepreneurship (the mainstream/economic/normative and the 'European'/creative process) has much to offer, and at the level of particular chapter topics yet other 'middle-range', empirically-specific perspectives also show their utility (see for example Edwards et al. 2006 in Chapter 5). The way we look at the world and its problems and puzzles depends on where we are standing in relation to it. If you take one thing from this book, it is to accept that it is worthwhile to move around a bit and look at things from different angles, and try to see the whole in its context.

The story of the 'Blind men and the elephant'*

In the farthest reaches of the desert there was a city in which all the people were blind. A king and his army were passing through that region, and camped outside the city. The king had with him a great elephant, which he used for heavy work, and to frighten his enemies in battle. The people of the city had heard of elephants, but never had the opportunity to know one. Out rushed six young men, determined to discover what the elephant was like.

Figure 12.1   The story of the 'Blind men and the elephant'

From Holton, M.A. and Curry, C.M. (1914) *Holton-Curry Readers*. Chicago: Rand McNally & Co.

[The six young blind men make their own limited assessments of the creature – see Gartner 2001 for the full story.]

But finally, an old blind man came. He had left the city, walking in his usual slow way, content to take his time and study the elephant thoroughly. He walked all around the elephant, touching every part of it, smelling it, listening to all of its sounds. He found the elephant's mouth and fed the animal a treat, then petted it on its great trunk. Finally he returned to the city, only to find it in an uproar.

Each of the six young men had acquired followers who eagerly heard his story. But then, as the people found that there were six different contradictory descriptions, they all began to argue. The old man quietly listened to the fighting. 'It's like a wall!' 'No, it's like a snake!' 'No, it's like a spear!' 'No, it's like a tree!' 'No, it's like a rope!' 'No, it's like a fan!'

The old man turned and went home, laughing as he remembered his own foolishness as a young man. Like these, he once hastily concluded that he understood the whole of something when he had experienced only a part. He laughed again as he remembered his greater foolishness of once being unwilling to discover truth for himself, depending wholly on others' teachings.

But he laughed hardest of all as he realized that he had become the only one in the city who did not know what an elephant is like.

*As used by William Gartner in his article 'Is there an elephant in entrepreneurship? Blind assumptions in theory development', 2001, *Entrepreneurship Theory and Practice* 25(4): 27–39.

So much of what you read in the social sciences is aimed at unification and producing general theories about this or that behaviour or process. Yet so much of behaviour in society and the economy is fragmented and subject to ever increasing degrees of specialisation. Understanding what all 'people' are doing and why is often very difficult to establish. Science has a strong tendency to want to generalise, whether it be through statistical aggregate trends or through the search for underlying processes. This text has shown the diversity of enterprising behaviour, because it *is* diverse. I have stressed the importance of seeing human behaviour as something that is situated in a time and place, not reducible to general theories of all 'people' or all 'entrepreneurs'. As a result this book has taken a particular stance in current conversations about what the study of enterprise, entrepreneurship and small business knowledge is and should be. I have characterised this somewhat dualistically and simply as a conversation between a dominant, normative school of entrepreneurship (one strongly wedded to economic and individualistic ideas about human nature) and a 'European', creative process approach. This is not because an economic, statistically-oriented approach that sees enterprise predominantly as a tool for material enrichment adds nothing to our knowledge about enterprising behaviour. This would be ridiculous and is not my point at all. But, it is fair to say that knowledge about enterprise, if it is to be useful, needs alternative perspectives: better to have some choices if you are making important decisions. The blinkered horse might win the race, but are we in a race?

As I concluded in Chapter 2, a science of entrepreneurship with general theories and universal laws is impossible, and to my mind undesirable. This is not least because of the growth of enterprise, entrepreneurship and small business as an academic discipline. With growth comes increasing specialisation and fragmentation, and the emergence of what Gartner has termed 'informal communities' (2001: 35). It is perhaps ironic that just as enterprise education is becoming a normal part of the business school curriculum, and its journals more broadly respected, the prospect of textbooks inevitably failing to cover all the topics in the discipline grows. Here, I have tried to emphasise an intellectual journey over comprehensiveness (so there are some topics that are missing – there is for instance no chapter or section on social enterprise, female entrepreneurship, enterprise education, business start-up, or green entrepreneurship).

What then, can you do with what you have learnt? In offering alternatives rather than certitude I have been encouraging you to question the ideas, concepts and theories you have read about. Academic research offers *competing* explanations of the world; they can't all be right. In this sense I have asked you to engage in critical thinking. This way of thinking is important for many reasons, but chiefly it offers a means by which to question knowledge claims; to think for yourself. This is a generic skill for life, not just a tool to question and examine knowledge about enterprise. As a result I hope that this text has improved your ability to detect bullshit. A skill which, given its ubiquity, should come in quite handy (Frankfurt 2005; Mears 2002).

Regardless of whether you yourself will engage in enterprise activity directly through your career – and many students will indeed become self-employed, start up your own organisations, or act as change agents in one form or another – the majority will work in environments that will connect you to entrepreneurial activity of one sort or another. This is the case whether you work in the private or public sectors (or the ever growing zone of public-private partnership, in quangos and the like). Enterprise is an integral aspect of the way our societies operate, and is difficult to avoid. In this sense then the knowledge read in this text and discussed in your enterprise course has given you a broad insight into the way your future career will be organised. You have learnt about how to study enterprise (Chapter 2); economic, social and psychological theories of enterprising behaviour (Chapters 3–4); what people do when they manage, and work in, smaller enterprises (Chapters 5–6); you have learnt about entrepreneurship in corporations (Chapter 7); different functional practices that are vital to running businesses (Chapter 8); and the economic, social and political contexts in which enterprise takes place (Chapter 9–11).

What you will remember from the text will depend on what essays and exam questions you answered as part of your course, and what you do after you have finished university or college. If you are anything like me, you'll probably forget most of it quite quickly. Knowledge is kept alive by using it. This is another reason not to focus on facts independent of their context. What you have learnt about knowledge itself and how it is produced, and that there are competing claims to knowledge, will probably last the longest. What will hopefully also last is an attitude that will help you interpret and analyse the world as it throws challenges, decisions and opportunities your way. More than this is up to you.

Anderson, A.R. and Smith, R. (2007) 'The moral space in entrepreneurship: An exploration of ethical imperative and the moral legitimacy of being enterprising', *Entrepreneurship and Regional Development* 19(6): 479–497.

Baumol, W.J. (1990) 'Entrepreneurship: Productive, unproductive and destructive', *Journal of Political Economy* 98(5): 893–921.

Gartner, W.B. (2001) 'Is there an elephant in entrepreneurship? Blind assumptions in theory development', *Entrepreneurship Theory and Practice* 25(4): 27–39.

Goss, D. (2005) 'Schumpeter's legacy? Interaction and emotions in the sociology of entrepreneurship', *Entrepreneurship, Theory and Practice* 30(2): 205–218.

References

Abercrombie, A., Hill, S. and Turner, B.S. (2000) *The Penguin Dictionary of Sociology*, Harmondsworth: Penguin.

Acs, Z. (2006) 'Innovation and the small business', in S. Carter and D. Jones-Evans (eds), *Enterprise and Small Business: Principles, Practice and Policy* (2nd edn), Harlow: Prentice Hall.

Acs, Z. and Audretsch, D. (eds) (2003) *Handbook of Entrepreneurship Research: An Interdisciplinary Survey and Introduction*, Boston/Dordrecht/London: Kluwer Academic Publishers.

Acs, Z. and Preston, L. (1997) 'Small and medium-sized enterprises, technology, and globalisation: Introduction to a special issue on small and medium-sized enterprises in the global economy', *Small Business Economics* 9: 1–6.

Ahl, H. (2006) 'Why research on women entrepreneurs needs new directions', *Entrepreneurship Theory and Practice* 30(5): 595–623.

Aldrich, H. (1979) *Organizations and Environments*, Englewood Cliffs, NJ: Prentice Hall.

Aldrich, H.E. and Argelia Martinez, M. (2001) 'Many are called, but few are chosen: An evolutionary perspective for the study of entrepreneurship', *Entrepreneurship, Theory and Practice* 25(4): 41–56.

Aldrich, H.E. and Cliff, J.E. (2003) 'The pervasive effects of family on entrepreneurship: towards a family embeddedness perspective', *Journal of Business Venturing* 18(5): 573–596.

Aldrich, H. and Ruef, M. (2006) *An Introduction to Organizational Evolution and Entrepreneurship*, London: Sage.

Anderson, A.R. and Smith, R. (2007) 'The moral space in entrepreneurship: An exploration of ethical imperative and the moral legitimacy of being enterprising', *Entrepreneurship and Regional Development* 19(6): 479–497.

Anderson, A., Drakopoulou Dodd, S. and Jack, S. (2009) 'Aggressors; winners; victims and outsiders: European schools' social construction of the entrepreneur', *International Small Business Journal* 27(1): 126–133.

Anderson, P. (2007) 'Russia's managed democracy', *London Review of Books* 29(2): 3–12.

Anglund, S.M. (2000) *Small Business Policy and the American Creed*, Westport, CT, US and London: Praeger.

Aoyama, Y. (1999) 'Policy interventions for industrial network formation: Contrasting historical underpinnings of the small business policy in Japan and the United States', *Small Business Economics* 12: 217–231.

Arnold, J., Schalk, R., Bosely, S. and van Overbeek, S. (2002) 'Graduates' experiences of work in small organizations in the UK and the Netherlands: Better than expected', *International Small Business Journal* 20(4): 477–494.

Audretsch, D. (2006) *Entrepreneurship, Innovation and Economic Growth*, Cheltenham: Edward Elgar.

Audretsch, D. (2007) *The Entrepreneurial Society*, Oxford: Oxford University Press.

Bacon, N., Ackers, P., Storey, J. and Coates, D. (1996) 'It's a small world: Managing human resources in small businesses', *International Journal of Human Resource Management* 7(1): 82–100.

Baron, R.A. (1998) 'Cognitive mechanisms in entrepreneurship: Why and when entrepreneurs think differently than other people', *Journal of Business Venturing* 13(4): 275–294.

Barratt, E. (2003) 'Representing enterprise: The texts of recruitment and change in the UK banking Sector', *Culture and Organization* 9(3): 145–160.

Barrett, R. and Rainnie, A. (2002) 'What's so special about small firms? Developing an integrated approach to analyzing small firm industrial relations', *Work, Employment and Society* 16(3): 415–431.

Baumol, W.J. (1990) 'Entrepreneurship: Productive, unproductive and destructive', *Journal of Political Economy* 98(5): 893–921.

Beard, M. (2003) 'Bosses gather for audience with Enron admirer', *The Independent* 29 March.

Beaver, G. (2003) 'Editorial: Management and the small firm', *Strategic Change* 12: 63–68.

Becher, T. and Trowler, P.R. (2001) *Academic Tribes and Territories: Intellectual Enquiry and the Cultures of Disciplines* (2nd edn), Buckingham: Open University Press/SRHE.

Beck, U. (2000) *The Brave New World of Work*, Cambridge: Polity.

Becker, H.S. (1993) 'Theory: The necessary evil', in D.J. Flinders and G.E. Mills (eds), *Theory and Concepts in Qualitative Research: Perspectives From the Field*, New York: Teachers College Press, pp. 218–229.

Birch, D. (1979) 'The Job Generation Process', Unpublished report prepared by the Massachusetts Institute of Technology Program on Neighborhood and regional Change for the Economic Development Administration, U.S. Department of Commerce, Washington, D.C.

Birkinshaw, J. (1997) 'Entrepreneurship in multinational corporations: The characteristics of subsidiary initiatives', *Strategic Management Journal* 18(3): 207–229.

Birkinshaw, J. (2003) 'The paradox of corporate entrepreneurship: Post-Enron principles for encouraging creativity without crossing the line', *Strategy and Business* 30(1): 46–57.

Birley, S. (1982) 'Corporate strategy and the small firm', *Journal of General Management* 8(2): 82–86.

Blackburn, R.A. and Smallbone, D. (2008) 'Researching small firms in the UK: Developments and distinctiveness', *Entrepreneurship Theory and Practice* 32(2): 267–288.

Boje, D.M. and Rosile, G.A. (2002) 'Enron whodunit?', *ephemera* 2(4): 315–327.

Brockhaus, R.H. and Horwitz, P.S. (1986) 'The psychology of the entrepreneur', in D.L. Sexton and R.W. Smilor (eds), *The Art and Science of Entrepreneurship*, Cambridge, MA: Ballinger, pp. 25–48.

Brooksbank, D. (2000) 'Self-employment and small firms', in S. Carter and D. Jones-Evans (ed), *Enterprise and Small Business: Principles, Practice and Policy*, Harlow: Pearson.

Brooksbank, D. (2006) 'Self-employment and the small business', in S. Carter and D. Jones-Evans (eds), *Enterprise and Small Business: Principles, Practice and Policy* (2nd edn), Harlow: Prentice Hall.

Brush, C.G., Manolova, T.S. and Edelman, L.F. (2008) 'Separated by a common language: Entrepreneurship research across the Atlantic', *Entrepreneurship Theory and Practice* 32(2): 249–266.

Bryman, A. and Bell, E. (2007) *Business Research Methods*, Oxford: Oxford University Press.

Buckley, P.J. (1997) 'International technology transfer by small and medium-sized enterprises', *Small Business Economics* 9: 67–78.

Burgelman, R.A. (1983) 'Process model of internal corporate venturing in the diversified major firm', *Administrative Science Quarterly* 28: 223–244.

Burleigh, M. and Wippermann, W. (1991) *The Racial State, Germany 1933–1945*, Cambridge: Cambridge University Press.

Burns, P. (2007) *Entrepreneurship and Small Business* (2nd edn), London: Palgrave.

Cardon, M.S. and Stevens, C.E. (2004) 'Managing human resources in small organisations: What do we know?', *Human Resource Management Review* 14: 295–323.

Carr, E.H. (1972) *What is History?* Harmondsworth: Penguin.

Carter, S. and Bennett, D. (2006) 'Gender and entrepreneurship', in S. Carter and D. Jones-Evans (eds), *Enterprise and Small Business: Principles, Practice and Policy* (2nd edn), Harlow: Prentice Hall.

Cassar, G. (2004) 'The financing of business start-ups', *Journal of Business Venturing* 19(2): 261–283.

Cassis, Y. and Pepelasis Minoglou, I. (eds) (2005) *Entrepreneurship in theory and history*, Basingstoke: Palgrave, Macmillan.

Casson, M. (1991) *The entrepreneur: An economic theory.* Oxford: Oxford University Press.

Casson, M. (2005) 'Entrepreneurship and the theory of the firm', *Journal of Economic Behavior and Organization* 58: 327–348.

Chambers Dictionary (1993) Edinburgh: Chambers Harrap Publishers.

Chell, E. and Baines, S. (2000) 'Networking, entrepreneurship and microbusiness behaviour', *Entrepreneurship and Regional Development* 12(3): 195–215.

Chell, E., Haworth, J.M. and Brearley, S.A. (1991) *The Entrepreneurial Personality: Concepts, Cases and Categories*, London: Routledge.

Chua, J.H., Chrisman, J.J. and Steier, L.P. (2003) 'Extending the theoretical horizons of family business research', *Entrepreneurship Theory and Practice* 27(4): 331–338.

Clarkin, J.E. and Rosa, P.J. (2005) 'Entrepreneurial teams within franchise firms', *International Small Business Journal* 23(3): 303–332.

Clinard, M.B. and Yeager, P.C. (2005) *Corporate Crime*, Somerset, NJ: Transaction Publishers.

Cohen, L. and Musson, G. (2000) 'Entrepreneurial identities: Reflections from two case studies', *Organization* 7(1): 31–48.

Collins, J. (2002) 'Chinese entrepreneurs: The Chinese diaspora in Australia', *International Journal of Entrepreneurial Behaviour and Research* 8(1/2): 113–133.

Collinson, E. and Shaw, E. (2001) 'Entrepreneurial marketing – a historical perspective on development and practice', *Management Decision* 39(9): 761–766.

Collis, J. and Jarvis, R. (2002) 'Financial information and the management of small private companies', *Journal of Small Business and Enterprise Development* 9(2): 100–110.

Conway, S. and Jones, O. (2006) 'Networking and the small business', in S. Carter and D. Jones-Evans (eds), *Enterprise and Small Business: Principles, Practice and Policy* (2nd edn), Harlow: Prentice Hall.

Cooper, S. (2006) 'Technical entrepreneurship', in S. Carter and D. Jones-Evans (eds), *Enterprise and Small Business: Principles, Practice and Policy* (2nd edn), Harlow: Prentice Hall.

Cope, J. (2005) 'Researching entrepreneurship through phenomenological inquiry', *International Small Business Journal* 23(2): 163–189.

Curran, J. (1990) 'Rethinking economic structure: Exploring the role of the small firm and self-employment in the British economy', *Work, Employment and Society* Special Issue (May): 125–146.

Curran, J. (2000a) 'What is small business policy in the UK for? Evaluation and assessing small business support policies', *International Small Business Journal* 18(3): 36–50.

Curran, J. (2000b) 'Small and medium enterprise development: Borrowing from elsewhere: A research and development agenda – A comment on Allan Gibb's paper', *Journal of Small Business and Enterprise Development* 7(3): 212–219.

Curran, J. and Burrows, R. (1986) 'The sociology of petit capitalism: A trend report', *Sociology* 20(2): 265–279.

Curran, J. and Blackburn, R. (1994) *Small Firms and Local Economic Networks: The Death of the Local Economy?* London: Paul Chapman.

Curran, J. and Blackburn, R. (2001) 'Older people and the enterprise society: Age and self-employment propensities', *Work, Employment and Society* 15(4): 889–902.

Curran, J. and Stanworth, J. (1999) 'Colas, burgers, shakes, and shirkers: Towards a sociological model of franchising in the market economy', *Journal of Business Venturing* 14(4): 323–344.

Curran, J. and Storey, D. (2002) 'Small business policy in the United Kingdom: The inheritance of the Small Business Service and implications for its future effectiveness', *Environment and Planning C: Government and Policy* 20(2): 163–177.

Curran, J., Jarvis, R., Blackburn, R.A. and Black, S. (1993) 'Networks and small firms: Constructs, methodological strategies and some findings', *International Small Business Journal* 11(2): 13–25.

Davidsson, P. (2003) 'The domain of entrepreneurship research: Some suggestions', in J. Katz and S. Shepherd (eds), *Advances in Entrepreneurship: Firm Emergence and Growth*, Vol.6, Oxford, UK: Elsevier/JAI Press, pp. 315–372.

Davidsson, P. (2004) 'Review of Scott Shane, *A General Theory of Entrepreneurship: The Individual–Opportunity Nexus*, Cheltenham: Edward Elgar', in *International Small Business Journal* 22(2): 206–216.

Davidsson, P. and Wiklund, J. (2001) 'Levels of analysis in entrepreneurship research: Current research practice and suggestions for the future', *Entrepreneurship Theory and Practice* 25(4): 81–100.

de Bruin, A., Brush, C. and Welter, F. (2006) 'Towards building cumulative knowledge on women's entrepreneurship', *Entrepreneurship Theory and Practice* 30(5): 585–594.

Dennett, D.C. (1993) *Consciousness Explained*, London: Penguin.

Dennett, D.C. (2003) *Freedom Evolves*, London: Allen Lane.

Diamond, J.M. (1997) *Guns, Germs and Steel: The Fates of Human Societies*, London: Jonathan Cape.

Doolin, B. (2002) 'Enterprise discourse, professional identity, and the organisational control of hospital clinicians', *Organization Studies* 23(3): 369–390.

Down, S. (1999) 'Owner-manager learning in small firms', *Journal of Small Business and Enterprise Development* 6(3): 1–14.

Down, S. (2001) 'The use of history in business and management, and some implications for management learning', *Management Learning* 32(3): 395–417.

Down, S. (2006) *Narratives of Enterprise: Crafting Entrepreneurial Self-identity in a Small Firm*, Cheltenham: Edward Elgar.

Down, S. and Reveley, J. (2004) 'Generational encounters and the social formation of entrepreneurial identity – "young guns" and "old farts"', *Organization* 11(2): 233–250.

Down, S. and Warren, L. (2008) 'Constructing narratives of enterprise: Clichés and entrepreneurial self-identity', *International Journal of Entrepreneurial Behaviour and Research* 14(1): 4–23.

Downing, S. (2005) 'The social construction of entrepreneurship: Narrative and dramatic processes in the coproduction of organizations and identities', *Entrepreneurship Theory and Practice* 29(2): 185–204.

Drakopoulou-Dodd, S. (2002) 'Metaphors and meaning: A grounded cultural model of US entrepreneurship', *Journal of Business Venturing* 17(5): 519–535.

Drakopoulou Dodd, S. and Seaman, P.T. (1999) 'Religion and enterprise: An introductory exploration', *Entrepreneurship Theory and Practice* 23(1): 71–86.

Du Gay, P. (2000) *In Praise of Bureaucracy: Weber, Organization, Ethics*. London: Sage.

Dundon, T., Grugulis, I. and Wilkinson, A. (2001) 'New management techniques in small and medium-sized enterprises', in T. Redman and A. Wilkinson (eds), *Contemporary Human Resource Management: Text and Classes*, Harlow: Pearson Education, pp. 432–449.

Edwards, P. and Ram, M. (2006) 'Surviving on the margins of the economy: Working relationships in small, low-wage firms', *Journal of Management Studies* 43(4): 895–916.

Edwards, P., Ram, M., Gupta, S.S. and Tsai, C. (2006) 'The structure of working relationships in small firms: Towards a formal framework', *Organization* 13(5): 701–724.

Edwards, P., Ram, M. and Smith, V. (2008) 'Introduction to special issue: Workers, risk and the new economy', *Human Relations* 61(9): 1163–1170.

Emerson, R.W. (1998) 'Franchise terminations: Legal rights and practical effects when franchisees claim the franchisor discriminates', *American Business Law Journal* 35(4): 559–646.

Fadahunsi, A. and Rosa, P. (2002) 'Entrepreneurship and illegality: Insights from the Nigerian cross-border trade', *Journal of Business Venturing* 17(5): 397–429.

Fenwick, T.J. (2002a) 'Transgressive selves: new enterprising selves in the new capitalism', *Work, Employment and Society* 16(4): 703–723.

Fenwick, T.J. (2002b) 'Lady, Inc.: Women learning, negotiating subjectivity in entrepreneurial discourses', *International Journal of Lifelong Education* 21(2): 162–177.

Fenwick, T.J. (2003) 'Transgressive selves: new enterprising selves in the new capitalism', *Work, Employment and Society* 16(4): 703–723.

Fletcher, D.E. (ed.) (2002) *Understanding the Small Family Business*, London: Routledge.

Fletcher, D.E. (2006) 'Entrepreneurial processes and the social construction of opportunity', *Entrepreneurship and Regional Development* 18(5): 421–440.

Foss, K., Foss, N.J., Klein, P.G. and Klein, S.K. (2007) 'The entrepreneurial organization of heterogeneous capital', *Journal of Management Studies* 44(7): 1165–1186.

Frankfurt, H. (2005) *On Bullshit*, Princeton, NJ: Princeton University Press.

Freel, M. (2000) 'External linkages and product innovation in small manufacturing firms', *Entrepreneurship and Regional Development* 12(3): 245–266.

Galbraith, J.K. (1967) *The New Industrial State*, Boston, MA: Houghton Mifflin.

Gallie, D. (ed.) (2007) *Employment Regimes and the Quality of Work*, Oxford: Oxford University Press.

Gartner, W.B. (1985) 'A conceptual framework for describing the phenomenon of new venture creation', *Academy of Management Review* 10(4): 696–706.

Gartner, W. (1988) '"Who is an entrepreneur?" is the wrong question', *American Journal of Small Business* 12(4): 11–32.

Gartner, W.B. (2001) 'Is there an elephant in entrepreneurship? Blind assumptions in theory development', *Entrepreneurship Theory and Practice* 25(4): 27–39.

Gavron, R., Cowling, M., Holtham, G. and Westall, A. (1998) *The Entrepreneurial Society*, London: IPPR.

Geertz, C. (1973) *The Interpretation of Cultures*, New York: Basic Books.

Gibb, A. (2000) 'SME policy, academic research and the growth of ignorance, mythical concepts, myths, assumptions, rituals and confusions', *International Small Business Journal* 18(3): 13–35.

Gibb, A. (2002) 'In pursuit of a new "enterprise" and "entrepreneurship" paradigm for learning: creative destruction, new values, new ways of doing things and new combinations of knowledge', *International Journal of Management Reviews* 4(3): 233–270.

Giddens, A. (1991) *Modernity and Self-identity: Self and Society in the Late Modern Age*, Cambridge: Polity Press.

Gilbert, B.A., Audretsch, D.B. and McDougall, P.P. (2004) 'The emergence of entrepreneurial policy', *Small Business Economics* 22: 313–323.

Gilmore, A., Carson, D. and Grant, K. (2001) 'SME marketing in practice', *Marketing Intelligence & Planning* 19(1): 6–11.

Goffee, R. and Scase, R. (1995) *Corporate Realities: The Dynamics of Large and Small Organisations*, London: Thomson.

Goffman, E. (1959) *The Presentation of Self in Everyday Life*, Harmondsworth: Penguin.

Goss, D. (1988) 'Social harmony and the small firm', *The Sociological Review* 36(1): 114–132.

Goss, D. (1991) *Small Business and Society*, London: Routledge.

Goss, D. (2005) 'Schumpeter's legacy? Interaction and emotions in the sociology of entrepreneurship', *Entrepreneurship, Theory and Practice* 30(2): 205–218.

Granovetter, M.S. (1973) 'The strength of weak ties', *American Journal of Sociology* 78(6): 1360–1380.

Granovetter, M.S. (1985) 'Economic action and social structure: The problem of embeddedness', *American Journal of Sociology* 91: 481–510.

Granovetter, M.S. (1995) 'The economic sociology of firms and entrepreneurs', in A. Portes (ed.), *The Economic Sociology of Immigration: Essays on Networks, Ethnicity, and Entrepreneurship*, New York: Russell Sage Foundation, pp.128–165.

Grant, P. and Perren, L. (2002) 'Small business and entrepreneurial research: meta-theories, paradigms and prejudices', *International Small Business Journal* 20(2): 185–211.

Gray, C. (1998) *Enterprise and Culture*, London: Routledge.

Gray, J. (1998) *False Dawn: The Delusions of Global Capitalism*, London: Granta.

Greenspan, A. (2004) 'Alan Greenspan on the economic implications of population aging', *Population and Development Review* 30(4): 779–783.

Greve, A. and Salaff, J.W. (2003) 'Social networks and entrepreneurship', *Entrepreneurship, Theory and Practice* 28(1): 1–22.

Hamilton, E. (2006) 'Whose story is it anyway? Narrative accounts of the role of women in founding and establishing family business', *International Small Business Journal* 24(3): 253–271.

Hancké, B. (1998) 'Trust or hierarchy? Changing relationships between large and small firms in France', *Small Business Economics* 11: 237–252.

Harding, R. (2003) *Global Entrepreneurship Monitor United Kingdom 2003*, London: London Business School.

Harré, R. and Gillett, G. (1994) *The Discursive Mind*, London: Sage.

Harrison, B. (1994) 'The small firms myth', *California Management Review* 36(3): 142.

Harvey, M. (2001) *Undermining Construction: The Corrosive Effects of False Self-employment*, London: Institute of Employment Rights (http://www.ier.org.uk).

Heilbronner, R.L. (1961) *The Worldly Philosophers: The Lives, Times and Ideas of the Great Economic Thinkers*, New York: Simon and Schuster.

Hendry, J. (2004) *Between Ethics and Enterprise: Business and Management in a Bimoral Society*, Oxford: Oxford University Press.

Heneman, R.L., Tansky, J.W. and Camp, S.M. (2000) 'Human resource management practices in small and medium-sized enterprises: Unanswered questions and future research perspectives', *Entrepreneurship, Theory and Practice* 25(1): 11–26.

Henry, N. and Pinch, S. (2000) 'Spatialising knowledge: placing the knowledge community of Motor Sport Valley', *Geoforum* 31: 191–208.

Henry, N. and Pinch, S. (2001) 'Neo-Marshallian nodes, institutional thickness, and Britain's "Motor Sport Valley": thick or thin?', *Environment and Planning A* 33(7): 1169–1183.

Hindle, K. and Rushworth, S. (2002) 'Part Four: Indigenous Entrepreneurship in Australia', in *Sensis GEM Australia, 2002 focus report*, Swinburne University of Technology.

Hjorth, D. and Steyaert, C. (eds) (2004) *Narrative and Discursive Approaches in Entrepreneurship*, Cheltenham: Edward Elgar.

Hjorth, D., Jones, C. and Gartner, W.B. (2008) 'Introduction for "recreating/recontextualising entrepreneurship"', *Scandinavian Journal of Management* 24(2): 81–84.

Hobbs, D. (1988) *Doing the Business: Entrepreneurship, the Working Class, and Detectives in the East End of London*, Oxford: Clarendon Press.

Hobsbawm, E. (1975) *The Age of Capital: 1848–1875*, London: Weidenfeld and Nicolson.

Hobsbawm, E. (1985) *Bandits*, Harmondsworth: Penguin.

Holden, R. and Hamblett, J. (2007) 'The transition from higher education into work: tales of cohesion and fragmentation', *Education and Training* 49(7): 516–585.

Holliday, R. (1995) *Investigating Small firms: Nice Work?*, London and New York: Routledge.

Holliday, R. and Letherby, G. (1993) 'Happy families or poor relations: An exploration of familial analogies in the small firm', *International Small Business Journal* 11(2): 54–63.

Holtz-Eakin, D. (2000) 'Public policy towards entrepreneurship', *Small Business Economics* 15: 283–291.

Hoy, F. (1994) 'The dark side of franchising', *International Small Business Journal* 12(2): 26–38.

Hyman, R. (1987) 'Strategy or structure? Capital, labour and control', *Work, Employment & Society* 1(1): 25–55.

Jarvis, R. (2006) 'Finance and the small firm', in S. Carter and D. Jones-Evans (eds), *Enterprise and Small Business: Principles, Practice and Policy* (2nd edn), Harlow: Prentice Hall.

Jenkins, R. (1992) *Pierre Bourdieu*, London: Routledge.

Jones, C. and Spicer, A. (2005) 'Outline of a genealogy of the value of the entrepreneur', in Guido Erreygers and Geert Jacobs (eds), *Language, Communication and the Economy*. Amsterdam: Benjamins.

Jones, G. and Wadhwani, R.D. (2006a) 'Entrepreneurship and business history: Renewing the research agenda', Harvard Business School Working Paper, No. 07-007.

Jones, G. and Wadhwani, R.D. (2006b) 'Schumpeter's plea: Historical methods in the study of entrepreneurship', The AOM Best Paper Proceedings Series.

Katz, J.A. and Shepherd, D.A. (eds) (2004) *Corporate Entrepreneurship (advances in entrepreneurship, firm emergence and growth volume 7)*, Oxford: Elsevier/JAI.

Kautonen, T., Down, S., Welter, F., Vainio, P., Althoff, K., Kautola, J. and Kolb, S. (2010) '"Involuntary self-employment" as a public policy issue. A cross-country EU comparison', *International Journal of Entrepreneurial Behaviour and Research* 16(2): in press.

Keeble, D., Lawson, C., Lawton Smith, H., Moore, B. and Wilkinson, F. (1998) 'Internationalisation processes, networking and local embeddedness in technology intensive small firms', *Small Business Economics* 11: 327–342.

Kirchhoff, B.A. and Greene, P.G. (1998) 'Understanding the theoretical and empirical content of critiques of US job creation research', *Small Business Economics* 10: 153–169.

Kirzner, I. (1973) *Competition and Entrepreneurship*, Chicago: University of Chicago Press.

Koning, J. (2009) 'Singing yourself into existence; Chinese Indonesian entrepreneurs, pentecostal-charismatic christianity, and the Indonesian nation state', in J. Bautista and F. Lim Khek Gee (eds), *Christianity and the State in Asia. Complicity and Conflict*, London: Routledge, pp. 115–130.

Korunka, C., Frank, H., Lueger, M. and Mugler, J. (2003) 'The entrepreneurial personality in the context of resources, environment, and the start-up process – A configurational approach', *Entrepreneurship Theory and Practice* 28(1): 23–42.

Krueger, N.F. (2003) 'The cognitive psychology of entrepreneurship', in Z. Acs and D. Audretsch (eds), *Handbook of Entrepreneurship Research: An Interdisciplinary Survey and Introduction*, Boston/Dordrecht/London: Kluwer Academic Publishers, pp. 105–140.

Krugman, P. (2006) 'Incentives for the dead', *New York Times*, 20 October, http://select.nytimes.com/2006/10/20/opinion/20krugman.html?_r=1, accessed October 15th 2009.

Kuhn, T.S. (1962) *The Structure of Scientific Revolutions*, Chicago: University of Chicago Press.

Kuratko, D.F. (2007) *Corporate Entrepreneurship*, Boston: Now Publishers Inc.

Kuratko, D.F. and Goldsby, M.G. (2004) 'Corporate entrepreneurs or rouge middle managers? A framework for ethical corporate entrepreneurship', *Journal of Business Ethics* 55: 13–30.

Kuznetsov, A., McDonald, F. and Kuznetsov, O. (2000) 'Entrepreneurial qualities: A case from Russia', *Journal of Small Business Management* January: 101–107.

Landes, D.S. (1998) *The Wealth and Poverty of Nations: Why Some are So Rich and Some So Poor*, London: Abacus.

Low, M.B. and MacMillan, I.C. (1988) 'Entrepreneurship: Past research and future challenges', *Journal of Management* 35: 139–161.

MacDonald, R. (1996) 'Welfare dependency, the enterprise culture and self-employed survival', *Work, Employment and Society* 10(3): 431–447.

Marlow, S. (2000) 'People the Small Firm', in S. Carter and D. Jones-Evans (eds), *Enterprise and Small Business: Principles, Practice and Policy*, Harlow: Pearson.

Marlow, S. and Patton, D. (1993) 'Managing the employment relationship in the smaller firm: Possibilities for Human Resource Management', *International Small Business Journal* 11(3): 57–64.

McCartan-Quinn, D. and Carson, D. (2003) 'Issues which impact upon marketing in the small firm', *Small Firm Economics* 21: 201–213.

McClelland, D.C. (1961) *The Achieving Society*, Princeton, NJ: D. Van Nostrand Co.

McCraw, T.K. (2007) *Prophet of Innovation: Joseph Schumpeter and Creative Destruction*, Cambridge, MA: Harvard University Press.

Mears, D. (2002) 'The ubiquity, functions, and contexts of bullshitting', *Journal of Mundane Behaviour* 3(2): http://www.mundanebehavior.org/index2.htm, accessed 25th August 2009.

Meek, J. (2008) 'When the floods came: James Meek goes to Tewkesbury', *London Review of Books* 31 July, pp. 5–11.

Mitchell, R.K., Busenitz, L., Lant, T., McDougall, P.P., Morse, E.A. and Brock Smith, J. (2002) 'Towards a theory of entrepreneurial cognition: Rethinking the people side of entrepreneurship research', *Entrepreneurship, Theory and Practice* 27(2): 93–104.

Morse, C.W. (1986) 'The delusion of intrapreneurship', *Long Range Planning* 19(6): 92–95.

Moule, C. (1998) 'Regulation of work in small firms: A view from the inside', *Work, Employment and Society* 12(4): 635–653.

Munir, K.A. and Phillips, N. (2005) 'The birth of the "Kodak moment": Institutional entrepreneurship and the adoption of new technologies', *Organization Studies* 26(11): 1665–1687.

Nelson, J.A. and Winter, S.G. (1982) *An Evolutionary Theory of Economic Change*, Cambridge, MA: Harvard University Press.

Netter, J.M. and Megginson, W.L. (2001) 'From state to market: A survey of empirical studies on privatisation', *Journal of Economic Literature* 39(2): 321–389.

Nicholson, L. and Anderson, A.R. (2005) 'News and nuances of the entrepreneurial myth and metaphor: Linguistic games in entrepreneurial sense-making and sense-giving', *Entrepreneurship Theory and Practice* 29(2): 153–173.

O'Hagan, A. (2009) 'A car of one's own', *London Review of Books* 31(11): 3–9.

Ogbor, J.O. (2000) 'Mythicizing and reification in entrepreneurial discourse: Ideology-critique of entrepreneurial studies', *Journal of Management Studies* 37(5): 605–635.

Osbeck, L.M., Malone, K.R. and Nersessian, N.J. (2007) 'Dissenters in the sanctuary: evolving frameworks in "mainstream" cognitive science', *Theory and Psychology* 17(2): 243–264.

Peel, M.J., Wilson, N. and Howorth, C. (2000) 'Late payment and credit management in the small firm sector: Some empirical evidence', *International Small Business Journal* 18(2): 17–37.

Peredo, A.M., Anderson, R.B., Galbraith, C.S., Honig, B. and Dana, L.P. (2004) 'Towards a theory of indigenous entrepreneurship', *International Journal of Entrepreneurship and Small Business* 1(1/2): 1–20.

Piore, M. and Sabel, C. (1984) *The Second Industrial Divide: Possibilities for Prosperity*, New York: Basic Books.

Pittaway, L., Robertson, M., Munir, K., Denyer, D. and Neely, A. (2004) 'Networking and innovation: A systematic review of the evidence', *International Journal of Management Reviews* 5/6(3&4): 137–168.

Pollard, J.S. (2007) 'Making money, (re)making firms' microbusiness financial networks in Birmingham's Jewellery Quarter', *Environment and Planning A* 39(2): 378–397.

Prasad, S.B. (1999) 'Globalization of smaller firms: Field notes on processes', *Small Business Economics* 13: 1–7.

Rainnie, A. (1989) *Industrial Relations in Small Firms: Small isn't Beautiful*, London: Routledge.

Ram, M. (1994) *Managing to Survive: Working Lives in Small Firms*, Oxford: Blackwell.

Ram, M. and Edwards, P. (2003) 'Praising Caesar not burying him: What we know about employment relations in small firms', *Work, Employment and Society* 17(4): 719–730.

Ram, M. and Jones, T. (2002) 'Exploring the connection: Ethnic minority businesses and family enterprise', in D.E. Fletcher (ed.), *Understanding the Small Family Business*, London: Routledge.

Ram, M., Abbas, T., Sanghera, B., Barlow, G. and Jones, T. (2001) '"Apprentice entrepreneurs"? Ethnic minority workers in the independent restaurant sector', *Work, Employment and Society* 15(2): 353–372.

Rath, J. (2002) 'A quintessential immigrant niche? The non-case of immigrants in the Dutch construction industry', *Entrepreneurship and Regional Development* 14(4): 355–372.

Rehn, A. and Taalas, S. (2004a) '"Znakomstva I Svyazi" (Acquaintances and connections) – *Blat*, the Soviet Union, and mundane entrepreneurship', *Entrepreneurship and Regional Development* 16(3): 235–250.

Rehn, A. and Taalas, S. (2004b) 'Crime and assumptions in entrepreneurship', in D. Hjorth and C. Steyaert (eds), *Narrative and Discursive Approaches in Entrepreneurship*, Cheltenham: Edward Elgar.

Reveley, J. and Down, S. (2009) 'Stigmatization and self-presentation in Australian Entrepreneurial Identity Formation', in D. Hjorth and C. Steyaert (eds), *The Politics and Aesthetics of Entrepreneurship*, Cheltenham: Edward Elgar.

Reveley, J., Down, S. and Taylor, S. (2004) 'Beyond the boundaries: An ethnographic analysis of spatially diffuse control in a small firm', *International Small Business Journal* 22(4): 349–367.

Ricketts, M.J. (2002) *The Economics of Business Enterprise: An Introduction to Economic Organisation and the Theory of the Firm*, Cheltenham: Edward Elgar.

Roper, S. (2007) 'Review of David B. Audretsch *Entrepreneurship, Innovation and Economic Growth*, Cheltenham, UK and Northampton, MA: Edward Elgar, 2006. 512pp', *International Small Business Journal* 25(3): 337–338.

Rorty, R. (1989) *Contingency, Irony and Solidarity*, Cambridge: Cambridge University Press.

Rowlinson, M. (1997) *Organisations and Institutions*, London: Macmillan.

Rowlinson, M. (2001) 'Business history and organisation theory', *Journal of Industrial History* 4(1): 1–23.

Roy, W.G. (1997) *Socializing Capital: The Rise of the Large Industrial Corporation in America*, Princeton, NJ: Princeton University Press.

Russell, B. (1935/2004) *In Praise of Idleness: And Other Essays*, London: Routledge.

Sadler-Smith, E. (2004) 'Cognitive style and the management of small and medium-sized enterprises', *Organization Studies* 25(2): 155–181.

Sathe, V. (2003) *Corporate Entrepreneurship: Top Managers and New Business Creation*, Cambridge: Cambridge University Press.

Scase, R. and Goffee, R. (1980) *The Real World of Small Business Owners*, London: Croom Helm.

Schumpeter, J.A. (1934/1911) *Theory of Economic Development: An Inquiry into Profits, Capital, Credit, Interest, and the Business Cycle*, Cambridge, MA: Harvard University Press.

Schumpeter, J.A. (1962/1942) *Capitalism, Socialism and Democracy* (3rd edn), New York: Harper & Row.

Scott, A.J. (2006) 'Entrepreneurship, innovation and industrial development: Geography and the creative field revisited', *Small Business Economics* 26: 1.24.

Scott, M. and Rosa, P. (1996) 'Opinion: Has firm level analysis reached its limits? Time for a rethink', *International Small Business Journal* 14(4): 81–89.

Seeger, M.W. and Ulmer, R.R. (2003) 'Explaining Enron: Communication and responsible leadership', *Management Communication Quarterly* 17(1): 58–84.

Sennett, R. (1998) *The Corrosion of Character: The Personal Consequences of Work in the New Capitalism*, New York: Norton.

Sennett, R. (2003) *Respect: The Formation of Character in an Age of Inequality*, London: Penguin.

Sewell, G. (2004) 'Yabba-dabba-doo! Evolutionary psychology and the rise of Flintstone psychological thinking in organization and management studies', *Human Relations* 57(8): 923–955.

Shane, S. (2003) *A General Theory of Entrepreneurship: The Individual–Opportunity Nexus*, Cheltenham: Edward Elgar.

Shane, S. and Venkataraman, S. (2000) 'The promise of entrepreneurship as a field of research', *The Academy of Management Review* 25(1): 217–226.

Shaver, K.G. (2003) 'The social psychology of entrepreneurial behaviour', in Z. Acs and D. Audretsch (eds), *Handbook of Entrepreneurship Research: An Interdisciplinary Survey and Introduction*, Boston/Dordrecht/London: Kluwer Academic Publishers, pp. 331–357.

Simon, D. (2009) 'Senate committee on commerce, science, transportation. Sub committee on communications, technology and the internet. Hearing on the future of journalism', 6 May 2009, http://commerce.senate.gov/public/_files/DavidSimonTestimonyFutureofJournalism.pdf, accessed 1 July 2009.

Simon, S. (2003) *Sweet and Sour: Life Worlds of Taipei Women Entrepreneurs*, Lanham, MD: Rowman & Littlefield.

Singh, G. and DeNoble, A. (2003) 'Early retirees as the next generation of entrepreneurs', *Entrepreneurship Theory and Practice* 27(3): 207–226.

Slapper, G. and Tombs, S. (1999) *Corporate Crime*, Harlow: Pearson Education.

Smallbone, D., Leigh, R. and North, D. (1995) 'The characteristics and strategies of high growth SMEs', *International Journal Entrepreneurial Behaviour and Research* 1(3): 44–62.

Smeaton, D. (2003) 'Self-employed workers: Call the shots or hesitant independents: A consideration of the trends', *Work, Employment and Society* 17(2): 379–391.

Smith, A. (1776) *An Inquiry into the Nature and Causes of the Wealth of Nations*, Oxford: Clarendon Press.

Sorenson, O. and Stuart, T.E. (2008) 'Entrepreneurship: A field of dreams?', *The Academy of Management Annals* 2(1): 517–543.

Stanworth, C. and Stanworth, J. (1997) 'Reluctant entrepreneurs and their clients: the case of self-employed freelance workers in the British book publishing industry', *International Small Business Journal* 16(1): 58–73.

Stanworth, J. and Purdy, D. (2006) 'Franchising and the small business', in S. Carter and D. Jones-Evans (eds), *Enterprise and Small Business: Principles, Practice and Policy* (2nd edn), Harlow: Prentice Hall.

Stanworth, J., Stanworth, C., Watson, A., Purdy, D. and Healeas, S. (2004) 'Franchising as a small business growth strategy: a resource-based view of organizational development', *International Small Business Journal* 22(6): 539–559.

Steier, L.P., Chrisman, J.J. and Chua, J.H. (2004) 'Entrepreneursial management and governance in family firms: An introduction', *Entrepreneurship Theory and Practice* 28(4): 295–303.

Stein, M. (2007) 'Oedipus Rex at Enron: Leadership, Oedipal straggles, and organisational collapse', *Human Relations* 60(9): 1387–1410.

Steyaert, C. (2004) 'Entrepreneurship without entrepreneurs? Reclaiming a(n other) psychology of entrepreneurship studies', paper presented at the 18th RENT conference, Copenhagen, 24–26 November.

Steyaert, C. (2007) '"Entrepreneuring" as a conceptual attractor? A review of process theories in 20 years of entrepreneurship studies', *Entrepreneurship and Regional Development* 19(6): 453–477.

Steyaert, C. and Katz, J. (2004) 'Reclaiming the space of entrepreneurship in society: geographical, discursive and social dimensions', *Entrepreneurship and Regional Development* 16(3): 179–196.

Stokes, D. (2006) 'Marketing and the small business', in S. Carter and D. Jones-Evans (eds), *Enterprise and Small Business: Principles, Practice and Policy* (2nd edn), Harlow: Prentice Hall.

Storey, D.J. (1985) 'The means of management control', *Sociology* 19(2): 193–211.

Storey, D.J. (1994) *Understanding the Small Business Sector*, Oxford: Routledge.

Storey, D. (2002) 'Foreword', in D.E. Fletcher (ed.), *Understanding the Small Family Business*, London and New York: Routledge, pp. xi–xiii.

Storey D.J. and Van Stel, A.J. (2004) 'The link between firm births and job creation: Is there a Upas tree effect?', *Regional Studies* 38: 893–909.

Stuckler, D., King, L. and McKee, M. (2009) 'Mass privatisation and the post-communist mortality crisis: a cross-national analysis', *Lancet* 373(9661): 399–407.

Swedberg, R. (2000) *Entrepreneurship: The Social Science View*, Oxford: Oxford University Press.

Taylor, C. (1991) *The Ethics of Authenticity*, Cambridge, MA: Harvard University Press.

Taylor, M. (2005) '"Clusters": The mesmerizing mantra', paper presented at the Regional Studies Association conference, Aalborg, Denmark, May.

Terkel, S. (1974) *Working*, New York: New Press.

Van Maanen, J. (1995) 'Style as theory', *Organization Science* 6(1): 133–143.

Volkov, V. (1999) 'Violent entrepreneurship in post-communist Russia', *Europe-Asia Studies* 51(5): 741–754.

Watson, T. (1995) 'Entrepreneurship and professional management: A fatal distinction', *International Small Business Journal* 13(2): 34–46.

Watson, T.J. (1996) 'How do managers think: Identity, morality and pragmatism in managerial theory and practice', *Management Learning* 27(3): 323–341.

Weber, M. (1995/1930) *The Protestant Ethic and the Spirit of Capitalism*, London: Routledge.

Weick, K. (1996) 'Drop your tools: An allegory for organizational studies', *Administrative Science Quarterly* 41: 310–313.

Welsh, J. and White, J. (1981) 'A small business is not a little big business', *Harvard Business Review*: 18–32.

Welter, F. and Lasch, F. (2008) 'Entrepreneurship research in Europe: Taking stock and looking forward', *Entrepreneurship Theory and Practice* 32(2): 241–246.

Wenger, E., McDermott, R. and Snyder, W.M. (2002) *Cultivating Communities of Practice*, Boston, MA: Harvard Business School Press.

Westhead, P. and Storey, D. (1996) 'Management training and small firm performance: Why is the link so weak', *International Small Business Journal* 14(4): 13–24.

Williams, C.C. (2007) 'Small business and the informal economy: evidence from the UK', *International Journal of Entrepreneurial Behaviour and Research* 13(6): 349–366.

Williamson, O.E. (1986) *Economic Organisation: Firms, Markets and Policy Control*, London: Harvester Wheatsheaf.

Winter, S.G. (2003) 'Will economics ever change? Should it?', presented at the 'Sidfest', October 18–19, The Wharton School.

Witt, U. (1999) 'Do entrepreneurs need firms: A contribution to a missing chapter in Austrian economics', *Review of Austrian Economics* 11: 99–109.

Wolin, S.S. (2008) *Democracy Incorporated: Managed Democracy and the Spectre of Inverted Totalitarianism*, Princeton and Oxford: Princeton University Press.

Woods, A. and Joyce, P. (2003) 'Owner-managers and the practice of strategic management', *International Small Business Journal* 21(2): 181–195.

Zahra, S.A., Jennings, D.F. and Kuratko, D.F. (1999) 'The antecedents and consequences of firm-level entrepreneurship: The state of the field', *Entrepreneurship, Theory and Practice* 24(4): 45–65.

Ziegler, M., Rosenzweig, W. and Ziegler, P. (1992) *The Republic of Tea: Letters to a Young Zentrepreneur*, New York: Currency Doubleday.

Index